Of Women 'Inside'

Of Women 'Inside'

Prison Voices from India

RANI DHAVAN SHANKARDASS

Routledge
Taylor & Francis Group
LONDON NEW YORK NEW DELHI

First published 2012 in India
by Routledge
912 Tolstoy House, 15–17 Tolstoy Marg, Connaught Place, New Delhi 110 001

Simultaneously published in the UK
by Routledge
2 Park Square, Milton Park, Abingdon, OX14 4RN

Routledge is an imprint of the Taylor & Francis Group, an informa business

© 2012 Rani Dhavan Shankardass

Typeset by
Star Compugraphics Private Limited
5, CSC, Near City Apartments
Vasundhara Enclave
Delhi 110 096

Printed and bound in India by
Avantika Printers Private Limited
194/2, Ramesh Market, Garhi, East of Kailash
New Delhi 110 065

British Library Cataloguing-in-Publication Data
A catalogue record of this book is available from the British Library

ISBN: 978-0-415-53507-6

To my daughter Aditi — a salutation to her exemplary courage and fortitude in facing the unforeseen calamity in her life that should never have befallen her.

Contents

List of Plates

Meals — a time to relax?
JAIPUR AND HYDERABAD

Not for everyone

How happy can anyone be 'inside'?
CHILDREN IN HYDERABAD WOMEN'S PRISON

Children don't belong 'inside'
RAJAHMUNDRY AND LUCKNOW

Children don't belong 'inside' — ever
HYDERABAD AND JAIPUR

And then there are open prisons where families
can live as families
SANGANER OPEN CAMP, RAJASTHAN

Acknowledgements

The most invaluable contribution towards this work is that of the hundreds of women prisoners who gave a little bit of themselves to us as they shared and relived their lives' journeys with us. While they remain unnamed and faceless here, it is to them we owe the greatest debt of gratitude.

I thank the authorities and staff of the Prison Departments in various States of India who enabled us to move freely within the prisons we identified for our work and thereby made life easy for us. Among them, the authorities and staff at the Andhra Pradesh and Rajasthan Prison Departments deserve a special mention. No work in a prison can be done satisfactorily if the Department is 'out to get you'. We were lucky to get the cooperation of the staff in most of the prisons we worked in.

The contribution of my colleagues and research associates who have worked with me over the years in the prisons of several States also merits a special acknowledgement: this is their work as much as it is mine. Among them Vaidehi Reddy, Neelam Vishnoi, Jai Kirti Singh, Kanchan Sai Krishna, Jyothishree, Kavya Jyothsna, and Deepali Verma went all the way to work in prisons, big and small, in Central and District Jails, in Courts (High, District and Magistrates) and in police stations and shelter homes in several states to procure the kind of information and details that gave us the whole picture of the world behind the prison walls. Taking copious notes in all the different languages that the prisoners spoke (which I then translated for the purpose of writing this book) was no easy task, and their research and methodology was commendable. They put themselves out as they doubled up as counsellors in several prisons and helped the distressed women in multifarious ways. I am grateful for their spirited commitment. Without them this work would not have been possible.

Several members of the judiciary and legal fraternity have made invaluable contributions at the many workshops and seminars we organised to elicit public response to the problems in the criminal justice system particularly those in the area of legal and punitive action against women. Justices M. N. Venkatachaliah, J. N. Verma and A. S. Anand, in their official capacity as the Chief Justices of India and the Chairpersons of the National Human Rights Commission at different points of time, participated actively in our conferences and accompanied us to different locations all over the country as also Bangladesh and Nepal. There is nothing so treacherous for a society as a public that is ill-informed about and even vengeful towards those charged with crimes and lodged in prisons, but we did try desperately to set that right through public discussions in many Indian states. Of the prison officials all over the country that I have dealt with over the years, one who deserves a special mention is Riazuddin Ahmed, the then Andhra Pradesh D.I.G. (Prisons) and now the Director of the Academy of Prisons and Corrections in Vellore. His heart is in the right place and the prison reforms owe much to his enlightened attitude. His prompt responses to my queries for information all through the years have been of invaluable help in addressing our joint concerns.

Support from family and friends is always a great help when the going gets tough: to my immediate family (Vijay, Aditi, Anirudh, and Siddharth), my brothers Ravi and Rajeev, several close friends, and co-workers in the prison reform programme, I extend thanks and appreciation for putting in their 'many-pounds' worth! In particular, I would like to mention the contribution of many colleagues at the Penal Reform International (UK) of which I was the Chairperson till 2010 and where I got the opportunity to have a first-hand and deeper understanding of the several problems and issues discussed in the book in other parts of the world. The non-government organisation PRAJA (India), of which I am currently the Secretary-General, was shaped with the help of Baroness Vivien Stern who had also founded Penal Reform International (PRI) in the UK in 1989. Further, I have benefited greatly from my association with the International Centre for Prison Studies whose Director Professor Andrew Coyle opened (literally and figuratively) several prison doors for me in England and enabled me to take the camera inside to make a definitive film on prisons (*The Prison: Does It Serve them Right?*, 2000) that was used for several training programmes for prison officers in South Asia and elsewhere.

Someone who literally goaded me on to putting all the stories out in the open and kept the pressure up each time I saw her is my friend and author Namita Gokhale whom I have known since she was six and I, sixteen. If she hadn't pushed so hard, I might have still been resolving my moral dilemmas and wondering whether I had the right to expose what happens to women behind those walls. And once I started penning these stories, it was clear to me that the damage that was being done to women and entire families in our society through the misuse of many loopholes in the justice process needed to be addressed; and that the sooner alternative ways of punishing legal offences is found for those who pose minimal risk to society the better it would be for the moral health of our society.

I also thank Omita Goyal who has overseen a lot of my writing over many years in her capacity as publisher and editor. Once more, she made invaluable suggestions to make the book intense and thought-provoking.

Pictures tell a thousand stories all on their own. Angela Clay, Chair of Association of Members of Independent Monitoring Boards (AMIMB) UK, whose interest in Indian prisons brought her to us to enable her to capture the subject on camera has provided several images from her collection that tell their own stories. I am grateful to her for providing some poignant photographs for the book, including the cover picture.

My closest colleague and dear friend Saraswati Haider whose insightful approach to the subject of women prisoners helped our younger researchers get their act right prematurely left us for another world after she gave us the best of herself. Without her commitment and indefatigable energy much of what is revealed here would have lost its impact. She is sorely missed and the world is poorer for her loss.

Introduction

▣

The trajectory of a woman's life in South Asia is one of location, relocation and dislocation, not always in that order. Starting out located in the relative security of a parental home, as a girl child she is usually relocated either to a marital home, or in the event of a mishap, to a 'shelter home', or to a workplace and its alien environs. The changes that follow are sometimes trivialised because this relocation (particularly to the marital home) is seen as inevitable, except that it is not always of her choosing or indeed of her making. Then there is dislocation: this is the part of a journey for many women that can be most dramatic and often traumatic. It involves being uprooted and placed in disagreeable surroundings either by social agents or by the state. In the case of the former, a woman may be trafficked, forced into labour, pushed into sex work, or punished by her community for violating the social code; this is a space that is theoretically supposedly negotiated but practically has little room for choice and manoeuvrability. The other dislocation, the one discussed in this book, is the dislocation that follows when the state takes charge of aberrant or deviant behaviour on the part of a woman and, in dealing with it, takes her through the paces in a meticulously worked out criminal justice system that the state has formally put in place for stated goals and purposes — supposedly with the complicity of society. It is a neat fit wherein the state works almost on its own momentum to take care of all the untidy strands in social functioning.

This dislocation is the focus of our attention in these stories and while the institutional framework it boasts has worked like a charm for the state's purposes, it has not addressed adequately and effectively the subject of that dislocation — the woman's person. state institutions avowedly work for the betterment of society, and within it, of persons who constitute that society, but leave a gaping abyss where the connections and bridges between the two (society and state) should be. Most women in the environments we are looking at understand little of the connections of their social life and the state's overarching role in them. Their lives are made up of day-to-day existence determined by the roles that society (their own society) has drawn for them on the *social* drawing board. The state is not really in the picture they see but does enter every now and then with all its power to reveal whose writ really prevails should normalcy be disturbed (as the state envisages it). This is the site for contested allegiances, loyalties and priorities, and above all, the conflict between society's limits and the reach of the state.

The legacy of the overarching state system and its attempts to subordinate other socio-legal systems has had a chequered history everywhere and more prominently amidst the inheritors of the colonial state. In the seventeenth century, when the political philosopher Thomas Hobbes justified the need for a strong state (political order and law) to save society from the anarchy and chaos of living in a 'state of nature', he clearly did not envisage that the tussle between other (social) orders and the state would not be resolved as easily as his theoretical framework suggested. The 'Monster of Malmsbury' may have sought to make life less 'solitary, poor, nasty, brutish and short' by putting the state (even a sovereign) in charge of the well being of all, but what shapes the state could and would take in all contexts and contingencies was not for him to predict.

Most crucial for individuals and communities is how all this has played itself out in defining who and what was to be regarded as falling foul of the state's system of order, and how the non-compliant would be controlled and subsumed in the larger whole. The legacy of this conflict lives on with vigour in the everyday lives that we are seeking to portray in the narratives in this book. If the legal and political order sought by the 'contracted' state is a means towards the end of enhancing individual and group living, then it must be admitted that on many counts this has not happened. Ordinary, everyday lives are as ordinary and everyday as they always were. They do not alter with the abstraction called the state. Old vested interests conflict with the new to produce new victims of change so that no matter how well-intentioned the state system, the attempts towards relegating other systems to a subordinate status result in newer altercations and newer victims of these altercations. Most often, it is women who are the casualty.

For our purposes here, the concern is the state's exclusive power to punish offenders who violate the writ of the state in the area of criminal laws and procedures. While conceding that punishment did exist in the pre-state community, and that the punishment was often ruthless and brutish with an agenda that worked against the vulnerable, the state's power to punish still causes greater concern on account of its absoluteness and its unfulfilled promises of non-arbitrariness and uniformity. In either system the most vulnerable have been the greatest sufferers (women, poor, disadvantaged, elderly and the very young), leading analysts to investigate why each system fails to deliver. If the state takes on the role of delivering the justice that the social order failed to deliver, what do we do when the state and its functionaries become the deliberate or negligent perpetrators of injustice? If the modern state's justice system was the remedial measure that would safeguard what earlier socio-legal systems could not address (arbitrariness and discrimination), where is the remedy when the state itself becomes the Leviathan?

The trajectory of punishment systems in Indian society (and other ex-colonial and/or developing societies), rife with nuanced ramifications, unveils an untidy picture, but also reveals some patterns. Stoning women to death, parading them naked, mutilating their genitals, or severing other parts of the body are crude examples that have formed a part of the repertoire of punishments meted out within communities to offending women in this part of the world (and in earlier times, in other parts of the world as well). The offences and the punishments are designed for the maintenance of a social order constructed with gendered ideals for the preservation of a male-dominated society. The modern state sought to redesign this order by either eliminating it through state strictures (the law) or destroying it by substituting superior punitive systems that were then privileged with the quality of being called 'civilised'.

Punishment for offence is as old as human society and this is not the place to expostulate on theories of punishment (see Shankardass, 2000). Suffice it to say that the theoretical underpinnings of the punitive process have evolved considerably: from earlier punishments being the prerogative of the wronged, to punishment meted out by those given the authority to do so (in the community or earlier state orders), and finally, to the stage where we are today with the abstraction called the modern state and its formally enacted laws and machinery of justice. The state has the authority to decide: (*i*) what constitutes an offence, (*ii*) what should be the punishment for it, and (*iii*) how it should deal with the wrongdoer, and the state takes charge of the punishment process and procedure: crime is an offence against the state. In any historical trajectory of punishment in most societies, the vital feature is the principle that dictates the specifics of the punishment — retribution has been the most popular guiding principle but there are others too.

Ideas developed in Europe (Enlightenment, Humanism, Utilitarianism) from the late seventeenth and eighteenth centuries were transported through colonisation to other parts of the world and India duly received its colonial package comprising codes, institutions, theoretical formulations (on law and justice), and procedural apparatuses and mechanisms. These, more often than not, fit awkwardly with already existing forms of punishment that were an intrinsic part of traditional and customary community living. This uncomfortable fit of the 'superior' form over the 'inferior', according to colonial logic, continues to plague post-colonial criminal justice to this day. Nowhere is this more apparent than areas where the community writ still prevails, albeit often to the detriment of the under-privileged, hapless and ill-equipped in the society. The reality is that the overarching presence of a larger-than-life formal, equal, neutral state system of justice has still not managed to equitably sever the communities' links with traditional social justice that continues to govern the lives of simple people. Punishment is one area where the conflict of law and tradition is stark, and nowhere are the scars from this conflict more visible than in the area of punishment for women.

Imprisonment is the colonial state's 'civilised' answer to the uncivilised punishments of the earlier social order. In everyday life, more people are likely to have experienced non-state than state punishments. The fact that these are often more ruthless and, above all, arbitrarily dispensed, gives the state's power and methods of punishment the pride of place it has. But that could equally be questioned. The state takes the clinical path with its faith in uniformity and, therefore, equality, and sends people (all people) to prison for most offences on the assumption that this will deter them from committing it again. Mothers may have slapped their children all through time; it may not be an appropriate response towards indiscipline among children, but when the state takes charge of making 'slapping' illegal, two questions arise: (i) how does the state address this question of indiscipline at the ground level, and (ii) how does a punitive response to the mother help solve the problem faced within the mother and child equation. Equally, the state took a long time to take cognisance of several sexual offences and molestations against women, including domestic violence and rape: did they become reprehensible offences only when the state stepped in or was rape always a lowly and dishonourable act? Clearly, nothing is a criminal offence unless the state deems it so, and clearly too, that means that the state's agenda (and we believe states do have agendas) would prevail over all others. While according a higher status to the state's ability to decide what constitutes offences and what kind of measured punishment should be meted out to those who commit these offences, the problems and issues do not disappear. The old and the new conflict, and the new simply absorbs many of the perceptions of the old order, not the least among them being gender bias.

Very simply, the conflict is attributable to the fact that men and women are viewed differently in terms of the expected codes of conduct (a feature not exclusive to traditional India). The offences and the prescribed punishments would logically then be different. Punishment for women (in Hindu and Islamic traditions) had socio-moral overtones because it addressed breaches of a law or code as well as violations of moral strictures for daily life, the latter being considered more unacceptable than the former.

Left unpunished, such conduct was seen as destroying the very fabric of a community or society, for the world-view of communities was based on a vital link between a person and the larger whole. Punishment could be cruel and merciless — deterrence, retribution, reprisal, retaliation, all rolled into one. The state's presumption that it could change all that was often misplaced.

Two factors have strongly affected the way we deal with women offenders today: (*i*) historical perceptions of women and women offenders, and (*ii*) constructed theories about women offenders (Shankardass, 2000). Older forms of punishment were visible and ruthless for all, but for a woman there was always a reason to be more strict and unrelenting. The anxieties and misgivings that surrounded her sexuality and the mysteries surrounding her fecundity gave rise to many apprehensions about her power. The emerging images were a bundle of contradictions: from *devi* to demon, she could be anything. In Greek and Roman myths, powerful goddesses are attributed less sexuality, implying that in her sexuality lay the dangers of the female human form. With women's own voices conspicuously absent in historical corridors, many of the reasons for and causes of women's subordination have been worked through from chronicled tradition, oral tradition and collections of socio-legal and religious commentaries. The significant element here is that the social and legal codes of the lawgivers of most ancient civilised societies drew special portraits of the ideal woman and then made extraordinary provisions for punishing the fallen woman who transgressed the ideal. The hypocrisy of this logic has survived the state's neutrality.

There are some vivid accounts of the roots of savage punishment for women in the now 'civilised' Western world — accounts that reveal why man chose to inflict humiliation and suffering on a section of society without economic and political power. Impaling on sharpened stakes for punishing abortion (Hammurabi's Code) to burning at the stake for killing a husband (medieval England) to ordeals by fire and water — even later the tales of horror and barbarism are unending (Burford and Shulman, 1992).

So, while punishment is a social institution with a long history, the modern state has clothed it in legal rules and strictures that derive sustenance from principles that are grand but confusing. One of the principles presenting as many problems as it solves when it relates to punishment is 'justice'. That is probably because there is after all 'justice, justice and again justice!' (Dhavan, 2003).

The manner and measure of punishing offending behaviour reflects how each society perceives those it seeks to punish (in this case women). Punishment may be part of a justice system but it is one that is based on existing power relations in the first instance. What happens when a supposedly dramatic change occurs in the apparatus of the system?

Enter the colonial model. Its operative principles of equal and fair justice could be portrayed as laudable for unequal societies (ours *and* theirs), but the chances of successfully replacing with one stroke the powerful and legitimate (albeit often oppressive) living models of community justice with those that were alien, unfamiliar and fearful were slender. Yet change came with the territory. The superior colonial model of punishing had every intention of addressing social issues (regarded as aberrations) in Indian society and therein lay the seeds of a confusing interface.

The resulting mixed bag of do's and don'ts played havoc with the lives of those who were either ill-equipped and unwilling to, or simply unprepared to, handle the dramatic changes (and promises) that new laws, codes, procedures and processes brought. The majority of women in South Asia (and other regions where women have been divorced from equal opportunities) constitute that unprepared group. In any case, they hardly formed a priority in any agenda for change. How that affected their lives at the ground level is what emerges in some of our stories.

No list of criminal laws is ever exhaustive; it continues to change (mostly expand) as the state deems necessary and adds more and more offences to the list. The 150-year-old Indian Penal Code (Act 45 of 1860) is the major (colonial) document that decides what is a criminal act and the punishment for committing such an act. The handiwork of Lord Macaulay and his colleagues, it was submitted as the Report of the Law Commission on the Penal Code. Before 1860, English criminal law was administered in the Presidencies of Bombay, Calcutta and Madras, and in the moffusil, the courts were principally guided by the Mohammadan criminal law. The judicial system of Bombay was the first to undergo change in 1827 when a regulation defining offences and specifying punishments was set out. In Calcutta and Madras the change from Mohammadan criminal law came with the Indian Penal Code.

The authors of the Report saw no reason to examine indigenous systems that were considered inferior ('foreign and introduced by conquerors different in race, manners, language and religion from the great mass of the people'). The underpinnings of the new recommendations ('innovation in penal legislation') were that the future of the Empire depended on it.

The true reasons for change notwithstanding, the imperious and cavalier nature of the Code could not be disguised under its declared principles. The significant thing about this change is what the Code sets out at the beginning (section 2): '*Every* person shall be liable to punishment under this code *and not otherwise* for every act or omission contrary to the provisions thereof of which he shall be guilty within India' (emphasis mine). Submerging any other identities of the natives was a prerequisite for efficacious rule. Punishments were also meant to instil fear, and unfamiliar punishment was the most effective way to control the eccentric Indian. The equal and uniform punishment clause offers an equal discrimination-free justice for every person and like punishment for like offences. Caste, class, gender, race, religion, status — all the features that formed an intrinsic part of the earlier system of justice would be eliminated through this uniform Code. There was no room for any conflicting realities, no more cultural or other identity. Creating a neat approach to crime and its symmetrically constructed counterpart — punishment — was the promise. However, real life never is neat and symmetrical and the conflicts soon become apparent.

The Indian Penal Code (IPC) has 511 sections. Of them 330 are punitive provisions (the rest being definitions and explanatory provisions), of which 319 carry a prison sentence from one, three or six months to one, two, three, five, ten and fourteen years, or 'life'. Fifty-one sections of the IPC provide for the sentence of life imprisonment, and eight offences carry the death penalty. It is curious how the punishments are measured — so many months for this and so many years for that. How are these determined and decided? Why three months and not four? Why ten years and not more or less? The state adds and takes away offences as well as the accruing punishments from its list. I have in my possession an edition of the Indian Penal Code dating back almost a hundred years that was given to me many years ago by a judge of the Allahabad High Court. Chapter III (Section 53) of the Code provides for six punishments therein for which offenders are liable: Death, Transportation, Penal Servitude, Imprisonment of two descriptions (Rigorous, that is with hard labour, and Simple), Forfeiture of Property and Fine. In a paragraph in the *Comment* is a further clarification:

> To the six kinds of punishments in the section two more are added by subsequent enactments, viz., whipping, and detention in reformatories. In the Madras Presidency the punishment of stocks is inflicted on offenders of lower castes.

There is a further explanatory comment relating to Penal Servitude.

> The punishment of penal servitude which is a substitute for transportation is applicable only to Europeans and Americans under Act XXIV of 1855. By reason of the difficulty of providing a place to which Europeans and Americans can, with safety to their health be sent for the purpose of undergoing sentences of transportation or of imprisonment for long terms, it has been expedient to substitute other punishment for that of transportation.

Clearly, during the course of his judicial career the list of punishments had changed and the judge (who had used the book in his judicial capacity) had penned in the appropriate corrections: imprisonment for life substituted transportation for life and penal servitude was crossed out as not applicable throughout the document.

I have laboured this point for three reasons that perplex and intrigue any analyst of the justice process. Historically, with changing social circumstances and/or ideas, there have been additions and subtractions in the stockroom of offences and punishments. When codified laws with neutrality, objectivity and impartiality as their hallmarks are substituted for uneven, unequal legal systems, it is assumed that the distinguishing characteristics of the new systems will be what they promise — equal and impartial. Are 'exceptions' considered equal or unequal? In providing for penal servitude for Europeans and Americans to exempt them from transportation and life imprisonment, and introducing stocks for lower castes, was the *uniform* Penal Code living up to its reputation? Was the punishment equal or equivalent, or simply unequal?

Historically too, the authority systems of earlier societies have recognised *difference* in punishment and believed that that was just. And when the new legal order brought uniformity through codified instruments and processes, ways were found to accommodate difference — legal exceptions and exemptions. So, what happened to the difference factor for women whereby a case could be made for viewing them *differently* should circumstances require? The question can provide contradictory answers. From 'but they *are* viewed differently' to 'but that would be unequal'; either way they are disadvantaged.

The third reason for dwelling at length on the colonial model's bestowal of the Code and the subsequent developments is that while the state (colonial and post-colonial) continued to add new offences to the 'list', rather like Koko's 'little list' in the opera *Mikado,* the punishments for them were still picked out from the catalogue of punishments (the Code) that remained unaltered (but for the earlier changes brought through the colonial dispensation — removal of transportation, penal servitude, etc). Did the new republic of post-independence India not require and demand *any* changes in the ways we punish? Did we run out of ideas in the punishment list, but not in the offence list? The colonial implant had a colonial agenda. What was/is our agenda?

The process in the inherited colonial system is that when any criminal law is alleged to have been violated the accused is apprehended (by the police) and presented before the judicial agency empowered to deal with the (alleged) offender and take appropriate action according to the substantive and procedural law. There is a presumption of innocence until proven guilty. If innocent, the accused is set free; if guilty, she is penalised according to the punishments in the prescribed rulebook in which prison dominates. Once 'inside', a fresh set of rules become operative. These are the rules that determine the standards and guidelines for the handling and treatment of prisoners. In India, the prison rulebook varies from State to State, and in some States, it is antiquated. The Prisons Act of 1894 and the Jail Manuals of various States (not all have been revised) determine what happens to prisoners inside. There are international minimum standards for custodial institutions that all countries have subscribed to and whether in police stations, courts or prisons, State officials/functionaries are required to protect the alleged offender from abuse or arbitrary treatment while in custody. Our stories give some idea about the observance, or non-observance, of these standards.

Our concern here is two-fold: one relates to the problem of state functionaries themselves being the abusers and violating not just the laws that protect citizens and their rights, but also those rules that have to be followed in the discharge of their functions relating to the criminal justice process. The other concerns the subjects (women) who are a mere statistic in the scheme of things: no attempt is made to address the prisoner as person, much to the detriment of the system's own goals. There is permanent damage being caused to incarcerated women *and* their families: the nature and extent of the damage has not been factored into the procedural processes at any point (neither arrest nor adjudication).

The procedural rules are set out in a definitive document and without dwelling at length on the history of this document — the Code of Criminal Procedure — some features of its evolution need to be recounted. A uniform law relating to criminal procedure applicable to all criminal proceedings (except certain specified areas) was consolidated in 1898. The Code of Criminal Procedure has been amended from time to time by several acts of the central and state legislatures, and of these, the amendments of 1955 were important for two reasons: they sought to simplify procedures and speed up trials as much as possible. Subsequently, various law commissions were engaged in the exercise of a general revision of the Code to remove anomalies and ambiguities, and to further consolidate laws wherever possible in the interests of as much uniformity as was possible.

Some important features of the considerations (of the Law Commission) that influenced the revision of the earlier Code are being highlighted to help ascertain in our narratives whether they are observed and whether they provide the intended help and assistance to vulnerable groups.

> — *fair trial* according to the principles of *natural justice*
> — *avoidance of delay* in investigation which was considered harmful to the individuals and to society
> — a *less complicated procedure* that would ensure a fair deal to *the poorer sections of the community* (emphasis mine).

Reversing the practice prevailing from colonial times, there was a separation of the judiciary from the executive with new criminal courts so that legally qualified and trained judicial magistrates would perform the judicial functions once performed by ordinary magistrates. Other changes in the Code of Criminal Procedure included legal aid to an indigent, adequate payment of compensation to the victim, and representation against a punishment before it is imposed.

Penal and Procedure Codes and Acts notwithstanding, the ambiguities and near lack of precision surrounding some issues continue to plague both implementers and experts in the quest for real justice. The Criminal Procedure Code sets out several offences (in Section 320) that are compoundable. Simply stated, a compoundable offence is one that can be settled privately and the result may be the same as that of an acquittal. Offences are listed as being compoundable by the persons against whom the offence has been committed with a specification for some that they may only be compoundable with the permission of the court. The principle behind compounding offences attempts to address issues of justice that lie beyond the mechanical logics of punishment. Implying, as they do, some form of reparation, they throw open questions that relate to overlaps between civil action and criminal process. Why should particular offences be compoundable? Can there be others that may be put on the list, and if so, is that to be done by a fresh statute or may the court before which a prosecution is pending permit the compounding of an offence? Can a judge exercise his power to deny the compounding of a compoundable offence? Apart from interrogating some issues relating to the distinction between civil and criminal matters/courts, these questions have recently assumed importance in the area of offences relating to women because judges send out fresh messages for re-examining the law on compoundable offences, particularly in the area of domestic violence, dowry-related offences and other domestic problems (see note at the end of the chapter).

Against this backdrop the second concern raises an inevitable question: can one do something about the irregularities in the institutional frameworks where all these women are brought for careful handling and 'safe keeping' (police, courts, prisons)? Maybe one can only highlight the malfunctions and recommend improvements. Perhaps someone will listen. And yet it is somewhat obvious that the prisoner as statistic and the prisoner as person can almost be two different things. Any focus on one without due consideration to the other is counter-productive. Pretending that there is nothing before and after imprisonment and that the prisoner's persona becomes irrelevant the moment she enters the prison gate is damaging for the person and the institution. Surely someone wants to know how and why the incidents (earlier) in these women's lives occurred, only in some and not in others' lives. And if that is so, can these persons really be treated with clinical sameness, or do they need specialised help when in the custody of the formal justice system? Our observations are that they are neither treated with sameness nor with special expertise. They are treated with (negative) difference and indifference — depending on how far out they are of the ideal constructs of women in the social groups from which they come. So, the social stays with them regardless of the 'superior' colonial logic of equal, neutral, uniform justice. With that scenario our agenda began to fall into place with each exploratory visit.

Above all, these were the underlying issues that plagued our work in women's prisons. Nothing was as neat as the state would have us believe. No offence was capable of being tidily carved out of its context to reveal the straightforward link between Offence and Punishment. 'Abstract' state offences and punishments still need to be brought face to face with real (flesh and blood) contexts to determine whether their boast of being universal/uniform and rational can be sustained in the real world.

Women constitute that group in society where the symmetrical logic of the punitive policies of the state runs into problems. This has been theoretically addressed elsewhere and what is unfurled in this book is the 'flesh and blood' manifestation of the flawed logic.

> When women commit crimes are they/can they/should they be viewed in exactly the same way that men are viewed as offenders? Or are they/can they/should they be viewed differently *because* they are women? Or is there a third way? The historical treatment of women offenders whose offences are viewed as more than just offences against a legal code (there is always an accompanying moral and social charge) has oscillated between greater concession and greater condemnation. Women are accused of being either typically woman, too woman or not woman enough (Shankardass, 2000: 298).

Women constitute a small percentage of imprisoned populations all over the world (between 3 and 5 per cent). Women's prisons in India are relatively less overcrowded, misleading the public into believing that the state does not really imprison women all too readily and that the problems of overcrowding that are the bane of the penal system do not plague women's prisons. There are many reasons for the seemingly low figures in women's prisons: women commit fewer and different crimes compared to men, and they receive more punishments in the community than men do. Moreover, the administration's statistic for women prisoners, a number recorded for a particular day, is a misguided way of judging how many women (and accompanying children) have actually had a prison experience in a month, a year or ten years; that number could be twenty times the official figure recorded for the Bureau on one particular day. These details are not unimportant for the big picture.

Women's areas of engagement in life are different (sometimes more numerous) in comparison to those of men. Their offences are different but less numerous. The most prevalent (differing from State to State and dependent on the kinds of punitive laws each state has) form a list of approximately ten offences: dowry harassment and dowry death, murder, prostitution, Excise Act offences (illicit liquor), NDPS (Narcotic Drugs and Psychotropic Substances Act 1985) violations, terrorism and disruptive activities, cheating, theft, abduction, kidnapping, and abetting suicide. In some cases they are arrested in groups (e.g., in raids and family fights) and consequently numbers rise in some prisons; they languish as pre-trial prisoners while the justice machinery takes its course.

While in prison too, their experiences are different from those of men in the men's prison. Most prisons have not been designed with women in mind: that women manage to survive as well as they do is a tribute to their resilience. But our investigations revealed that they barely survive. They may come out with their limbs and bodies intact, but the effects on their mind and spirit is another story. This is related, among other things, to the most devastating aspect of their imprisonment — the separation from their families and their concerns about their children, both of which are the defining feature of their lives outside. Hailed as prime carers and nurturers 'outside', they are suddenly almost dramatically shorn of their womanhood 'inside'. Subjected to rules that are baffling and meaningless, most women find themselves unable to express their sense of helplessness in being so totally redefined once they enter prison. Many become victims of ailments, physical and mental, that make the prison experience intolerable. Any assessment of their condition is only possible when their voices are heard in first person; only then can one see their personalities and their lives in entirety rather than their criminal status and procedurally determined futures.

Not too long ago, Kevin Warner, a prison educationist and coordinator of education in the Irish Prison Service for thirty years, addressed a conference of European Directors and Coordinators of Prison Education, making a few salient points relating to how prisoners are perceived. His words struck a chord for I had been struggling to express similar ideas for the Indian situation, ideas that I have tried to underscore in these narratives: whether we view the prisoner as a whole person or an offender, whether we see the full personality or take a narrower view that dwells on her crime, and whether we see the prisoner as a member of society or accept a stereotype that regards the prisoner as 'other' than ourselves. In short, is our view 'inclusive' or 'exclusive'?

> The crime and the criminal are brought to the fore; other aspects of the person and their life recede into the background. We are expected to see them as 'offenders', an offensive term that is negative and one-dimensional. And often they are expected to carry this mark forever as 'ex-offenders' like Jean Valjean in *Les Miserables*.
>
> (Warner, 2010)

From arrest to adjudication and then incarceration, the law and justice machinery functions with a one-dimensional picture of a woman. Essential features like details relating to her family background and particularly her children are not part of the procedural repertoire of variables that enter the process formally. An enlightened officer of the system may show concern out of compassion but an inquiry into these aspects of the woman's life is not required when the legal machinery starts to roll. It is this lacuna that has prompted us to delve into these women's lives in order to determine how each agency of the criminal justice system treats women offenders. Presenting the woman prisoner as the person she is first and foremost is difficult when she begins life behind bars so completely defined by her status as offender or criminal. The prison, as the institution it is and has become, scarcely makes room for the *person* of the prisoner — her life before she was arrested, intricately intertwined with her family and community, disappears sometimes never to return.

The penal rulebook underscores the need for well-run institutions in which security and order are priorities *and* the safety and well being of those inside is also ensured. All custodial institutions demand an equal measure of both these features. Experientially, drawing the balance seems to pose a problem and the tilt has always been towards discipline and order. All rhetoric to the contrary notwithstanding, it is a fact that offenders and criminals have few if any entitlements. We forget that they are still people. They still need food, clean water, decent living space, hygienic surroundings, links and contact with their families, and meaningful activity to spend the hours and days and months and years. Deprivation of *liberty* is their punishment, not deprivation of all their *human rights*.

Unfortunately, that is not how it works in this, the most opaque of all the state's institutions. And who would object if it is not run the way the 'Standard Minimum Rules' require? If the underlying aim is to 'put people away' and warehouse them in lock ups, from where would the ethos of improving the lockups or the lot of the prisoners emerge? The contradictions of the institution become apparent soon enough. The state's attitude seems to suggest that if someone is being locked up there has to be something very wrong with him/her as a person in addition to the offence committed. Women stand no chance in this convoluted logic for reasons already stated.

A discussion about prisons and prisoners is difficult at the best of times. There are too many assumptions, misdirected questions and shaky answers. Even the most basic question addressed to ourselves — 'why are we here' — defies explanation. Why did we pick this spot — a prison — of all places? There are other places of gross deprivation in our country where no one has committed felony. People here have killed and stolen and peddled drugs and committed 'immoral' and illegal acts for which they have to be punished by the state and imprisonment is that mandated punishment. We gave the state that power, so why are we so concerned about these wrongdoers: are we questioning the basic premise of punishment? What is it that my colleagues and I are doing among these supposedly 'sub-standard' women? Is it that we want to go where others don't and do what others don't want to? Or is there something that is far more important than mechanical equations like crime–punishment, punishment–prison, etc.

These are not idle questions — they are often put to us in some form or other in one prison or another. And they are not easy to answer. For more than fifteen years I have been in and out of prisons all over the world, observing and analysing prison populations, prison conditions, laws and procedures. After all this time I am still not able to pronounce with any profundity or certainty on some of the very fundamental questions relating to prison as punishment. But one thing gets clearer with time: this is not a civilised institution and each person, each corner and each day in this, the most opaque of the state's institutions, confirms that. When I first stepped into these legitimate penal institutions, women of all ages walked past me and saw me as an intruder, which, in a manner of speaking, I was. This was their domain and I really had no business being here, their attitude suggested. Did I think this was a zoo where curious creatures were on view? Would I get them out of the jail and send them back to families? If not, what was my mission if I did indeed have a mission? Valid questions these, not always spoken but indicated through their eyes and rebuking gazes.

The staff too had difficulty understanding exactly why we were working in prisons and with women prisoners. 'Do you think all of them are angels? Do you know how wretched some of them really are? For every ten prisoners you meet, how many do you think are hapless creatures, victims of circumstances and how many are hardened felons? And do you know what our problems and lives are?

'I don't know', was my answer when I started out. What I did know was that there were two elements in this scenario that needed critical examination: the *legalities* that determined prisoners' guilt (or otherwise) and the *realities* of the before and after relating to them. Doing the homework on the legalities is only one part of the story of crime and punishment; the rest is comprised of flesh and blood issues of the persons and their problems and that is what constitutes the discourse. The state has a set of laws and rules for regulating citizens' behaviour, duly enacted by legitimate authorities, and when there is violation of the rules, a prescribed process begins its course whereby designated persons arrest, investigate, charge and then sentence the offender. What happens to the offender thereafter depends on the sentence — and he/she is punished according to the laws of the state. This is the relatively simple part. The complex part relates to the interface between the clinical (sometimes alien) rules and the actual lives of the players that constitute the operative elements of the criminal justice process.

There are two aspects of this undertaking: one that relates to prisons (conditions) and the other, to those (prisoners — they may or may not be offenders — and staff) who occupy it. Unfortunately, the two aspects were out of sync. The underlying question in most discussions was, 'Why should it be a pleasant experience for these criminals?' Our contention was: 'It can never be a pleasant experience. A cage is still a cage even if gold plated'. Thus the prison becomes the site for a contest between two schools of thought. Increasing transparency and the changing (high) profile of prison populations does bring the institution under some kind of review. People with a degree of vision promote better standards and improved conditions. There are reports and recommendations time and again, but implementation does not always logically follow. People 'outside' don't want to hear about people 'inside'.

The second aspect of this undertaking relates to the prisoners: it took almost two years to only partly resolve the particular (moral) dilemma that we faced as researchers and reformers, and that relates to our entitlement to use information about other people's private lives to be able to say what we have wanted to for many years. It was Urvashi's experiences that resolved some of the questions we had battled with: she almost wished for the world to know (without revealing her identity) that there are all kinds of girls who have got enmeshed in 'sex work'. 'Why do people put all women in a manageable category — is it to make it easy for themselves?', she had asked. She also wanted us to highlight the duplicity of another supposedly innocuous institution called an *ashram* (care institution) for women. She had been disillusioned with both institutions and bore the scars of both.

Urvashi's permission to tell her story still did not make it easy for us. Even after we convinced ourselves that all of it needed to be said, some part of the predicament continues: to justify what we were doing we told ourselves that people 'outside' knew nothing about what was happening 'inside' and they needed to (as Urvashi believed they should). But then again, why do they need to know what happened to Hasina, or Saloni, or Rukhsana, or Mumta, or Bina, or Shobhavati, or whoever is the subject of our investigation and research. These are 'criminals', offenders who are supposedly spoiling the equilibrium in society — why would one want to publicise objectively and without condemnation the life histories and experiences of offending women? They committed acts that have had adverse repercussions on entire families — how can they be given space or attention of any kind. Do they deserve such focus? And how does it affect the indifferent 'outside' to know what is happening 'inside'.

What these women inside deserve or don't deserve is a difficult question to answer. It would have to start with whether they deserve the lives they have had from childhood? Did they deserve to be as poor, ignorant and powerless as they were? Even those who deliberated the offences they had committed did not really have the opportunity to tell us why they did what they did. Like the woman who said: '*Such* a long punishment because my daughter-in-law died? Eleven members of my family are locked up for a dowry death — is that fair?' With no sympathy for those who harass daughters-in-law I was hardly likely to say, 'You poor thing!' My instinctive response was 'You should have stopped yourself from being so greedy for dowry that you bullied a young girl who leaves her own family in good faith so badly that it eventually *results in her death*.' She questioned my acceptance of the fact that eleven persons would set about the task of planning to kill the daughter-in-law. I remind her that that was the judge's verdict not mine and that I had simply said that what had resulted in her death was reprehensible. She also lectured me on how customary traditional practices like dowry were followed by everyone but only 'we of the lower classes' are penalised when something untoward happens in a household. How do we handle our customary life? Should we disregard it, the colonial way, or embark on redefining and reconstructing the juxtaposition between the real and the legal.

The stories of the yesterdays, todays and tomorrows of the women inside are unsettling; they are also long and tiring to follow because even as we have fitted each into a few pages, there are complexities and nuances that get blurred in the legalities of criminality. But all this needs to be known without the prejudice of one's own ideological leanings. This one peddled poppy husk or illicit liquor. This one worked in a dance bar. This one stole from her employer. This one killed her drunken husband. This one sacrificed a child because a local Tantric told her to. This one harassed a daughter-in-law for dowry and made life so unbearable for her that it led to her death and the imprisonment of the mother-in-law and her family. This one is a Naxalite. There are others as well who have committed offences and are incarcerated here, incarceration being supposedly the most appropriate punishment out of a repertoire of punishments deemed suitable by the state.

These are *real* stories of *real* people, *real* events with *real* outcomes. Actual names of persons and places have been changed for confidentiality and out of respect. Specificity about time and place has often been glossed over for the same reasons: many of these women are still 'inside'; many are still caught in the webs they were trapped in and many who are 'outside' are struggling to get back on track, any track. It seems only fair to disguise identities and locations. Though guilty of probing the interstices of people's lives, the least one can do is to protect their privacy and future prospects. Each event and incident is narrated as it happened and as it was lived, and every story has been told as accurately as possible without embellishment. The sequence may have been altered for brevity, but nothing here is false, fictitious or fabricated. If anything, some sordid details may have been toned down for reasons of delicacy. Some poetic license in methodology has been taken: if two or more women had very similar experiences of life and adversity, details of their stories have been merged and combined to cover the wider range of experiences that overlap and intertwine. None of this compromises accuracy in any way.

Each chapter focuses on a different criminal offence and the story revolves around both the person and the offence. The stories have been selected to present the most prevalent offences found to have been committed by women in prisons in India. An explanatory note at the end of each chapter provides details of the legal provisions and the history of the specific offences that relate to the story, primarily to acquaint the reader with the status of the law or statute and the political beliefs related to it. Interrogating the adequacy or inadequacy of the law relating to the offences and the procedures accompanying the justice process has proved essential in many cases. Contesting oppressions (the social and the legal) becomes a site for more regressive behaviour among individuals, providing further reasons for authoritative restraint by the state.

Whether these narratives, chronicled presumably for a reason, will achieve any purpose depends on the reader. If, each time we encounter a woman with a chequered past and a depressing and unpromising future, we can try to be less dismissive about her and try to discover the minutiae of her life before condemning her to the dustbins of society, and then to the warehouses designed by colonisers, we might achieve something. Labelling the unwanted and then warehousing them is not the counsel of a democratic system. Offending women get labelled faster than other categories: the clubbing process is based on social stigmatising and legal pigeonholing. The vocabulary of criminal charges is itself condemnatory — theft, fraud, murder, indecency, immoral trafficking or prostitution, adultery, drug addiction, narcotics peddling: there is little room for negotiation. Ill-equipped to deal with and overawed and terrorised by the legal machinery, women are easy targets for being apprehended and portrayed as (socially) guilty. Finding them legally guilty thereafter is a relatively easy task. Bina (who allegedly threw two children into a well at the behest of a local *ojha*), whose journey through the system we followed closely, is a case in point. Even when the law has space for it, little or no cognisance is taken of the victim's status or adversities faced before the offence. Nor is there room for their horrific experiences at the hands of the agents of the criminal justice machinery (Mumta in the police lockup in Andhra Pradesh). Many attributes of the ethos of punishment that inspired the colonial Penal Code still present difficulties that can be surmounted only if there is a fundamental rethink about goals, aims, purposes and, above all, attitudes.

Several questions are being asked through these narratives, not the least among them being the purpose behind punishment. These stories are being told not for compassionate responses to horrendous experiences; they are stories that are lost to the world 'outside' because they happen 'inside' — an 'inside' that is hidden from view and so intended. The system's reliance on such opaqueness needs to be questioned.

To tell the stories as they happened is simply to remind oneself that there are lives being lived in ways that differ from ours, that things happen to people that do not happen to us, and that as women we need to know what these occurrences are. Just as men need to know what happens to women, all women, not just the women of our ilk. An underlying statement is that labelling individuals as criminals, or defining them according to their offences downplays the part that society plays through its indifference to the social conditions that foster much of the aberrant behaviour leading to 'crimes'. Excessive focus on individual responsibility in what the state recognises as crime, criminality, offending behaviour, and 'crimogenic factors' are all part of its method and plan of taking enough control to demonstrate state efficiency in creating a crime-free society for a supposedly larger collective. That the collective itself may have flaws that lead to certain behaviours is easily overlooked, not to mention the arbitrariness with which the state views certain social wrongs and the accompanying punitive steps taken (or not taken) to address those wrongs. As one legal expert put it, 'What is criminal is what suits the mood of the contemporary status quo' (Shankardass, 2000: 264).

Will all this information contribute to a realisation that leads to change? The real question is whether change is really desired. The justice package is neatly and tidily stitched up by 'experts' and reopening its seams is a formidable and arduous task not to be undertaken lightly, especially when vested interests are content with the status quo. The punitive part of this package, repressive and oppressive for the vulnerable, is where a status quo approach is damaging for many who just have to accept the rules they had no hand in making. We felt as though were peeling an onion, trying to get to the core layers, observing all the while how neatly the onion was packed, each layer sitting tightly on the other and yet distinct enough to be seen on its own. Layers and layers later, at the core, we found the woman waiting to speak and waiting for us to get through to her.

Peeling away the layers exposed things that were uncomfortable and unacceptable as part of the punitive process no matter which way one viewed it. There were visibly debilitated elderly

women who clearly did not belong there: pronouncements to
that effect (about persons over the age of 60) have been made
by judicial minds to no avail. There were women with cataract,
arthritis, depression, and not always because of a callous prison
administration, but because the policy on elderly prisoners was
deemed unclear and therefore not focused upon. The question
of children was another problem that baffled theoreticians and
practitioners alike — children locked up with mothers till the age
of six and sometimes beyond if there were disability problems.
The staff had their own problems. Just as the woman prisoner
had a life before she came to the prison as an offender, the women
who came as jailors and warders had 'normal', decent lives before
they adorned the 'khakhi' uniform and picked up the baton.
Not all of them were the demons they were often portrayed as it
was the system itself that was flawed. And it needed more than
an overhaul.

A final reason for this work is, above all, the quest for alternatives. The 'prison package', a hallowed colonial inheritance that
appears tidy and neutral, is neither one nor the other. If locking
people up serves a purpose, perhaps the purpose needs reviewing.
And if locking up is not the answer for *all* offenders, regardless
of whether they are a danger to society or not, then other ways
need to be explored. Have we run out of ideas that we cling to
something as brutal as incarceration? Is it because we believe it
is the most civilised way of dealing with people, all people, who
have offended against the 'Code' (and we have already that the
Code too had an agenda). Is imprisonment civilised just because
it enables us to say that we did not hang them, or beat them, or
mutilate their limbs, or stone them to death?

Our quest has been to suggest that prison as a place of punishment is nowhere near being as innocuous as it may seem. For a simple
and better understanding we have set it out thus: that there is the
body of the prison and there is the *spirit* of the prison. The former
relates to the physical facilities and amenities that prisons have
(or don't have) that make for the dignity for all those inside
(including staff). The latter, the spirit of the prison, is the relationships, the atmosphere and the management of the place that is
either conducive or not towards enabling prison to be considered

a civilised institution meant for decent human beings who have had far from decent lives (outside). Clearly then, if there is a special focus here, it is 'the mind and soul' of the institution and of the persons occupying it. Along with the body (the physical), this is an area (mind, personality, spirit) that has been grossly neglected in all the rhetoric that forms the substance of penal reform. It needs to be analysed, understood and addressed so that the fracturing of the mind, and/or the handling of already fractured minds, becomes a vital part of the debate for change and transformation.

It would be an incomplete treatise that did not take stock of the positives that have been attempted, albeit in recent times. For once it is possible to assert with a degree of satisfaction that some of the best ideas and recommendations to address many of the flaws and drawbacks that we highlighted have not been handed down from the west. Every feature of prison reform that one can think of has been cogently and clearly set out in the Indian Bible of prison reform — the Mulla Committee Report of 1983. Supplemented with Justice Krishna Iyer's renderings in the Report on Women Prisoners, nothing more remains to be said to set much of the old obsolete record straight. From physical prison conditions, rules and regulations, routines and practices to cases of special treatment, nothing has been missed. Recommendations to the judiciary relating to bail for women and a clear statement to the effect that alternatives to imprisonment are necessary have all been taken note of in these reports. More than twenty years on they form a vital part of the reformer's reference list and the policy-makers' quotable quotes. Meaningful implementation, however, is still a far cry.

Inevitably, our narratives reveal our own reactions, reflections and disillusionments: the stories would be incomplete without the perspectives and explanations of the interviewer about this 'closed' world removed from the everyday lives of most of us. No value judgement or high moral ground is intended in these reactions: it is a quest for understanding. If it betrays a subjectivity that should be avoided, it is so because most of the complexities of the situations are indeed subjective — for the narrator and the listener. It is as much about the subjects as about us, as part and parcel of the society that (mis)handles these subjects. Without further apology an admission should be made that perhaps there is an agenda after all in placing these stories before the world: the belief that prisons damage people, some more than others, and that those who are already damaged in society need recovery and rehabilitation and not imprisonment in harsh and insensitive environs, is the most vital feature of this work. If they are to be sent back to society two things need to happen: first society must be educated on the fact that they are not sick and abnormal, and are from amongst us and that they had experiences that we did not and they snapped. Secondly, if in paying the price for what we have defined as the ultimate blunder of their lives, they lose the nerve to live or to return to society as 'damaged goods', we would have lost more than we gained.

Do we have the courage to try and understand the complex problems associated with penal questions in all their ramifications? If the pointers show that we might be wrong in our contention that prison is best for *all*, are we ready to look for other ways? Does the law always get it right? The questions that emerge through the lives of these women are relevant in many parts of the world and without doubt in most countries of the developing world. Our starting point would have to be to concede that we haven't asked the right questions and therefore not arrived at the right answers. If the dilemmas posed in these narratives serve some remedial purpose by bringing us closer to the search for alternatives to imprisonment as punishment, then it may have been worthwhile after all.

▣

Note

The Supreme Court recently sought an amendment in the Indian Penal Code through a judicial order stating that dowry harassment be made a compoundable offence that allows willing families to settle their disputes and related problems outside court (Supreme Court, July 2010). The Court protested the excessive burden on the courts arising from matters that could easily be settled out of court but were not because the Penal Code stipulated that they were criminal matters to be decided by the criminal justice system's existing laws and procedures.

Dowry harassment (Section 498 A of the Indian Penal Code) is a non-bailable, non-compoundable offence under the Penal Code and carries a punishment of imprisonment for three years. The debate on dowry as a social malpractice that has affected women negatively has had a chequered history. The intervention of law has brought its own share of problems as the 'victims' and their relatives misuse the provisions of the statutes relating to dowry harassment and deaths to extract their own pound of flesh in marital disputes and their aftermath. Protagonists and antagonists of the laws and enactments relating to dowry line up on opposite sides to suggest the importance of law in handling social malpractices, only to back-track when pronouncements of this kind (Judicial Order of July 2010) are made by the highest judicial authorities, not on grounds of principle, but for reasons of convenience related to reducing the case load and unburdening the judicial machinery. Would such mechanically determined objectives obfuscate the real location of those problems in society that cause more damage to some than to others? The lives of these women are being shared to suggest what really happens to them, and why and how the formal system that addresses societal malfunction, whether individual or social, takes account of the differentials in society. Systems are set up for reasons that do not relate equally and similarly to everyone. When changes are sought they should be thought through to remedy earlier flaws of principle, rather than be speedily and expediently engineered to surmount awkward problems of functionality and pragmatism. Real people, real problems, real solutions — they can only be addressed through a logic that is agenda-free.

1

Saloni's Choice

◙

She's young; she's pretty and she seems sure of herself. She stands there in a well-fitted *kurta* — yellow, with a dark red patterned border on the sleeves, neck and hem-line. Her *dupatta* is maroon with a small yellow *bandni* print. She has it draped across her bosom and repeatedly adjusts it as she moves across the room to the chair I have indicated. Her fingernails and toenails are painted bright red and she seems to have spent time trying to look good. Somehow if a woman tries to look attractive in jail she is asking for trouble, particularly from the staff. She gets more than her share of distasteful adjectives from one and all, delivered in downbeat muted tones, and she either grins and bears them, or brazenly retorts.

I know that Saloni has been arrested under the Prevention of Immoral Trafficking Act (see note at the end of the chapter). So, I also know that if a woman is in prison for a 'sexual offence' or, as the law would label it, 'immoral trafficking', she doesn't stand a chance of being accepted. Prisons may classify prisoners according to their legal offences but a prison's social grouping, especially in a women's prison, is not all about legal offences: it's about them having crossed the barriers of social and moral taboos set out over the ages by custom, tradition and often religion, and are expected to be a stronger sanction than the law. Such offenders just don't fit in with the others — whether they are viewed through the eyes of those in charge of them, or those who are locked up with them. Every nuance of their behaviour is noted — how they dress, how they talk, who they move about with, whom comes to visit them, what they eat, how they eat; the scrutiny is constant.

I look at Saloni curiously without betraying any emotion at all. She still hasn't sat down; I ask her to sit and offer her some water.

She declines with a shake of her head. She is so young and really quite attractive. Dark, almost beautiful, she has a rich crop of hair, neatly braided, and she keeps fiddling with the braid as it hangs across her left shoulder, down her waist and almost into her lap.

It seems that Saloni is not about to start her conversation the way that many others do. She sits there determined to be a little resistant.

'How old are you Saloni'? I ask.

She looks at me almost indignantly. 'Does it matter', she replies almost cockily. 'Why should my age be your concern? I'm here aren't I and you probably want to know what I was booked for, how did they catch me, what I do in the prison and so on. I might tell you that, but other things are really irrelevant to your work and I am not interested in a long conversation with you the way other persons here may be. You will probably be interested in preaching to me about morality assuming that I have no clue about such issues. But I am not here to be converted.'

I do feel the need to protest. 'No Saloni, I think you have it all wrong. I am not about to make you a guinea pig in my project. Yes, my objective is to set up counselling units in our jails, especially for vulnerable prisoners, but I am not here just to make you a statistic in my book. And for us counselling does not mean preaching, moralising, or judging. This is intended to be confidential activity conducted without judgement and with utmost professionalism. It might help us all understand why people do the things they do and above all, my colleagues and I want to understand, as women, the compulsions that structure women's lives. It might also enable you to express what you may have kept bottled up inside because there was no one to listen.'

'I really am not interested', Saloni retorts. 'I do what I think I have to do when I have to do it. And my reasons and compulsions are neither important nor comprehensible for you. So, forget about helping me. Just leave it. You asked all of us to come once to your room, so I have come. I am not likely to come again. I know how everyone views our types. Yes, and we are a "type" because you call us a type; the law calls us a type. So, let's just leave it at that.' She makes her way to the door, and I still beseech her to stay. But she is gone before I utter another word. Clearly, she is bitter.

This was not how I had seen myself conduct the conversation. I was concerned about how I would have a dialogue with someone whose world was so removed from mine. How was I going to try to build Saloni's confidence in me and my colleagues? As it is, I was having a problem with intruding into prisoners' lives, having asked myself repeatedly how I would like my private life probed by a stranger. But then, how can anyone ever really know the 'why' of the offences of all those persons dumped into 'lock ups' and forgotten about by the rest of the world that has decided simply that they are criminals and prison is where they belong.

Two days pass and I get a chance to talk to several other women in the jail, about their experiences here, where they come from. A handful (five or six) of women visit the room each day as they have been told that I am here with my colleagues to listen and to 'chat'.

Mid-morning on a rainy Tuesday, the curtain of the room is lifted and Saloni steps in. There is an elderly woman already with me at the time and I don't want to send her away. So, I ask Saloni to wait outside or come back in an hour. She winces and goes out and I am desperate to get her back. Perhaps I should have let her come and asked the elderly woman to go and come back later. But that wouldn't be right. So I wait in hope.

I finish my conversation with the older woman and assure her about confidentialities again. I ask her to come back whenever she wishes but with a proviso that she must not lie to me at any point: the session has seen more than a fistful of lies. She leaves and I am just about to get up to make a round of the jail when Saloni steps in. Clearly, she had been waiting for the other woman's departure. She comes in, and as I beckon her to sit I notice she has a slight limp. She pulls up her knee slightly to assume a comfortable sitting position, and then gives me a glance. She then quickly lowers her eyes. This is certainly a change from her previous visit.

'I'm sorry that I was so sharp the other day. I really get so tired of the inane questions people ask of me. Anyone whose offences have anything to do with sexual activity seems to arouse not just curiosity but a prying inquisitiveness that borders on disdain and contempt. It is as if they want to hear what they want to hear. There is such a burdensome background to everything — how can one explain to those who are not likely to understand.'

'And you thought I was yet another one of those. No reason for you to think otherwise', I say.

'No, now I do have reason to think otherwise — that is why I have come. Otherwise, I would have stayed away. I have heard people in the prison talk about you all and they seemed happy, so I wanted to unload my burdens too.'

I smile and think that she almost did too. 'So, are we going to have a free and frank chat then? Or am I still a suspect?'

'I really haven't had a free and frank chat in years, so I don't even know if I know what that means anymore. But I still need to know why you are interested', she insists.

'You know even I don't really know why I am interested. But I am, that I do know. And I am passionately interested, that too I know. Is it because I am a woman? May be. Is it because I have a daughter not much older than you, I think and I wonder. May be. And it may also be that after I talk to you, I can even tell you why I am so interested in you, your life, and your reasons. Right now I can't really answer your question with honesty because I am at a loss, just as you are when I ask you questions that you may find awkward.'

'What do you want to know then? And how much time have you got to listen to my pathetic story?'

'What I want to know is more about you, and I have all the time to listen. I must warn you also that it is possible that lurking inside me are all those innate prejudices and the built-in biases that come with my 'baggage': I can tell myself that I have got rid of them, but they may sneak in from time to time. So, let's just say we need to be patient with each other and you need to see me with the same openness that I wish to see you with. Right?'

I look at her, quizzing her with an expression of assurance that may or may not register.

'You wanted to know my age? I am twenty-two.'

'Holy Moses', I whisper to myself.

'*Jee? Kya kaha aapne?* [What did you say?] Are you horrified or what?'

I have obviously interjected inappropriately. She is too young and I *am* horrified. But I needn't have been so quick to express the horror. Just what I had promised I would not do. But it did hit me.

'No', I say sheepishly. 'Not horrified. Just a little saddened. You are younger than my children and I assume that all mothers wish the best for their children.'

'Nonsense! That is not so at all. I only wish people didn't take all these things for granted. How do you assume that every mother is looking at things that way? Well, here's the horror part if you wanted to be horrified. My mother sent me into this work, if work is what one calls it. Is that horrifying enough for you? So, you see — so much for you people's assumptions.'

I sit silent with my head bowed for several moments. She can see I am perturbed. I am disturbed, and yes, I am now truly horrified. I can feel her silent stare and she clearly knows my thoughts. As I lift my head I see tears in her eyes. There is no need for me to say anything, this is the moment signifying a feeling on both sides that I had to be excused for my ignorance even if I needed to be humbled for that brief minute. I was humbled and felt from that point on that we were equal, for I was not in any way superior in my understanding or so-called knowledge of the world. I had made some fundamentally erroneous assumptions and I was truly and rightly put in my place — me and my middle-class morality.

'I can't pass judgement on your mother. But I am interested to know how such a thing came to pass. I must know — I must know what passes through a mother's mind when she feels she has to suggest to her daughter that her body can be a source of living not by working it for what is conventionally called "work" but for sexual work. There has to be a reason that is very compelling even if repelling.'

'I don't know all these intricacies: If you say "work" is legitimate then this is treated by some as "work". You people refer to us as "sex-workers". So, what is all this about conventional work? You need to earn and you find the quickest way — so long as it is not thieving or robbing from other people does it matter? All I know is that when a family desperately needs money, they set about ensuring that all those in the family who are able-bodied somehow, anyhow, work and get that money. In our case this had to be done on the basis of urgency.' She is getting a bit agitated about the fact that she is having once again to justify to someone why she does what she does: addressing again that semi-moral plane. This is work, that is not. This is good work, that is not. Why does she have to do this? While I can feel her frustration and know what is passing through her mind, she is distressed and uneasy.

I apologise. 'I didn't intend to take you on this "explain yourself" path. Yes, it is about earning, but you can't blame me if questions arise in my mind and I just wonder if they arrived in someone else's mind as well, someone like your mother or you for that matter. That is all. No, I am not judging. I am baffled beyond my own belief. What prompts a mother of a twenty-year-old to send her daughter down this path of earning money? *What?* Am I so wide off the mark to ask the question?'

I am obviously sounding concerned and perplexed to the point of being angry, an emotion I am trying hard to suppress. But she detects it before I am able to conceal my querying eyebrows and my puckered lips, and before I remove the hand that has touched my forehead in dismay. How shall I tell her how desperate I feel that I am unable to turn the clock back and wipe out all that had happened, or offer some alternatives that would remove the 'label' that she must carry for all her life — and label it is. Those in jail for violating the PITA (Prevention of Immoral Trafficking Act) regulation find the proverbial finger pointing viciously at them. The moral condemnation and social ostracism that destroyed these 'criminals' (or 'victims') follows them in here as well.

I need a rest from this conversation: I have (erroneously for a counsellor who proclaims a certain neutrality from partisanship and emotion) started getting entangled in the sensitivities and subjectivities that inevitably accompany my own ideas of motherhood and womanhood: I am looking at this girl as if … clearly I am going along another route!

I take a break and offer her water and have some myself. I ask her if she would like to carry on, or would she like to come back later, may be even tomorrow. This is a risk I am taking but there is a moment, a juncture, at which such a dialogue must stop and be resumed later.

She smiles. 'I may not be here tomorrow. After all we do get bailed out you know. So, I can take a break if you wish: but then there are even chances that we [and there are more here for the same 'offence'] will get bail in a day or so and whereas I am not usually glad to talk to people, I have learnt about you from others here and I do believe you want to know and you are not about to condemn us for life.'

She is right. I have more to lose than she if I don't take this opportunity. I need to keep the exchange going. There are many girls in the jail for the same offences. But disregarding her earlier attempts at being cocky, this girl actually believes our conversation might be of use. Others were cocky and rudely dismissive; assured of being out in a few days they were less interested in interacting politely with anyone.

'Yes. You are right. You could be out on bail tomorrow and far be it from me to grudge you that. And I will always regret the fact that I would not have learnt from you why this happens and how you and your mother feel about it. I wish I could meet your mother — but perhaps it is best I don't for I may betray the same accusatory tone that I might have adopted with you had we not had the candid exchange at the beginning of our conversation. In fact, I may have been more accusatory towards her for I am a mother and would have difficulty concealing my maternal indignation if I faced her. So, let it be between you and me then.'

'So, tell me about you. How many brothers and sisters are you? Where is your father? What does he do for a living? How educated are you? What kind of life did you have? Were you a happy child? Was there unpleasantness in your home?' I had to stop even though I could have lined up another half a dozen questions for her: I didn't want to inundate her with so many queries about her past unless and until I had had a glimpse of that past.

It's always difficult to find a delicate way of getting into someone's life, someone's past. I couldn't stop reminding myself that this was an intrusion at the best of times, and in cases like this when there is such a baggage of mistrust and prejudice on both sides, one always seems to need greater doses of delicacy and acceptability than I was managing to muster up. The need to measure the words and the silences was clear enough and yet one wished for a certain amount of freedom in the exchanges but treading cautiously was probably a wiser choice and that is what I needed to do.

'If you don't want to answer something, tell me and I won't press you: it is your personal life and you have a right to keep it personal.' I am hoping I will elicit something extra if I start with the reassurances. There is no telling, but I somehow feel she will say something; how true all of it is will be for me to evaluate.

'My father left us for another woman when I was about eight; my brother and sister were five and three. He was a mechanic and worked at a garage and earned enough to feed us. For a couple of years I went to a local primary school . I loved school and made friends and thought I would be able to work in some half-decent place after a few years in school. Then all the problems started. There was a teashop across the road from the garage where my father worked where people in the locality had tea. It was "run" by a couple, and the routine was that twice a day the wife would cross the road and serve the tea to the garage employees. She often just sat down while they drank tea and chit chatted with them.'

'Over time, I believe, my father became attracted towards her and she too responded by hanging around longer in each tea session. It is not difficult to surmise what followed. I was too young to know what triggered off the unpleasantness at home and what shape and form it took. These details of the whole story were only told to me by my mother a couple of years ago.'

There is a long pause and I am not about to interrupt it. She is fiddling with her *dupatta*, then with her braid, and then looks up and says somewhat impatiently and desperately, 'Why should I be remembering all these things when so much has happened to *me* since then?'

I don't want to rush in, so I stay quiet for a moment. The silence continues. Do I break it or should I wait till she might? She answers that for me by saying, 'I suppose I have to face these realities from time to time, otherwise I will become a cog in the machine and won't even rethink what I am doing.'

That is what I want to hear — the part about the rethink. This is the feature that, for me, is so crucial and I wonder how we came to it so soon. But there is a pause again.

And then she speaks, very softly, 'My mother worked in the house and was a hard-working woman. She slogged each day to make sure that we were all well-fed and clothed and had dreams that all of us would go to school. I went to school for two years or may be three, and I remember her making my braids and sending me off with a black slate and chalk pieces and some notebooks. My siblings stayed at home and she went about her house-keeping and errands.'

'One day she was on an errand and passed by the garage and found my father cosily seated with the lady from the tea shop, merrily having tea and *samosas*. She went home unnoticed and was uncomfortable about the incident, but did not say anything to my father. Evidently, she decided to visit the garage area again and then accost him about his relationship with the woman.

'Unfortunately, her next visit was only a week later and meanwhile the relationship was fast becoming something that even the other woman's husband was worried about. When my mother went the next time round my father was not there. She asked his workmates where he was and they smiled and said, "You don't want to know". But she did, and pushed them into revealing where he was. They said he was probably at the house of the tea-stall owner. But the tea-stall owner was sitting right there selling cups of tea across the road. So, my mother decided to go to his home anyway. She entered his cottage and clearly was aghast by what she saw; she ran back to the house hastily and cried and cried and cried.'

There is a long pause again, and then Saloni says, 'I will come back and tell you the rest. It is getting too much for me and I want to stop, please.'

I watch her leave the room limping and remember that I wanted to ask her how she developed that limp. Next time I think, and hope there is a next time.

Saloni doesn't come the next day and I fear she might have been released on bail. And then I feel guilty for grudging her the freedom that she is legally entitled to. So, I dismiss it all from my mind for then.

A few other women come for short sessions — some come primarily to suggest that I apprise them of their legal rights because they are not well-informed, and others to say that visits by family and friends are sometimes not permitted even though they come from long distances. I ask them to report these to the Welfare Officer who is the person to be told of these failings in the system.

I make some notes and also record Saloni's visit in detail. As I pen them down, I am again foxed by the statement she has only cursorily made about being sent into 'sex work' by her mother. What does it take for a mother to send a daughter into this 'occupation' for the money? It proves too baffling for me, and I feel exhausted by the questions I start to ask myself. Is it because one is on the brink of a crisis — of survival? How many more mothers are there who might have done the same? Are there more? I find myself going round in circles. Clearly, I am looking at the world, everyone's world, with my rose-tinted glasses, and no answers will be forthcoming if I continue to do that. So, I leave it at that; let's see what tomorrow brings I tell myself.

She comes the next day: this time in blue. There is a smile on her face. 'We have been given bail and I will go tomorrow.'

'Good.' I am genuinely pleased, perhaps because I feel assured that she has come to talk despite the fact that she knows she will be gone the next day. I still don't want to push the talking session. I feel remiss about expecting her to conclude what she had started with me. But fortunately, she breaks the silence herself.

'Aunty', she says to me. 'I have a feeling you are really disturbed by what I have said to you so far. I am assuming that you are truly concerned for me. Unfortunately, I can't say that I will be able to extricate myself from this way of earning my living. But who knows.'

I am not sure how I should respond to this and decide to carry on eliciting the story of her beginnings. She has come back to reassure me and perhaps also expects some kind of understanding of her circumstances. I am not sure.

'So, when your mother discovered just how far gone your father was with this relationship, what did she do? Was she bitter, angry, desperate, saddened? Or maybe all of these.'

'She confronted him that very day and there was a big fight. She abused him and called him all kinds of names. He was also abusive and when things got out of hand he struck her and she fell. I still remember the day because she fell on the floor and was bleeding and I didn't know what to do. Then he picked up his things and left the house. My mother struggled to her feet and sat for hours weeping. Nothing was cooked in our house that evening and all of the next day, I think. We were so hungry and my siblings were crying all the time (perhaps from hunger). The following day my mother suddenly got up and cleaned the gash on her arm and tied it with a clean cloth, and then with superhuman energy swept and tidied the whole house and cooked a meal. We had so much food that day it was incredible. I can still remember what we ate: *daal, aloo-gobhi ki sabji, paratha*, mango pickle and some *raita*. Then she cleared the things away and asked me to sit and watch over the younger children and not to open the door to anyone while she was away. And she left the house presumably on an errand.'

Saloni has a faraway look in her eyes as she reminisces and she seems tired. I offer her water; she drinks it and wants to finish her story.

'My mother came back after sunset and I know I was petrified because it was getting dark. But she sat down, drank water, and said to me: "From today you will have to take care of your brother and sister: I have got myself some work and I will have to go for some hours each day to earn for our food. I'm afraid you will have to stop going to school and will have to help me manage the house. Your father has let us all down and I cannot forgive him. If I had done something like that he would have killed me without thinking twice. But that is the lot of women." And she wept and wept. I too wept that day because I was not going to be able to go to school. That was the last day I went to school and I was miserable.'

'So, you can read and write a little', I ask her.

'Yes, but hardly enough to be of any use.'

And she continues, 'And so the years passed and my sister and brother grew older. My sister turned six and then seven and I decided to teach her a little. By the time I was thirteen my brother was almost ten years old and my mother figured he really should go to school to be able to earn a livelihood in the future. So, he was sent to school. Of course, all this cost money and we didn't have enough. So, I told my mother I would also earn something. She said "No" and I was angry.

'Why my father did what he did, and just what effect it had on my mother and indeed all of us at that time were really questions that only arose in my mind in a very fundamental way when I was older, not then at the time of the dramatic events. But I know that it dramatically and drastically changed our lives forever.'

I sit listening to a life unfolding before me and know that this is how it happens to many. But the crucial part is still to come. What events pushed her (or pushed her mother) into the situation that ensnared Saloni the way it did. And that bit about the limp. Clearly, there is more in the intervening years and things only get worse.

'When my brother went to school I started to take my [seven-year-old] sister along and began asking around if someone wanted me to do some jobs that they could pay me for. My sister was sworn to secrecy and finally I did find something: someone not too far from where we lived wanted me to come and clean her house and wash her dishes each day for two hours and was willing to pay ₹75 a month. I had no clue whether it was right or not but I took the work and each day carted my sister with me, did the work and came back well before my mother or brother did.'

'Plucky girl', I think to myself. And she proceeds.

'One day I was washing the woman's dishes and a large glass bowl slipped from my hand and broke. I was so frightened I couldn't breathe. The woman came into the kitchen and was red with rage. She said it was a very expensive bowl ('cut glass' she called it) and was I blind or what. She picked up a *danda* and beat me so hard on my back and legs I couldn't stand. Then she threw me out of the house and I saw I was badly bruised especially on my legs: there was no blood but my back and legs ached all over and I could not move. I was unable to walk and at that point my sister rushed home to see if someone could help bring me back. There was no one. An hour or more later my mother came and took me home and was so angry I thought I was going to get another thrashing. While she scolded me she kept crying and saying, "Did you think I would let you all starve? Why did you go and start working, you silly girl?"'

Clearly, that is when she got the injury that left this limp. Must have been a vicious thrashing administered with uncontrolled anger. And all because a glass bowl broke. You broke my bowl I'll break your limb — is that how the logic goes, I ask myself? But who's to answer such questions that fade into nothingness with time, that great healer that is supposed to heal everything. But does it heal a broken limb — clearly not.

Nor do things necessarily get better with time. Reassurances abound about things getting better, but they never do. Saloni continues her story and it reinforces my belief that these are only mollifying myths about time being a great healer.

'Some more time passed', she said, 'and things only got worse. My mother kept working hard, but as we grew older our needs increased. Books for my brother, more clothes and other things for all of us — we lived from hand to mouth but carried on like that for a few years.'

I am waiting for the critical point in her narrative that was going to spell disaster. And it came.

'One evening my mother returned from work and said, "I have no job from tomorrow, they asked me not to come back. Someone else eased me out of my job and unfortunately the employers did not respond to my pleas — they were very casual and said they would like to engage the other person". That was a depressing night for all of us, and my mother and I were particularly disturbed. There was no light at the end of the tunnel. None at all.'

'Many days passed, and one day a lady who lived near the place where my mother had worked came to visit. She and her husband ran a guesthouse and had seen my mother come in and out of the house. They learnt that she had been fired and wanted to know if my mother was interested in working for them. They might also have a job for me, but about that they would talk later. My mother readily agreed and soon enough she was earning again. They paid reasonably well and we were back on our feet at last.'

'But good times don't last, do they?', she said. 'Another catastrophe had to come: my mother got run over by a car while returning from work and sustained serious injuries on her legs: broken bones and all that. She was hospitalised for weeks and when she did come out there was no way she was going to be able to walk without an aid. That was the end of that. The guesthouse owners had paid for her hospitalisation and treatment so that was a blessing. But there was no work awaiting her.'

Something tells me that the bolt is coming just about now. I almost don't want to hear it.

'Soon after, the lady of the guesthouse came to see my mother one day. I was sent to make tea for her and she talked to my mother. She asked about her health and assured her that if there was a problem she would help out, so she need have no worries. Then she said that there was work for me at the guesthouse. After that she lowered her voice and I couldn't really hear what she was saying. She did all the talking and my mother was absolutely quiet.'

There is a silence and a tense moment for both of us. She knows and I know: She is fiddling with her *dupatta* and I, with my pen. Where can one hide reality even if one wants to? And how does one face it when it stares you in the face. Is life really full of choices? Or are choices the prerogative of the well off? All the while that she has been telling me the story that has to come to this moment of truth I have been thinking about how I would react to such a choice even if it was not identical to that faced by Saloni's mother. But the question is so unreal and I almost mock myself for making the comparison.

'You see', she says at last, breaking an awkward silence, one of many that follow, 'the guesthouse is one of many that have sprung up with the expanding small-time businesses that so many people are doing now in developing cities. There are guests from outside the city who come and stay and conduct their businesses. They are not big-timers like those who stay at five-star hotels but middle-of-the-range businessmen. They come almost regularly because this is their business beat and they frequent the same guesthouses.

In the evening they need to be entertained and that entertainment is what she was arranging; clearly, she convinced my mother that I would be 'safe' and that it would be very rewarding.'

Safe. Everyone has a different notion of what is safe. What is safe? I am not even sure whether I expressed my anger under my breath, or was audible enough because the next thing Saloni is saying to me is: 'One would imagine that a woman can hardly be safe with alien men around. And alien they were because they were from out of town, so there was a certain anonymity assured for them. But I am from around here — clearly she had assured my mother about my safety.'

'When my mother spoke to me about it the next day, I was numb. I was old enough to know what was being suggested here and although my mother kept saying "They want you to serve these guests drinks and then dress nicely in clothes that they will provide, and you have to keep the guests company in the evenings and that is all." I knew it was not really respectable even in my mother's eyes. I wouldn't be calling the shots, so what is my mother thinking. I was so baffled, so confused and so sceptical, but just didn't know how to express what I was thinking.'

Was she naïve, I say to myself? What was she thinking, this mother? While Saloni talks I feel agitated and physically sick: nausea and a fast pulse rate. But I have to stay calm. I manage, but I feel flushed and restless. I increase the speed of the fan and drink some water. She is quiet again.

She resumes, before the thought of prompting her comes to my mind. It is clear she has not delved into these memories for a long time and wants to get some things off her chest. She heaves a sigh, one that says so much, and carries on.

'First I begged my mother to let a few days pass and then we can talk about it. But my mother said, "They want you to start two days from now and they want you to move there for a few days. They will pay you ₹10,000 each week. Ten thousand, Saloni. It would take me six months to make that were I to resume working, which I can't. They will buy you fine things and then you can come home from time to time. As a gesture of good faith she will give us the first ten thousand before she takes you. Think

about it Saloni, think!" That was my mother. She was so earnest
I wondered if she had lost her mind, or was she really so simple
that she was letting her nineteen-year-old-go where, in less dire
straits, she would never dream of sending her.'

In a word, the mother was suggesting that only Saloni could
get them out of the mess they were in — the mess that left them
without food, and perhaps even shelter, and without a future. I
have an urge to burst into indignation. It is not my place to, and
I hold back again. This is not a moment for indignation. There
are complex issues involved here and simple emotional reactions
would be out of place.

'So, you see the whole process of deciding was not melodra-
matic, and yet it was dramatic alright. There was no hysteria,
oddly enough. That is what made it worse: It made me squirm
and led to a whole series of struggles within myself. My mother
was posing it as a choice, but actually there was no choice really,
was there?'

No, there wasn't really a choice. You need to kill your soul and
spirit to keep your body alive — that was the proposition and
the answer was almost being provided. So, where does she go
from there? It was an unimaginable amount of money for the
family no doubt — ten thousand rupees a week — forty thousand
a month, and the promise of more to come. This was a dream at
one level, but at another it was a nightmare. It was putting all
beliefs and convictions of womanhood to the test surely. All of
a mother's life is spent protecting daughters from 'wolves'; here
was a daughter being sent into the wolf's den. What was the
mother thinking?

Yes, she was incapacitated and hence unable to provide for
the family. Choices are a luxury and not everyone is lucky enough
to have them. But this? Or was she in denial about what really
happens when girls are employed to provide company for male
guests as part of their social entertainment? Or had the guesthouse
owner made the whole proposition sound so innocuous that
Saloni's mother genuinely believed it was not something that
could be labelled 'bad' by society on the one hand and illegal by

the state at another. Clearly, all this had not formed part of the thought process then, or perhaps at any time. It was certainly engaging my thoughts, including the thought that perhaps we of the privileged classes think too much.

Saloni senses the plethora of questions and wanderings engaging my mind. She looks in all directions and her eyes are brimming. Perhaps she is thinking of the day when she actually left home for this 'assignment'. All those memories and images are probably clouding her mind and this is naturally not a pleasant walk down memory lane. I look at her and can see her at the age of eighteen or nineteen — girls go to college at that age with hopes of a bright future; she went to a place where only desperation leads.

'I have viewed my mother in so many different lights I can't tell you. As a child she was my sense of security. She fed me, sheltered me, cared for me and was what all mothers I saw around were. As I grew older and my father left us after that incident, I pitied her and therefore loved her differently. I felt she needed something special to compensate for the hardships that had resulted from my father's misdemeanours. So, I pitched in at every turn and that was the spirit in which I went out and found myself a job and worked at that house where I broke a glass bowl and got beaten up.'

The brimming eyes are overflowing now and she is visibly distressed. She isn't so sure she should be baring all and yet feels choked because she is so full of emotion. I get up and close the door so that I don't have any visitors while I am with Saloni.

Saloni continues: 'When my mother got fired in her first job it was difficult for her. The guesthouse people employed her and she was relatively happy again. Then she had the accident and that turned our world topsy-turvy. She was so depressed I could not bear it. We spent a hard time, even though, fortunately, her medical treatment and care were paid for [by the guesthouse lady]. But she went through a rough patch and I only looked at her helplessly all that time. I was desperate to see her normal again but that wasn't going to happen. So, I viewed her as an invalid almost — and with a feeling of impatience.

'And then I was presented yet another view of my mother — and this for me was the most perplexing. I knew the anxieties and difficulties of her life, and yet it was not possible for me to understand this turn in her thinking. I can't say I hated her then. I was just confused, perhaps because I myself only had a vague idea of what was in store for me. But later, as I lived the life I had been pushed into, I developed the strangest feelings towards my mother.'

It is not easy or pleasant for her to say what she is going to say. I can see we are on the verge of either a collapse of communication or an unravelling that is going to be devastating.

'Have you any idea how we are enticed into doing things that we may not want to do at these places? There are usually at least half a dozen girls in each guesthouse. Some cooperate all too well. They are "seasoned" it is said. It is their job to get the likes of us in line — if one method doesn't work try another. We are given fineries to wear and good food to eat with cold drinks [I had my first ever Pepsi Cola at the guest house]. There is excitement all round on the first day when someone joins. The cynical ones know what is coming and give hints to that effect to newcomers; the ones in charge present a more than rosy picture.'

'You don't start meeting the guests till the second day after your arrival. Once you are settled in, you are told a few things. How to dress, how much make-up to use, how to talk, where to be, and then you are shown a few dance steps. It is exciting *and* scary. The guests come in groups and eat and drink. Sometimes we are around the tables and at times a floorshow is arranged. The lady in charge is aware of people's intentions. Some of the men indicate their preference for particular girls and they are brought to the men. Some just chat. Some see how things are progressing and before you know it have booked their rooms for the night and take the girls "upstairs". Their financial transactions are with the in-charge who submits all accounts to the owners and together they apportion the earnings. Clearly, they make a good profit and we are given relatively minuscule amounts compared to their earnings.'

I must appear visibly uncomfortable and Saloni is prompted to say: 'Ma'am the worst part is still to come and you are already so disturbed.'

How shall I tell her that for me now this is for real: it is not some imaginary scenario. I am looking at her in all the roles she has described and feeling bad for her.

'For a week I was simply attending to the guests as a hostess — moving around as they ate and drank, some of them talked to me and some did try to put their arms around me. Then came the real thing, what I had dreaded all of that week. There was a man who had come from Bangalore on business: he was in the shoe business and was there for new markets. He was about forty and wore a thick gold chain I remember. He carried a packet of cigarettes in his hand all the time. I was asked to look after him. That meant ensuring that he ate and drank what he wanted and was generally kept amused through the evening. He had a friend with him and they were busy among themselves too.'

'I first thought I could handle that much and that was all it would be. I even made an effort to be pleasant and congenial. Then he went to the in-charge and whispered something and she came to me and said I should accompany him to his room. I said I really wasn't well and could I be excused that night: "please, please", I kept saying. But "no" was the answer. So, I was taken upstairs and he took me inside his room. He sat me down and said he would be back in a minute. He came out of the bathroom changed into a kurta-pyjama, all perfumed, and started pouring drinks for both. I said I did not drink. He carried on anyway. He then gave me the glass and almost forced me to have a few sips. Then he said have more and took the glass and forced me to have it. He then came and sat beside me and started to fondle me. I moved away and he came closer. I was doomed. You see we had been told that if on account of any of us the guesthouse lost any clients, then not only would we NOT get any payment we would be asked to leave.'

'And that was the day I crossed over. He turned on the music — loud enough to smother any protestations I might make — and forcibly took off my garments. I clung to my blouse but there was no stopping him. He exposed his sexual organ and said luridly "Have you seen this before? It is a special thing that women crave"! I was in a stupor. I think, I passed out when he pushed me on the bed and raped me. Isn't that what it was?'

Am I meant to answer that question: I hope not because I am speechless. This is not some explicit movie I am watching: it is a young girl's first-hand *real* experience. But Saloni is not waiting for a reply.

'He was sexually quite violent and just carried on and on and on', she said. 'I had never had sex before, naturally, given my upbringing, and apart from the trauma it was painful and unpleasant. I was in a daze, perhaps from the drink and also from the shock. I hated him for it and then I started hating myself. I sat there afterwards in a trance with some clothes on and some off and he lay there pleased and smoked a cigarette and soon I heard him snoring. I dressed and left and I don't think I have wept like I did that night. That is the night I first had a feeling of hate for my mother. Why, I kept saying, why did you do this to me?'

'The next day was my day for going home to see my mother and the lady who ran the guesthouse gave me the money she had promised. I was not really keen to go home, but she said she had promised my mother the money and it should be done, adding, "You know how much difficulty your mother is in". I felt outraged. Difficulty? Mother? What about me? Do you know what you just subjected me to? Have you got a daughter, I wanted to ask her? Would you have put her to this if you were in a bad way? But that was again a hypothetical question. It was not going to happen, so why would she take herself through the paces of figuring that one out.'

'I went in an auto-rickshaw to my home. I hurt so much between my legs and felt so sore, I could hardly walk straight. My sister and brother were overjoyed to see me and I burst into tears when they hugged me. They had no clue where I had gone and where I was coming form, and wouldn't let go of me. I took refuge in their hugs because all I wanted to do was cry and cry and cry, and I did. And they had no idea why I was weeping so much because to them I looked good, well-dressed and smartly turned out.'

'Then we went inside where my mother was sitting and I wished her. No, I did not give her a hug and she didn't ask for one either. It was the strangest meeting between a mother and daughter and one that I am not likely to forget. I went to her reclining chair and sat down near by. I asked her how she was and she said, "Well!" She didn't ask me how I was. How could she? I then dipped into my bag and gave her an envelope with the ten thousand rupees. She looked at it but didn't put out her hand for it. I got up and put it in her lap and sat down again.'

'"Are you hungry?", she asked after a long pause. "I have some food in the kitchen. It is your favourite *paratha*!"'

'No. I am not hungry.'

' "Let me give you some tea". She limped precariously towards the kitchen to make tea that I didn't really want. As I saw her limp her way across many thoughts came and went inside my head. The first emotion as always was one of pity, soon overtaken by so much bitterness I wanted to scream out aloud. I was so bewildered with contradictory thoughts that I didn't hear her limp back with the tea precariously balanced in one hand and her stick in the other.'

'Why did you do it mother'? The words just came to my lips as she handed me the cup. 'Why?'

'She couldn't look me in the face and went and sat down, slumping into the chair for fear of falling if she did it slowly. She sat there and then placed the *saree pallu* across her face and wept. I don't think I have ever seen my mother weep so much — not even when my father walked out on her. She was so full of remorse, and guilt and shame — and what was paining her is that she had put me on a road of no return; I stood beside her, rigid and dazed. I was too stunned by all that had happened to me over the last twenty-four hours and she probably knew it too.'

'That was the last time I saw my mother. I don't know if she even knows I am in jail after the police raid on the guesthouse. The things that had started happening there were not really acceptable at all. I was caught in a storm of unpleasantness every day.

The people who came were so weird I couldn't bear it. But what could I do? I am condemned for life. I think people in this prison who have committed crimes that involve taking another's life are not so condemned as I am. I hear staff say of them, "There were compelling circumstances under which she killed. She will never do it again." But no one will ever say that of me. All that I hear is *dhandha karti hai* [She is in *that* business]. It is supposed to be unspeakable, unmentionable and I am scarred for ever.'

Yes, I thought, you are, and there's nothing that can wipe away *that* past. Then she catches me unawares: 'Will nothing wipe that slate clean?' (I am now hearing in my mind Lady Macbeth's lines: What, will these hands ne'er be clean?) I am hoping, I don't really have to answer that. For those around her have already done that: No, the answer is no.

'When I was arrested along with three other girls you should have seen how the arresting police persons handled us. One treats stray dogs on the street better. I am now told that women have to arrest women because there has to be decent handling. Well, there were two men and a woman. They came armed with their batons and barged into the rooms. Fortunately I was not in a compromising position just then, but other girls were. They actually said to one of them: "Hey, you prostitute, are you going to get dressed or shall I take you to the Station naked?' When the girl said something like "have some shame", the woman constable said to her, "Shame! You are talking of shame? Do you know what shame is? Look at you with your breasts and private parts exposed, you are talking of shame!" Then both constables [the man and the woman] pulled her up physically and made her stand in front of the others as she was. Even my eyes went down but not those of the two constables.'

'When we reached the police station they opened the registers and took our details. "Hardly worth asking their names just put them down as 'prostitutes'." The little caution they had to exercise at the guesthouse vanished and all kinds of taunts began. "Hey", said the male constable, "how about me? I'm available too, you know and we are almost alone here. No one will even know. Oh, but you will want to be paid. Well, I can give you a few bucks. Will that do? Or do you work for higher rates?" I could go on and on with the kind of heckling we were all subjected to. It was almost a relief to be brought to the prison the next day.'

Somehow what she says doesn't shock me. It makes my stomach turn that those who are supposedly the protectors in society can be so base. Having faced women with similar stories of their treatment at police stations I can only lament that this is how it is. Over the years that I have been associating with jail officers and prisoners I am told again and again that many women are brought here under the PITA law. Police personnel almost enjoy bringing them in. What is more, they know that being a 'bailable' offence, the women would probably be released in a short time. There have been cases where police personnel have been vicious enough to stick "drug dealing" charges along with PITA, knowing the latter to be a non-bailable offence. Saloni is lucky that a drug charge has not been clubbed along with the immoral trafficking charge. She could have been here for ages.

She spent a little over two years at the guesthouse: I shudder to think how each day passes for her and for all those girls who have left home, not for another home but for a hell-house that has to be called 'home' because they have lost all sense of belonging to a real home. These are thoughts that cloud the mind; there is no clarity and that is frustrating for a person who actually believes (perhaps erroneously) that perhaps there is some room for reversal, some alteration in these rigidly set patterns. It is going against the current, but is that so impossible?

Will she go back to the guesthouse? Will she return home first and then see how things go? Will she give life a rethink? How will the rest of her life play itself out? What will happen to her when she is older and not as physically attractive as the new recruits at such places? Will she be shunted out and be out on the streets again? How will she look back on all this when she is old? I almost don't want to think about these things, but think I do, and she senses it too.

'I know that you are quite upset with all that I have told you. What will happen to me is probably what you are asking yourself.

But bear this in mind, Aunty, I have lost that advantage of choice in life. If there are no choices then that is the end of real living, isn't it? Even I know that, though I am not educated, choice is what makes human beings special and makes life worth something. I don't have choice in my life anymore.'

I know just what she is talking about. It is that moribund stage in life when nothing matters because there is nothing *else*. It reminds me of the poet Kabir's couplet which suggests that a *babool* tree can hardly lament that it cannot produce mangoes. Saloni is that *babool* tree — there can never be anything except thorns and certainly no dreams of mangoes. But, why do I look at her with such pessimism? Surely, I can't be so accepting of the reverses that happen in someone's life because she had no choice. Or did she? That is what bothers me about Saloni's choice.

'You know I can't go back home. In fact, you know I can't go back, *any* back. I know what you are thinking. I can see it in your eyes. You are figuring out a choice for me — you don't want to accept I don't have one, at least not this time. But I am not so sure. You see, Aunty, this thing about choice: it is not just about me. It is about you also: I mean the larger you, the people around that constitute society. They are the ones that cut off the choice. Once I am labelled [a prostitute or call girl or sex-worker or whatever name society has chosen to give me] then that thing you call choice is not mine — society closes the door so tight I can't even begin to try to open it. Society decided it has no choice but to exclude those it will not accept — so society has no choice — it is bound by its own rigidity.'

I am awestruck by the girl's acuity. She knows what has happened to her life. Branded, is what it is. Labelled for life. And it's not of her choosing either. Does she want to get de-labelled?

'In some things there is no such thing as getting de-labelled, Aunty', she says almost with a conscious profundity. 'This is like a tattoo. It is for life'.

回

Note

The Indian Penal Code derived from British laws and practices does not have a specific provision relating to prostitution per se. In the nineteenth century English law, sex-workers were charged with 'public nuisance' or 'public indecency' which covered indecent exposure and sexual acts committed in public. The provision often included public urination. Slavery was a greater concern than prostitution and the buying and selling of slaves was punishable with life imprisonment in the Indian Penal Code (Indian Penal Code [1860]).

Legal historians, familiar with the trajectory of the laws on prostitution in Victorian England, show up these laws as hypocritical due to the exemption of prostitutes' clients from the punitive action list. Related acts in the same period show similar double standards and hypocrisy. According to the Contagious Diseases Prevention Act of 1864, women suspected of being prostitutes in towns with large military populations had to submit to involuntary periodic genital examination, and if they refused they were imprisoned. If they were diagnosed with an illness, they were hospitalised until cured. The decision to subject women to examination was left to police officers who were happy to round up as many women as they wished and subject them to the humiliation this examination involved. Men were not subjected to examination lest it tarnish their image of respectability. The Act was finally repealed in 1886.

Prostitution is mentioned in Sections 372 and 373 IPC in relation to selling, hiring, or otherwise disposing of persons under the age of eighteen 'with intent that such person shall at any age be employed or used for the purpose of prostitution or illicit intercourse with any person or for any unlawful and immoral purpose'. The section applied to males and females and to girls who were of 'the dancing girl caste'. The dedication of minors to the service of a temple as *dasis* amounted to 'disposing of persons' who were minors 'knowing it to be likely that they would be used for the purpose of prostitution'. These punitive sections were directed at those who were 'buying, hiring, or otherwise obtaining possession' of minors; relatively little was said about the 'prostitute'. The subsequent history of the 'offence' is a fire-fighting exercise at best as it is unable to deal with a subject that has more ramifications than instrumentalist law-making can handle. Blatantly exploitative features like use of minors for sexual purposes, or crude violations of standards of decency in respectable society by running brothels as a business were easier to handle through the nominal use of the law than issues of voluntariness and social compulsion that were claimed as reasons for girls going into sex work.

In pursuance of the International Convention for the Suppression of the Traffic in Persons and the Exploitation of the Prostitution of Others, signed in New York in 1950 and ratified by the Government of India, the Suppression of Immoral Traffic in Women and Girls Act 1956 was enacted. Much of the emphasis continued to be on keeping the social environment decent. Section 8 (seducing and soliciting) was also more concerned with prostitution causing obstruction or annoyance to persons residing nearby or offending against public decency. Voluntary and privately conducted sex work was not illegal. Amendment Act 46 of 1978 was introduced with the principal objective to prevent commercialisation of trafficking among women and girls. For mobilising adequate manpower, a special police was to be appointed. Provision was also made for summary trials in addition to the regular trial procedures. Continued dissatisfaction with the enforcement of the Act produced yet another Amendment (Amendment 44 of 1986).

The current Prevention of Immoral Trafficking Act is a 1986 amendment of the 1956 Act and its main features are set out under different heads below:

Re: sex workers: Prostitutes who seduce or solicit shall be prosecuted. Call girls may not advertise phone numbers, etc., to the public (imprisonment of up to six months with fine).

Clients: Clients would be guilty of consorting with prostitutes and can be charged if they engage in sex acts with a sex worker within 200 yards of a public place or 'notified area' (imprisonment of up to three months). Clients would be punished with imprisonment (seven to ten years) if the sex worker is a minor, i.e., below eighteen years of age.

Pimps or live-in lovers who live off a prostitute's earnings and adults living with prostitutes unless they prove otherwise are guilty of a crime punishable with imprisonment of up to two years with a fine.

Landlord and brothel keepers could be prosecuted and imprisoned (one to three years) with fine and detaining someone at a brothel for the purpose of sexual exploitation could lead to prosecution (imprisonment for more than seven years).

Persons procuring or attempting to procure and persons moving someone from one place to another for trafficking could be prosecuted (three to seven years with fine).

Rescued women: The government is legally obliged to rescue and rehabilitate sex workers who require assistance in protective homes.

For purposes of the Act, 'public place' includes places of public religious worship, educational institutions, hostels, hospitals, etc. A notified area is a place declared 'prostitution-free' by the state government under the Act. Brothel means a place where there are more than two sex workers. Prostitution itself is not an offence under this law but soliciting brothels and pimps are illegal.

The principal objective was to prevent commercialisation of trafficking among women and girls. Advocacy groups had pressed for making the penal provisions more stringent and also for providing for certain standards for correctional treatment and rehabilitation of the victims in addition to medical examination of all persons removed from a brothel after a search. Once again the emphasis on public order was evident. Seducing and soliciting were punishable by imprisonment and fine.

Clients, pimps, persons living off the earnings of sex workers, and adult males living with prostitutes were all deemed guilty and could be imprisoned for a term ranging from three months to seven years depending on the offence (seven to ten years if the sex worker was a minor).

In most cases of raids and searches carried out by police for uncovering commercial sex locations, girls are arrested and brought to police stations and, pending proceedings, are put into prison, often in groups. What is disconcerting is how clients or customers of the sex workers and those who own or run the premises where the girls operate slip through the net. Following the trajectory of prostitution laws, it becomes clear that the rhetoric of reform is the outcome of pressures from reform groups who demand action against 'buyers' and 'sellers'. Women's groups have agitated vociferously for penalties against the brothel owners. The ground reality is that there is a far greater focus (and sense of horror) on the declining standards of morality brought about by 'fallen' women who supposedly perpetuate the problem of prostitution rather than on curtailing the problem by coming down heavily on traffickers who bring young girls into prostitution forcefully and without their consent. Tackling the problem by punishing the 'fallen' women reveals an age-old mindset.

What is interesting here and has an impact on the case being discussed is that whereas most of the provisions of the above Acts (and amendments) nominally admonish the user/promoter (brothel owner, client, enticer, middleman) and have more stringent punitive provisions to deal with them, one does not catch a glimpse of any of them in any men's prison. While women's prisons have several sex workers at any given time, men's prisons have no offenders caught under this Act, raising few, if any, eyebrows, or causing no discomfort to anyone. The relative absence of cases of the 'user/promoter' category being brought before the courts sends out the same message of social cleansing as that imbibed from Victorian England — double standards and a warped idea of sexual morality.

2

Rukhsana Doesn't Belong Here!

Three women with two accompanying children are locked up for a case of dowry (death). Nothing unusual about that in today's women's prisons: sometimes up to one-third of a women's prison in India comprises those imprisoned for dowry deaths and/or dowry harassment. Despite several enactments — (Dowry Act of (28) of 1961 and the subsequent Dowry Prohibition (Amendment) Acts of 1984 and 1986 — aimed at abolishing the practice, cases of dowry death (and harassment) still abound. Whether such laws have helped address some of the problems associated with the age-old tradition of dowry begs two questions: has it always been the malpractice it has now become? And, can and does the law really address all the issues surrounding dowry? The question of social change through legislation competently addressed by legal and other experts is complex and cannot be elaborated here, but the problem is alluded to in this and other stories to suggest the misuse of the law at several levels — by families of alleged victims and by the implementers and executors of the law.

Sometimes, there are more members of a single family lodged in prison for a dowry death for long periods of time than one can imagine. The highest count in my experience is eleven, all con-victed for *one* dowry death; this includes the men locked in the men's prisons. Without minimising either the havoc caused by the misuse of a traditional social practice, or difficulties that a law seeking change would face in attempting to address the malpractices associated with the tradition, one thing becomes apparent from the cases of persons incarcerated for violating dowry related acts — that the law in this case has not been a success.

In India's Vedic scriptures *kanyadaan* (giving away the bride) is traditionally associated with *varadakshina* (gifts in cash or kind given by the guardians of the bride to the groom). The practice was intended to be voluntary without coercive overtones. But as with many innocuous or well-intentioned practices, these too acquired odious overtones and became the menace that they are today. The subject is a discussion site for many complex issues that relate to property rights in the traditional Hindu society. Disenfranchisement arising out of male inheritance customs, status building for daughters in their marital homes, or pure palliatives in patriarchal societies — all these get intertwined until finally the practice takes a contemporary form that has little to do with these customary reasons and manifests itself in the sheer greed and exhibitionism of modern monetisation and post-colonial globalisation.

It only needed modern society's insatiable greed and the gratification derived from flaunting wealth coupled perhaps with malevolence on the part of the groom's family for *varadakshina,* to become the curse it has become today. And with new laws relating to dowry having become part of a robust repertoire of criminal laws in society's march towards progress, it didn't take long for any personal grievances of a bride and/or her family to become an opportunity to slap a criminal accusation of dowry harassment against the groom and his family.

Apart from some glaring shortcomings and pitfalls in the law on dowry, there are accompanying problems relating to the manipulative use of the law that often result in gross miscarriage of justice in unrelated areas. The particular case being highlighted here is one such case that would have gone unnoticed for all of the subject's life if someone had not taken the pains to look into the crevices. These three women in prison for a dowry death span three generations: a mother with two daughters and two young children belonging to the elder daughter. All five stick together and stand out because of their appearance: they are good-looking, well-groomed and poised. They have all been convicted and wear the white 'uniform' *sarees* with pink borders worn by convicts. So, what's unusual here? If dowry deaths are on the increase and sometimes make up almost 50 per cent of women offenders, what is odd about this family being imprisoned for a dowry-related offence? (See note at the end of the chapter.)

From the time I enter the prison on this particular visit the family catches my eye. The daughters Farzana and Rukhsana look so like the mother — relatively light and pale skin compared to the other women and something mysteriously attractive about them. I talk with all of them and they are ever so polite and courteous — the right intonations, the right gestures, no raised voices, no excited tones, quietly angry when asked about the nature of the offence and the events surrounding it, and seeking help for many things that are wanting in the prison. The mother may be worldly-wise and has puckered lines between her brows — lines of displeasure and bitterness, but the daughters seem soft and benign. Or are they?

Why am I intrigued by this family? As my conversations with them continue, so does my knowledge of them; and the more I know of them the more I see how families work as families even in prison. There are facets of prison life that reveal how different groups devise strategies for dealing with the struggle for survival inside: family unions, regional and religious bonds, caste alliances, personality-type clusters, offence-related groupings, and the inevitable class alignments.

In the case of women in for dowry death or harrassment, there is a bond of 'denial', and nothing is more intriguing than a dialogue with women accused of having burned their daughters-in-law. A daughter-in-law dies (and she is young) and family members are suspected of 'foul play'. Two explanations are usually provided by the alleged perpetrators of the crime: that it was a genuine accident that happened while she was cooking (the gas was faulty or spilt kerosene from the stove caused a fire), or that she had problems, perhaps another love interest, and committed suicide because life was hopeless. That she was hounded for dowry and did not meet their demands, or that she was harassed enough to take her life and that this could count as leading her to suicide are not even considered as probabilities.

I sit with the mother for a while, and of course, she denies that any of them was guilty of harassment and certainly not of killing their daughter-in-law.

'Why would we kill our son's wife? After all, we are the ones who chose her for him and married him to her. And he too is in the jail for this? Why would we cause such an upheaval in our family?', the mother says to me.

I smile and she says, 'You don't believe me do you? I know because you have talked to all these women in this jail who are here for dowry deaths, so you think everyone is equally guilty. But is there a possibility that some of us are here unjustifiably?'

The first set of the questions could elicit a host of responses from me: But this is only my first encounter with the family and I am not yet ready to have a long argument or even a discussion with them. I have strong views on the subject and I would rather not give vent to them just yet. Why would you kill your son's wife? I could think of so many reasons and all of them might hold good in your case, I feel like saying. But another time, I tell myself. I move on assuring them that we would bring their requests relating to their needs, and especially of Farzana's children, to the notice of the staff and officers.

While the mother talk about the offence and how ridiculous it is to accuse them of it, and the older daughter talks about her children's needs not being adequately met, I keep looking at Rukhsana. She is impish in her responses and keeps skipping around restlessly, trying to engage in something that might amuse her. Then she cuddles Farzana's children and tickles them, adjusting her *saree* that she doesn't seem easy in. She is endearing as well as smart all at once.

But there are other prisoners who need to be talked to and addressed, for this is only round one of many for collecting 'grievances' from the women and children inside that they are reluctant to tell the staff for fear of being reprimanded, brushed aside and sometimes even victimised. Passed on through us the grievances are likely to get some attention from staff who are anxious to prove to us their compassion and sensitivity. Most unmet needs are clear: food, sleeping arrangements, toilet facilities, family visits, ignorance (among prisoners) of their most basic rights, health problems, including mental health, a much-neglected area in almost every prison.

Pre-trial prisoners are separated from convicted prisoners, unlike many other prisons where they are often kept together, thereby creating problems given the differences in the rules relating to their routines and privileges. Two long rows of small cells on either side of a large courtyard (about a dozen cells in all) are originally meant to have one pre-trial prisoner in each, or two at most. The 9 × 9 foot cell with a small enclosure in the corner for toilet facilities could hardly house more than one person with dignity. But there is no cell in this row where the rules of accommodation have been observed. One of the cells have nine women, all housed together because they have been collectively rounded up for the same offence under the Prevention of Immoral Trafficking Act (PITA). They stick together. The arrangements seem quite straightforward in the day time: they are allowed to sit in the *verandah* along the barracks and the courtyard is also accessible where they could sit in winter to get some sun and air. But it doesn't need too much imagination to ask about their sleeping arrangements. How do they manage? I am curious. I ask them to demonstrate to me the angles and positions in which they all sleep in that cell at night. I couldn't have worked out the geometric puzzle myself even if I tried. One of the girls designed the jigsaw for me and she could sense my indignation from the reluctant smile on my face: nine in a cell meant for one or at best two was a gross violation if ever I saw one.

'Oh Ma'am, we are used to all this: they think we should all be together and you know what, so do we, because for them we are a breed apart. Even murderers don't get the looks we do when we are brought here. Other prisoners also have a quizzical look on their faces when they look at us: "How do you do what you do?" So, it is just as well we are kept together. But yes, when we have to sleep it is disgusting, because the toilet facility is right here [that partially enclosed corner] and at night nine people using the toilet that cannot really be cleaned with water until the next morning is revolting. But they tell us, 'It is a prison, not a guesthouse! And you are prisoners not guests!" So, there we are — you don't know and surely don't want to know our stories nor our plight wherever we are.'

Yes, I do want to know and no, I don't know. And that is what I am here for because I am so ill-informed about how half the women around me actually live. And how bound by other people's attitudes and mindsets these women really are.

'I don't want to encroach on your personal lives, and nor do I have any rigid position about other's lives and how they have to live it, but I am sure that you would want to give a thought to your long-term future, and without expressing any prejudice I would be happy to have you come to my room and discuss any aspect of your lives and your future that you would wish to. I am not a preacher or a converter but I am a listener, and if I can assist in formulating and structuring your own thoughts, I am more than willing.' I say this and already sound like a pedagogue!

But I move on and the girls are silent, probably pondering what I have said and why I'm so bothered about their lives.

I go back to my room to make notes about the morning's encounters. An hour or so later someone peeps in and I say, 'Who is it?' Our young and sprightly Rukhsana asks, 'May I come?' And before I answer she is there looking around and smiling.

'I'm Rukhsana,' she says. 'I just wanted to come and chat, so here I am. No particular reason. Just came.'

'OK Rukhsana. How are you? And what is it that you have in your hand? Come and sit down here in front of this table.'

'Oh this: it is the sweets you left for my sister's kids. They weren't having them, so I took two," and she smiled again, feeling a little sheepish.

'No problem', I said, 'I'll get some more for them tomorrow.'

'How long have you all been here in the jail, Rukhsana?'

'Oh, I think about two years. We have met with your associates earlier and talked to them. They know all about us.'

'Yes', I said. 'I know, I have had a talk with my team and have some idea about your family history. But why don't you tell me about yourself?.'

'Oh, nothing much to tell. I was at school and then these things happened and before I knew it I was brought here with my mother and sister. I wasn't even told why but my sister-in-law had died and they said all of you have to go to jail. They first sent the elder people and then after some days I was told I would also be sent.'

'So, how did you feel when you were told you were going to be living in a prison. How was your first day here?'

'I hated it. The first day was admissions: they filled all kinds of papers and forms. They did a body search and examined our bodies for marks and identification. I didn't like that at all. They rummaged through our belongings, and then sent us to a barrack with some of our stuff and other things provided by them. For some time, I used to wear my own clothes, but then something happened and we were told to change into these white *sarees*. I hate this — but they said I had to wear them because now I was a convict. "What is a convict"? I asked them. And they said "You are a prisoner". But I was a prisoner before too: why the white saree now?' I asked them. And they said, "Now you are convicted for having committed an offence". I told them I had not done anything — I only came here because my mother was coming. They laughed.'

Is her naivety and innocence put on, I ask myself, or is it for real? She was fidgety and restless, but friendly and pleasant.

'How old are you Rukhsana?' I ask.

'I suppose, eighteen', is the casual reply. 'That's what they tell others, so I say the same.'

Suppose. What does that mean? The way she was conducting herself she seemed more sixteen than eighteen. And even if she is eighteen now, which is doubtful, she came to the prison when she was sixteen. A minor that belonged elsewhere.

'What class were you in when you were at school before you came here'?

'Seventh', she says again airily.

Most children in the Seventh Class (Grade) are about thirteen. Allowing for her social and/or economic background, give or take a year or two, she would be fourteen in Class seven. How could she possibly be eighteen years old! She has to be sixteen I figured, not more than that, which puts her at fourteen when she was brought to the prison. A perturbing thought.

Some personal questions had to be asked, albeit tactfully. So, I go on the roundabout.

'What do you dislike most about this place. Is it the food? Missing friends? What?'

'I miss friends and having fun with them. There are just grown-up people here and all with problems and sadness. And some are so old it is very disturbing: I think they are going to die any day and we will have a dead body in the barrack. Also, I don't like it that one is always being watched: when you dress and every-thing.

You have to expose your body in front of strange people. Sometimes they even pass comments when I ask them not to look and say, "do you think you are special — we are all the same".'

And now I need to know something that may answer more than one of my worries about Rukhsana.

'You are a young girl and these are older women. They probably think they have a greater need for privacy for bodily functions so they mock you. But I fully understand your anxiety, Rukhsana. I also think that this absence of privacy is not fair to women.' Then after a pause, I finally ask the question I want to and which is vexing me the most: 'When did you start your monthly periods, Rukhsana? Was it at home before you came here?'

'Oh no, Ma'am. I started just a few weeks *after* I came to the prison. My mother told me what happened on the day that I found I was all stained with blood. My clothes were soiled at night and I was so anxious. Then we had still not been told to be in the jail's white *sarees* so not everyone saw the stains on my coloured *kurta*. But I was petrified. When my mother told me what it was (and of course I had some idea because I remember seeing my sister's clothes stained sometimes when she was younger and I was a young child). It was at a time when the barrack was locked and there was only that much water in the bucket near the toilet area. My mother told me how I was to wrap something around for the few days. But it was unpleasant. Somehow I thought, "God what on earth is this rubbish?" But my mother said, "Thank God you have started menstruating — you have started late. Your sister started a year before you when she was thirteen and I was worried about you!".'

Thank God indeed is what I thought too, but for other reasons. So, there we are, I think in disbelief. *She is sixteen now,* just as I thought, and she was a mere fourteen years of age when they brought her in. They brought her into a women's prison as an offender when she was a minor! And add to that the fact that she knows little about the details of the offence. What happened here? What did they do and why? I was putting together the theories in my own mind — but whatever the reason, it was unjustified, unacceptable and illegal. She had not offended, she was a minor and someone had gone terribly wrong in bringing her here and giving her a prison record. What was happening here?

'So did your mother arrange for you to get your supply of sanitary pads each month regularly? And do you get cramps and pains each time', I ask, getting away from my real concerns.

'Oh, the first time it was all very awkward and nasty. Then I grew used to it. But then after some months the cramps came with the periods: It was unbearable and I would lie down and sometimes the staff person would say, "Get up why are you lying down early in the morning". If I said, "I am not well", she would say, "Don't behave like a softy, you have to finish your morning chores now".'

Suddenly her mother appears in the doorway. 'So this is where you are, Rukhsana. I have been looking all over for you.' Turning to me she says, '*Namaste* Ma'am. She probably came to have a chat with you. If she says something stupid please don't mind.'

Mind! I am relieved that she came and confirmed some of my fears, otherwise I would have contemplated these questions for days. I really need to talk to *you,* dear lady, I say to myself, so that I can get a few explanations before I spring into action to get to the bottom of how your minor daughter is a convicted prisoner in an adult women's prison.

'Nusrat', I say to the mother, 'Why don't you come and have a chat with me some day if you feel up to it. There must be things on your mind and may be we can resolve some issues if there is anything bothering you.'

'Yes, I will come. *Khuda Hafiz* [God be with you]'.

What a mess there is inside these walls. All kinds of people, each a person in her own right, with all sorts of apprehensions and concerns, all in need of attention and individual solutions, yet all clubbed together as if they are all of a type that can actually be dealt with en masse. Even members of a family cannot be treated identically, and prison is a place where people of all ages, backgrounds, personalities and problems congregate. Do we really believe they can be treated like peas in a pod? 'Unacceptable', I keep saying to myself. And my researchers are now fired up to solve 'the mystery of the minor', as they call it.

Rukhsana hasn't a clue about why she is here and for how long. She wants to get back to school and her friends, but she also wants to be with her mother. I watch her each day as she skips around the prison. This women's prison, unlike some others I have worked in, allows longer hours outside the cell. Rukhsana is thus able to stay out for a while in the *verandahs* and courtyards. She is self-conscious sometimes and carefree other times. She is in that no man's land: she is not a child like the six-year-olds who accompany their mothers into the prison and get the attention deserving of their status as children. She is a 'convicted' prisoner, biologically a minor and not mature enough to be considered, a thinking adult. She gets angry easily, but as easily softens when pampered. At best she is still a child.

So, what do we do about her? I have a chat with the head of the jail. On the books Rukhsana is an adult, and when she came in, her age was registered as eighteen. I smile and she says, 'I know but it is really not for us to question the orders under which she is brought to us. The arresting officer, the judge, and her family — they all put her age down as eighteen at the time of conviction. You would have to go into all these details to advocate a change here. We have no problem with your doing that, but we didn't decide this on our own.'

Then one day I meet Rukhsana in the *verandah* and she is in a frenzy. She is red in the face, pacing the corridor, and some of the prisoners are shouting at her to behave herself and not be rude to them. I approach her and ask her how she is. She is quiet but very agitated. Her mother comes up and says that Rukhsana has had a fever for four days and that she had asked the doctor to give her something. She prescribed tablets for two days and then said, 'I think she is better'. But she isn't. I touch Rukhsana's forehead and she is burning with a fever.

This is the last straw and something needs to be done immediately if we don't want a crisis on our hands. Someone whispers that Rukhsana locked herself in the toilet the evening before and would not come out. When she did, she fell to the ground. In her frustration she had swallowed all six tablets given to her by the doctor; 'I want to die', she said. A sixteen-year-old wanting to die, I thought. Something was very wrong here.

When the warden on duty was asked about Rukhsana, she said the doctor had examined her and prescribed medication for her two days ago. I had already been told by an inmate that the doctor never ever touches her patients, as though they were untouchables. I mentioned this to the staff, 'I just touched Rukhsana's forehead', I said 'and she is burning with a fever. How on earth can you treat someone if you are reluctant to touch her?'

Rukhsana was clearly delirious, hence her erratic behaviour. She needed rest and proper medication. Even her mother was getting impatient with her because of the pressure from other women who were angry with Rukhsana for her behaviour. Finally, Rukhsana was persuaded to go and lie down and try and get some sleep.

This incident didn't exactly help Rukhsana; she lost a lot of friends amongst the prisoners, especially the older ones who earlier had shown some maternal feeling towards her. Then something strange happened. A young radical group of prisoners (arrested for Naxalite activity) began warming up to Rukhsana and befriended her. They were nearer her age but it wasn't just that. They told how different she was from the others who were set in their ways and urged her to learn to stand on her own two feet and fight for her rights!

She tells me this when she comes to see me next. Some people in the prison, she says, are intolerant of her; they say, she is a spoilt brat and tell her mother to keep her in control and then her mother scolds her. What was she supposed to do? She says she is agitated all the time and has nothing to do. She can't be schooling with six-year-old children and she is not included in any activity with the adults, so how should she pass her time? A good question. What does a girl like Rukhsana do?

I ask her what she would like to do. Is there something that particularly interests her. Would she like some books, does she like sewing, or something else? She is too confused and unsure.

'I don't know,' she says, and I truly believe she has no clue about what she wants. There is really no one to guide people like her in jails. Doctors only look out for the physically sick, and if you demonstrate symptoms of mental illness you get sent away to a different prison as a mental patient. But all intermediary stages of being disturbed, over-anxious, depressed, nervous, or just confused are dismissed as whimsical flights of fancy. No one believes that such states of mind as 'feeling low' are important to address and not be brushed aside.

'I wish I could run away from here,' she finally confesses. 'This place is so full of people who can't tolerate anything that they don't do themselves. Sometimes, even when I laugh loudly I feel guilty. I have already been here two years and I feel it is a lifetime. How long is a lifetime anyway? If this is the way I have to be (and my mother says we have several more years to spend in here) then I won't be able to bear it and will continue to do things that people think are foolish and they will hate me more. And the more they hate me the more I will want to rebel.'

What is it about young girls who have a problem adjusting to difficult and demanding environments that makes one want to say to them, 'I sympathise my dear, but you haven't got a chance — not here and not anywhere, where there are people who want from you the prescribed behaviour that they and those before them have carefully delineated for you for all the stages of your life'. It is probably the bewildered and perplexed look on their faces that wants me to add, 'Wish you weren't here. But now that you are don't do too many foolish things otherwise there are those who will eat you alive.'

I look at her sitting there in her white saree, dressed like all the other women convicts, except she is not like all the other women and she is not a convict! I finally decide something needs to be done to put things right (and they have been so wrong). She needs attention immediately if her life is not to be ruined forever.

'Why don't you ask your mother to come and see me — if she is willing', I tell Rukhsana. 'She really needs to protect you, but from what I can make out she is getting irritated with you because others are getting irritated with her. This is what is making you unhappy. But in the meantime try not to upset anyone. You must understand that jail staff are not really concerned that people of different ages or different personality types need different treatment and handling. They are interested in maintaining order in the jail and if you disturb that order they will be looking for ways of disciplining you. And consequently, life will be more and more difficult for you as days go by.'

'You know, I don't even know what exactly happened between my mother and my brother's wife. If there are fights at home one thinks, "OK so there is a fight and the storm will blow over". But I don't know what happened this time. Before I knew it my sister-in-law had died and the police were all over the place. And I am here in this place. What did I do? I just haven't really understood to this day.'

Then she said something quite startling: 'Everyone said my sister-in-law was very unhappy in our house because people troubled her for things and she was so troubled that she died. I am also very unhappy here. If I die where will they send those who are troubling me? That day I nearly died because I was so sick and unhappy I wanted to die. So, if I had died who would be punished and where would *they* be sent?'

For want of a better answer, I said: 'Well, we wouldn't let you die, would we Rukhsana? Here everyone is unhappy because this is not a normal environment. So, the people in charge of this prison must make sure that unhappy people (and there will be many) are not driven to take such steps that are unpleasant and damaging to themselves and to others. That is their responsibility. Even in a family not everyone is equally happy? One has to find out why they are not happy and try and see if something can be done about it.'

'Well I am not happy here and I wish someone could do something about it. No one wants to; even my mother now gets very impatient with me. She thinks that because of my "bad" and unacceptable behaviour other prisoners and staff are not good to my mother and sister. So, she scolds me for little things all the time. That is really unfair.'

A day or two later, her mother, Nusrat, comes to my room. I feel I have to tread carefully since she was part of the arrangement to have both her daughters with her at all cost and knows that Rukhsana's age was fabricated. When I suggest that Rukhsana should not be here she gets agitated.

'How can I leave my "*javaan beti*" elsewhere?' she says. 'Do you know what would have happened to her if I had not brought her with me?'

'And do you know what will happen to her here, Nusrat,' I reply. 'This is not a place where she will gain anything. She will lose a lot because this is an unnatural environment and she will be affected almost invisibly and you won't even know what happened to your Rukhsana along the way. Her mind and spirit will be broken. In fact, it is already breaking because human beings like her should not be locked up.'

In the meantime I have also talked to some officers about Rukhsana being under-age when they admitted her to the prison. This was met with responses typically exhibited by prison administration in awkward situations.

'Well! You see we received papers that suggested she was eighteen and that is the age we wrote.'

'But you do your own medical examination: what did that say? If she was eighteen then, according to the official verdict, she is twenty now. Does she look like a girl of twenty to you?', I asked.

'The mother must have corroborated the age that was in the papers so it was taken at face value,' a staff member says.

'I'm afraid there is no way that the girl was a day older than fourteen. Clearly an error was made here and as a result she is totally maladjusted and suffering too. The mother may be guilty of complicity but the official machinery should know better, surely,' I protest.

'You see, Ma'am,' says one of the officials, 'if the whole family was going to be in jail who would take the responsibility of a minor. I think the mother preferred to have her daughter with her and hence there must have been some adjustments made in this case.'

'Adjustments! You call this adjustment. On other fronts you swear by the rulebook and won't give an ounce of extra food to someone even if she needs it. And now you are condoning adjustments? I am truly perplexed because I know of occasions when so many reasonable requests have been turned down and prisoners and their relatives have been shown the rule book — and you say that to lock up a minor in an adult jail because no one could come up with any other idea is an adjustment.'

'It wasn't our decision,' she retorts.

'Well, you know what? We will have to see whose decision it was and find a better "adjustment than this"', my fiery associate says promptly.

We march off to the offices of the senior administration. For every two, hardened rulebook-flaunting officials in an establishment such as this, there is at least one semi-enlightened officer who will listen with patience and try and give answers. Fortunately, this prison has just such a person. We have a long discussion about Rukhsana, and for all the previous declarations to the contrary, it is conceded that the mother's personal feelings about the daughter being safe and secure with her was not sufficient reason for putting a minor in an adult jail as a convicted prisoner. If she is guilty (and I wonder how that was determined — was it simply that she was present when it happened and hence her involvement assumed) then she must go to a juvenile facility. It was not right to change her age and house her with adult prisoners. If she has been recorded as guilty for the convenience of her mother, then that too is not right. We are talking, therefore, of all those involved in being a party to this (in our view) gross error of judgement.

It is decided then that a proper age assessment be done medically and professionally. The 'enlightened prison officer' promises to do just that. And he does. We end up with a result that contradicts everything the previous record showed: not only is her correct age determined and an admission that she was probably fourteen when she was brought in as a 'convict', but it is also conceded that she was *not* brought here because she was guilty and therefore a convict, but because it was thought best by 'all concerned' that as a young girl of fourteen she should be with her mother. Her age was put down as eighteen for the record to be 'straight'. How odd, I thought; if this is straight, what is 'crooked'.

We now have a fresh set of problems emerging out of our 'solution' of determining Rukhsana's correct age. Setting one set of things straight brings a fresh set of complex inconveniences, complicated primarily because it revolves around gender issues. If Rukhsana had been a minor boy I wonder what the approach would have been.

Nusrat is told of all this and naturally she is not surprised or horrified considering she was a party to it. The only difference between her role and that of the officials is that she was not committing an illegality: she said her daughter was fourteen but desperately wanted that she should somehow be with her otherwise she will 'be ruined'. It is the official machinery that had committed an illegality and clearly wanted to gloss over the situation as speedily as possible.

The question now is, where should Rukhsana be? Clearly, not here. Apart from the issue of irregularities and illegalities, Rukhsana is exhibiting signs of maladjustment and stress that have actually made her suicidal. Various locations for her placement are explored — relatives, institutions for young girls, boarding schools, but nothing concrete comes up.

Finally an NGO offeres to take Rukhsana under its wing: Nusrat gives her consent and so it is settled. Of course, Nusrat is not really happy with the new arrangement even though she has begun to grow increasingly irate with the way things have been going for her and Rukhsana as time goes on. She has no choice; this is not the first time one has felt just how devastating such lack of choice is for so many here.

'I am used to these kinds of choices in life. It has always been this way for me: Choice? What choice? Do we women really have a choice? I am not so sure. If you think so, tell me about it! My experience has been that we are made to believe (falsely) that something is of our choosing, but it never is. That is the way I am looking at Rukhsana's new fate. Let us see what happens. I have trepidations and fears and I can't say any more than that. I hope, we don't all live to regret this.' Nusrat is visibly angry as she says this.

Mission accomplished? I am not sure, and express as much to my colleagues who have taken the matter of age-deception seriously enough to want it investigated and put right. The mission has too many ramifications and we are lost in the maze. Rukhsana is free to leave, and before she does, she gives everyone a hug: there are tears as she takes leave of the family but also a strange sense of freedom that she is leaving behind a place where she was neither free nor accepted for who she was. Again, the same question — is she free now? We will find out and try and to keep track of what she does and what help she might need to settle in wherever she does.

Days later we see a tearful Nusrat. She says that there has been no word from Rukhsana. Where is she? The NGO said she was fine, but how come there is no direct communication from her? We promise to look into it and we do.

The young Naxalite girls in the prison had befriended Rukhsana when the 'whole prison' (as she put it) was against her and had decried her bad behaviour (*sara jail mere khilaf hai*, she had said). They have got in touch with her and have asked her to join them in 'worthier' causes. And she has. Is that a case of going from the frying pan to the fire? Her mother certainly thinks so. 'She was better off here — *allah* help her now. My daughter is lost forever.'

And then our colleague Veena gets a call one morning. It is Rukhsana.

'Ma'am,' she says, 'I am fine. Please don't worry about me. All these people are good to me and I think I am finding something that makes me feel responsible and may give a different meaning to my life. I know what my mother is feeling. She would hate me for joining these people. But then she also took me to prison with her. To what avail? I'd rather be a revolutionary than a jailbird. I hope you don't think I let all of you down. After all you told me that life must have a purpose and one should try and accomplish something that is not altogether selfish. Well, here I am, thinking of larger things than myself.'

Veena tells me about the phone call and I put my hands up in despair.

'What have we done, Veena? May be we should have let things be. Where have we led her? Does she really know what it's all about. Landless peasants, distribution of land, fair wages for workers, women's economic rights. Has she any idea where she's headed?'

Veena is equally puzzled. If anything, she is far more intolerant of radical politics and revolutionaries than I ever was, especially at her age, and is uncomfortable about this situation. But she goes on.

'Well there's only that much we can do,' she says. And she has the 'right' to say that considering she worked hard on

Rukhsana's case and tried everything in the book to get her out of the prison.

'Yes, Veena, there is only that much we can do.'

In our 15-year experience of working in women's prisons, in one capacity or other, there are two statements we have heard from every woman that we have spoken to: the first is, 'I didn't do it'. And the second is, 'Get me out of here please, I can't bear it.' Well, in this case we did. Rukhsana is out there, away from this claustrophobic place and away from the malicious aggression she was facing day in and day out. She is free. So, why are we faced with so many questions?

There were no two ways about the illegality of incarcerating an innocent person and a minor in an adult prison to suit the convenience of some people, mostly family and officials. So, why are we despondent? Are we regretting something? Are we questioning the wisdom of our decision and the steps we took? Is there a lament here? And if there is, why is it so? Is it because of a fear that this girl of a tender impressionable age is going to become a revolutionary? She feels good fighting for 'just' causes. Are we begrudging of her just cause? Aren't *we* doing just that: fighting for just causes? We are sitting here, questioning something that only a short while ago we were so sure of.

Veena speaks in a solemn voice: 'I think we sent her from the frying pan to the fire. I am convinced of that. The question is whether she would have endured the frying pan, or will she endure the fire. We don't know that yet — and that's what is eating me up. How will we ever know that we did the most correct, the best, and the proper thing for Rukhsana? Should this be viewed from her perception, even when we know and concede that she was vulnerable and still a minor, not able to make fully informed decisions? Are we judging from our perception, from the family's perception, or from Rukhsna's perception? We don't really know; we never will, but as Veena says, 'She sounded happy'.

Note

This story deals mainly with the question of the manipulative attempt of official machinery to solve a problem relating to a minor member of a convicted family who posed a dilemma: not being an accompanying *child*, nor a convicted adult, she had to be slotted somewhere to avoid the complications of leaving her uncared for. The system's implementers thought of an ingenious method: why not convict her as well and have her stay with the rest of her family in prison. That would take care of the predicament of where to send her. She would not be with unknown persons or in care, and her family fretting about what would happen to her if she were left outside, would be relieved. That was the solution arrived at by the criminal justice system.

Solutions of convenience raise further questions. While abhorring the system's easy way out, one is hard pressed to provide an alternative from the minor's point of view. Such quandaries have strengthened our case that government departments should look for solutions with the help of outside experts, rather than believe they have all the answers. We have time and again placed these suggestions before the concerned departments. In Nari Bandhi Niketan in Lucknow, we came across a similar predicament. Priti was a 12-year-old girl accompanying her mother in prison: in her case one did not have to ask why. The girl was blind and no family member was willing to take responsibility for her. We offered two solutions: (*i*) investigate the degree of blindness to find a cure, failing which (*ii*) take the help of child welfare groups to look for alternatives. The prison department's knee-jerk response to such suggestions is always, '*is baat kee to jaanch karni paregi. Tab tak yaheen theek hai*' [we would have to inquire into the matter, till then she is better off here]. Fair enough, but for months there was no '*jaanch*' and meanwhile the girl turned 13. How many Rukhsanas and Pritis will one have to rescue from the four walls of a prison even though they are not prisoners.

Shelter homes are not always beyond suspicion and having encountered ugly malpractices in several homes for hapless children, we have had reservations about recommending them too readily as suitable alternatives, especially for girls. Again the same dilemma: she is a girl, so the problem is different.

Before any analysis of the main offence for which the entire family was 'inside', it should be mentioned that had Rukhsana been 'guilty' of the offence the state would still not be entitled to send her to this prison with her adult family. As a 14-year-old her case would need to be dealt with by a different machinery altogether under the Juvenile Justice (Protection of Children) Act, 2000.

While this narrative highlights the gross falsification committed by one State in keeping a minor in an adult prison, it also reveals the problem of entire families being imprisoned in some cases (in this case dowry death), presenting problems that the rule book has no answers for. The family in question in this case was not a Hindu family. Condemnations of the practice of dowry in India are more often than not based on indictments of the Hindu tradition of giving gifts to a bride at the time of marriage. Today, for good reason the practice of dowry is seen as an indicator of the devalued status of women in Indian society. The term 'dowry' alludes to gifts in cash or kind given to the husband and his relatives by the wife and her relatives *in connection with marriage*. Ordinarily, giving gifts to a bride and/or her relatives would be the most natural of acts: that it is a part of social custom and tradition in many communities gives it the twist it has today. How did it change from gift-giving to the evil that it is today? The question needs to be answered along with the one relating to the best way of disallowing it. Society has developed and progressed in material ways, and goods and possessions are increasingly becoming symbols of status and respectability. Greed as the natural outcome of this development has redefined the custom or tradition of dowry, putting women into this untidy muddle.

One way or another, law as the instrument of change is not as simple as it may appear in societies where the majority look to tradition and custom for their basic understanding of life and human relationships. For women whose lives are not defined by the concept of the individual as an end, but rather of the collective, any attempt to redefine lives can only be successful if done without destroying the concept of the collective. Rights and liberation notwithstanding, life without the collective would be rudderless in much of society.

That the concept of the collective may be synonymous with male supremacy is the problematic here. Blatant condemnation of the imbalance of social equations in women's lives achieves little in practical terms. Sita Devi, a Rajasthani woman in prison for a 'dowry death', and who fits the stereotype of a bullying mother-in-law, was bitter about the ruthless manner in which the whole incident of dowry was handled by the legal machinery. 'Did it not strike the judge that the couple may have been unhappy and so the girl killed herself? *Apna pait nanga karoon?* [Am I expected to bare my own stomach?],' she asked. 'My son was a philanderer and they never got along. Yes he did taunt her about her parental home and I suppose we didn't support her. But the assumption that all of us ganged up and killed her is so preposterous.' Another woman who sat beside Sita Devi confronted me with a valid question: '*Ameer log bhee dahej maang maang ke lete hain. Unka parivaar jail*

mein kyon nahin hota is kanoon ko torne ke liye?' [The rich also give
and take lavish dowries — why are their families not behind bars for
violating the Dowry Prohibition Act?]. Another woman in a prison in
south India said that if this is a custom that puts women down and gives
men the benefits, then perhaps *raksha bandhan* and *karva chauth* and
other similar customs should also be suspect because these give sisters
and wives pride of place in lieu of granting the real rights and privileges
you are suggesting.

When exactly does a practice become a malpractice is difficult to
ascertain, and when it does, there is a flurry of activity to address the
problem. The fastest route is legislation whose greatest service is raising
awareness about the malpractice and offering a path of resistance. The
government promulgated the Dowry Prohibition Act in 1961 to deal
with the practice of dowry. This Act prohibits the request, payment or
acceptance of a dowry, 'as consideration for the marriage' — where
'dowry' is defined as a gift demanded or given as a precondition for
a marriage. Gifts given without a precondition are not considered
dowry and are legal. Asking for, or giving of dowry can be punished
by imprisonment of up to six months, or a fine of up to ₹15,000 or the
amount of dowry, whichever is higher, and imprisonment for up to five
years. It replaced several parts of anti-dowry legislation that had been
enacted by various States.

Amendments have been introduced in the Act to widen its net and
to make it stronger. This Act, as well as the penal statutes — the Indian
Penal Code, the Criminal Procedure Code and the Indian Evidence Act
— has been amended on more than one occasion to deal with dowry-
related violence. Section 498-A of the Indian Penal Code deals with all
cases of dowry-related cruelty and harassment of women. This section
made cruelty to married women punishable with imprisonment for a
term which may extend to three years and a fine.

Through the Amendment Act of 1983, Section 174 of the Criminal
Procedure Code was amended, empowering a magistrate to hold an
inquiry and making a postmortem essential when a woman dies under
suspicious circumstances within seven years of her marriage. A new
section —113-A — was inserted in the Indian Evidence Act, reversing
the presumption of innocence of the accused in the case of suicide by a
married woman. Two new sections — 304-B in the Indian Penal Code
and 113-B in the Indian Evidence Act — were added by the Dowry
Prohibition (Amendment) Act, 1986. Section 304-B in the Indian Penal
Code created and defined a new offence of 'dowry death':

> Where death of a woman is caused by any burns or bodily
> injury or occurs otherwise than under normal circumstances within

seven years of her marriage and it is shown that soon before her death she was subjected to cruelty or harassment by her husband or any relative of her husband for, or in connection with, any demand for dowry, such death shall be called 'dowry death' and such husband or relative shall be deemed to have caused her death.

Punishment for a person guilty of dowry death is a term of imprisonment which shall not be less than seven years but which may extend to imprisonment for life.

The law has tried to cover as many angles to prevent the ugly features of what was and can still be an innocuous custom. Despite the incremental toughness with which the state may intervene, the assumption that the demand and supply of dowry has decreased would be erroneous. Abundant wealth, often ill-gotten, is waiting to be flaunted and a marriage tie seems an ideal site for vulgar display. To boast that the law has been successful in eliminating 'dowry' is far-fetched. For as many as it punishes, sometimes rightly and sometimes wrongly, there are perhaps twice as many who get away because they belong to an 'untouchable' category — the over-privileged. Ground realities thereby highlight the weakness of relying on laws and the strength of customs. The law implicitly accepts this for the Act, while prohibiting dowry, recognises that it cannot be made completely illegal. Section 6 therefore sets out that any dowry shall be for the benefit of the wife or heirs.

Abuses associated with dowry giving and taking, violence, brutality, cruelty, killing, bride burning, are the dark side of the custom which need to be addressed through more than formal legal measures. Particular laws may address particular violations but would be impotent to face the assumptions of male supremacy that underlie so many customs. In fact, a failure to address the gendered assumptions that define roles and relations in society through additional ways may actually weaken the law's role in the limited areas where it could play a part. An Act would only be instrumental in the reform process up to a point: it may address particular cases and specific malpractices; it is unlikely to challenge some assumptions and values that underlie our social fabric and influence our acts. Law would have to be viewed as a site for more inclusive discourses that provide space and opportunities for voices outside the formal legal framework to be heard.

3

The Maiming of Mumta: 'Put Out Your Cigarette on Her Breasts Guys!'

回

Truth is stranger than fiction, it is said, and we are discovering this each day that we spend among the women here, delving into the real lives of real people.

Not having witnessed police violence and brutality ourselves, we assume it is the stuff that films are made of. It happens to someone else, and while we abhor the acts and wonder just what prompts those entrusted with our protection to behave as they do, unfortunately their misdemeanours are committed behind closed doors in the sanctity of their 'territory' where their writ prevails and where there is no one to stop them. But this we know: that what happened to Mumta was not a fabrication of her imagination. The scars (literal and figurative) were still raw when she came to the jail and there were others to vouch for her screams in the lockup — those others who dared not speak for fear of reprisal.

Mumta's experiences hit us the hardest immediately after they were recounted; but time fades the intensity of our responses and reactions and no one is ever really able to probe any logical end the reasons or insane motives that prompt such behaviour.

She is not pretty. She is not young either (how old does a woman have to be in order to be called young). She is ordinary in more ways than one: face, figure, fashion, style, elegance, culture or sophistication — nothing remarkable or noteworthy here. Just an ordinary woman who looks decent, plain, simple and unadorned. She is in prison for an offence and is a pre-trial prisoner in the women's jail. As this story relates to 'the woman' in a woman, the nature of the offence is not really the crucial feature of the narrative: indeed it is irrelevant to the happenings being recounted here.

She is limping and for the most part would rather lie down or stand, we are told, not sit. There is no question of her coming to talk to us in our counselling room, so we all go to talk to her in her cell. The young researchers have already had conversations with her and this time I accompany them because she wants to talk to me. Her name is Mumta; she is 45 years old. She is a married woman with married children. Her hair is beginning to grey and she is a little over-weight. She is in a pale blue *saree* with a printed design and a pale blue blouse (not in white because she is still a pre-trial prisoner). Her hair is dishevelled as she lies on a rug in the cell meant for one (but always occupied by at least half a dozen). She looks visibly weighed down by her experiences and emotions. As we enter, she tries to get up and we beckon to her not to move. We sit on the floor and she greets us, and then thanks us for taking the trouble to come.

'Don't thank us for that Mumta. We haven't done anything yet. And even if we had, the last thing you need to do is thank us. From what we are hearing about you, it is we who should be coming to apologise on behalf of some of our fellow-humans who brought you to the condition you are in.' These are the thoughts almost uttered but we don't want Mumta to think we have already been apprised of some facts about what happened to her. So, we don't say anything just yet.

'While we appreciate that you come regularly to this jail and your colleagues are here day in and day out to help everyone here and to try and make this a better place, I do wish that you could also come as regularly to that other place where people are kept locked up and where no one peeps in to see what is happening. That place is hell compared with this,' she says.

Of course, we know she is referring to the police station where she was kept before she was brought here, and compared to which this, she says, is a haven where she feels safe. I never thought I would live to hear that prison was a haven, but here it is.

'Unfortunately, Mumta, there are only a handful of us who have made this situation of locking up people our worry, so we thought we should start from the deep end [the prison] I suppose. We will get around to police stations soon enough.'

'Oh no Ma'am, this is not the deep end: *that* is. Once someone is locked up *there*, scarcely anyone can even vouch for the fact that you are still there. There is no prison population in hundreds there: there could be four persons over the day and suddenly you discover at night they have all gone and you are the only person locked up with a minimum staff in charge. So, while there is some safety in numbers here, there it is the fear of being almost alone. Believe me.'

'Of course, I believe you,' I say, 'it's just that everywhere in the world there is such dread and fear of a prison that to hear you refer to it as a haven is strange.'

'You won't think so once I tell you how things happen around there. And I don't need to tell you what fears a woman, any woman, has anywhere that she is alone.'

She then tries to get into a reclining position and lifts her *saree* above the knee. What is she doing, I think. Immediately, it becomes clear. On her thigh are reddish, pinkish, brown and almost raw, burn marks — several of them. Some have dried and crusted, others are still raw. Some areas of the thigh are purple. Clearly she still needs medical attention. My colleague tells me doctors are attending to her wounds and she is being given antibiotics because they think it could turn septic.

'There are more burns, Ma'am — on my breasts on my back and near my anus. And it hurts and smarts and ...' She tails off, not because she is beleaguered but because we are. And she can see it. Clearly, she has already been through this exercise of showing the sore and raw burn marks to others. In the first instance at the time of admission she would have shown them to the staff who are obliged to take down personal details and record any injuries on a prisoner's body. The record does have entries relating to Mamta's bruises which our younger researchers are able to confirm. Then, as this is something that needs to be treated, she would have already shown them to the doctor so that treatment can be started. Surely, as she gets settled in her allotted cell, she shows it to her cell mate(s) and perhaps some sympathetic staff. So we are at least fifth in the list. Someone behind us has already whispered, 'cigarette burns', followed by a disbelieving gasp. Mumta stops talking.

'Go on Mumta', I say softly, fearing what is coming and yet anxious to know it in all its horror.

'I never imagined such a thing could happen to me at my age. I thought the worst of my life's experiences were over, but clearly this was still left as part of my *kismet*. It is so humiliating for me with grown-up children to have suffered such degradation at the hands of those whom I should be running to if I am ever humiliated. But when the protectors become perpetrators there is no hope.'

I couldn't have put it better. We do have an expectation from agencies of the state which are there to protect us when we are under threat from anti-social elements. It is frightening when these same agencies turn on us.

'How did you get yourself into this? How did someone turn so viciously on you and treat you this way? Was your family not able to do anything?' I ask.

'My husband left me some years ago. In the case of men you don't even ask why they leave. It is funny how calmly society takes the fact of a husband leaving just like that and the wife is told to move on and make the best of what is left. But if a wife leaves she is called all kinds of names. Doesn't that tell us a lot about our status and our plight?'

'I have two married sons and an adopted daughter. One son has a scooter-taxi and the other, a spare-parts shop. After my husband left me I could not make two ends meet and I started working as a domestic help in a few houses. It gave me enough to eat but each time there was a health or other problem I was always seeking help from my employers and sometimes had to scrounge to get that help. It used to be demeaning.'

Thus far, the story was so familiar, I became a little impatient to get to the part where she had to actually face the kind of brutality her body was subjected to.

'One of my employers was a CI [Circle Inspector] in the police and when I asked him for extra financial help he said to me, "Look why don't you do a little business on the side? I can help you. You have to deliver some pouches every now and then and you will get extra money from me for doing that". Yes, I was tempted and agreed. He would send these pouches to my house with a constable and I would sell these to outlets that he had familiarised me with. If I made ₹ 5,000 a month with this he would take ₹ 3,000. I did this for almost five months. Yes, I knew this was really illegal because these were illicit liquor packets and while he was doing this side business with impunity I trembled each time I went to deliver.'

I am still groping for where her experience turns so sour that she is victimised the way she is. She soon enlightens me.

'One day he made the most absurd proposition. "Your son has just got married? I am told you have a pretty daughter-in-law. Send her to my house tonight. She seems a nice girl, she can spend some time here in the evenings. She can watch television and help around a little. I have guests coming so often, she could help out". My God! I thought — what does he take us for. Just because he has made me do this illegal thing, he thinks he has a hold over my family to use and misuse at his whim and fancy. I was numb for a while but knew there was no way I was going to be so helpless as to subject my family to his advances. I refused. From that day I also stopped doing the illicit liquor business for him. That was the turning point in my life and the beginning of my trauma.'

It is difficult to respond when someone tells you something you know is heading in an ugly direction. There are many ways that the local police can victimise a person and I have had some first hand experience of crude, abusive language from the police while helping friends and neighbours who faced police harassment and intimidation. That itself can leave one numb and unable to respond. A woman, of course, has so many vulnerabilities. Her family, her body, her lack of training and education, and of course her poverty. Mumta was vulnerable on all fronts. And yet I felt a bit angry: what does it take for a woman to realise all this, and at her age did she not have the wisdom to know where this would take her? Before my next thought she already addressed my concerns.

'My initial temptation for more money to live properly cost me dear,' she said. 'I hadn't a clue what I could do to seek help some place where, even if my mistake of doing an illegal business would be punished, I could at least have been saved from what I went through afterwards.'

That was her first vulnerability: poverty, I said to myself.

'The CI sent a police constable to my house one day and said I was required to clarify something and I better accompany him if I know what's good for me. I had to: as I said my one error of judgement was going to accompany me everywhere.'

'I went with the constable and was taken to a part of the house that looked somewhat empty, and I realised soon enough that there was no one else there. The CI shouted at me and rebuked me and said, "How dare you stop the selling of the pouches [liquor] just like that. Just because I asked you to send your daughter-in-law to me for an evening you thought I could be brushed aside. Just like that. Do you know whom you are dealing with? I could send you inside for so many illegal activities and you will spend the rest of your life grinding corn in the jail".' The phrase is *chakki peesogi* and alludes to the fact that images of women in jail are all about sitting with large stone grinders and rotating them to grind corn or wheat all day, each day, till their arms are close to falling off.

'I stood there believing that these were just hot words that he would give me and then maybe let me go. But I was told later I was foolish not to know that one does not confront those who have police power. It is not that no one will believe me — they might. But no one will ever disbelieve a police person. He will have his whole "force" behind him if he is in the dock.'

'I was desperate' [Mumta says], but clearly did not realise where my desperation was taking me. I then blurted: 'So what are you going to do with me?' 'Do you really want to know?' the CI smirked. He then unzipped his trousers and took out his male organ and forced my face on it shoving it into my mouth. I screamed and he pulled me aside and shut my mouth forcibly, saying if I breathed a word outside I had a lot to lose.'

Her second vulnerability, I thought — her sexuality.

'I was devastated', she continued. 'At my age to go through such a "dirty" experience. I could not even recount in my mind the lewd gesture I was faced with leave alone talk about it to someone. Of course, now with so many things having happened after that and my having had to narrate it so many times to persons I am able to talk about those horrible things. But at the time I was so sick I can't begin to tell you'.

I look at her with mixed emotions: her plight, her age, her circumstances — all of these were unenviable, but what had made her play into the hands of the man in the first place? I am not sure I was viewing her sympathetically at this stage. You are 40 years old, I keep thinking, young enough and old enough — contradictory as that may sound. Did you not know the ways of the world?

'Have you ever been so desperate', says Mumta, 'that you just clutch at anything to survive? That is how I was caught in this web. When I talk about it I am aware that all those persons who have not had to go through the coarse things that happened to me are either curious or simply aghast. But for me, it was so horrible. With grown up married sons and...', she trails off.

What can one say? I feel mixed emotions and reactions — including embarrassment. This is as unreal as it can get for a woman and there is more to come. When one gets on the wrong side of the police the consequences are grave, even I know that, secure and safe as I may be in my middle-class cocoon. And a woman who dares to think she can just say 'no'? That is not how it works. The first incident leads to another and another and so on, and that's how it was for Mumta. Still smarting, the CI sent a constable to Mumta's house with instructions to bring Mumta to the station. She questioned the constable and said she had no reason to go to the police station and besides, it was 8 pm and she really did not wish to go to the *thana* at that hour with anyone. It was too late an hour for her.

Her third vulnerability — powerlessness in the face of the *khakhi* uniform.

'Your son has been arrested for excessive drinking and misbehaviour and he is at the Station,' the constable said. 'So if I were you, I would go right now, 8 o'clock or not!'

And her fourth vulnerability — family.

She went to the station, and sure enough the son was locked up. Not that there was much she could have done about it, but the police knew she would come as soon as she heard about her son. And she certainly did. The *thana* was not exactly full of people; it was 8 pm and it was a Saturday. And there were no women (constables) present — even those assigned to be there when a woman is brought in for questioning (which is mandatory) are likely to have left for home at that hour.

'I sensed something fishy and trembled with fear. It is a strange feeling of powerlessness and you want the earth to swallow you up, as Sita wanted. But that never happens. They didn't even let me talk to my son, they just gave me a glimpse of him so that I knew what was at stake if I didn't do their bidding.

'I was taken to an interior room where there were five police persons (some sitting around a table and some standing). I stood there and asked why I had been brought there and one of them said, '*Abhi batate hain*' [we'll just tell you]. One of them approached me from behind and tied my hands behind my back and pushed me to the floor. I did shout but you know how sometimes when there is so much fear even your voice starts to fail you. One has that experience in one's dream, that you want to yell but the voice doesn't come out. Besides, they had pulled down the shutters of the police station. So who would hear anything? First they surrounded me and then slowly they approached: they had sticks in their hands and they beat me as I wriggled and turned on the floor to save my face and other exposed parts of my body. They didn't stop and went on and on and on! I could not believe where they were getting that energy — it was a non-stop lashing, first from one then another then another.....

'Within fifteen minutes I was almost unconscious and asked for water. One of the police persons who, after beating me, had sat down at the edge of the table, unzipped his trousers and I said disgustedly, "Oh no not that again, please". He took out his penis and urinated into my mouth saying, "You want water, do you? Here you are". It is at this point that I must have fainted'.

She stops talking and just as well. It was my turn to feel revolted. I need a moment — for what I am not sure. It's as if I'm going to be sick and know I won't, but I would rather not take a chance, so silence is an option. This is the stuff that nightmares are made of, and I couldn't believe that I was face to face with someone who had actually experienced these horrors. When we see such ghastly happenings in films we see them as exaggeration saying 'What drama, what sensationalism.' I remember seeing a film (*Meri Awaaz Suno*) a long time ago where the actor plays the pregnant wife of an upright policeman who stands up to corruption but is then so badly hounded that he decides to disappear for a while. The 'corrupt policemen' then turn to his pregnant wife. She is abducted on the street, locked up in a warehouse, thrown to the floor, and beaten and raped all night long in revenge. There is one scene in which the grocery bag that the woman is carrying falls from her hands and several eggs fall out and shatter to the ground, spilling yolk all over the floor. In the next scene the brutalised woman is unconscious and surrounded in blood: the symbolism being that the pregnant woman had just aborted. The scene upset me, as violent scenes do to any person, but I thought surely this is not real and only gross cinematic license — so much ruthless and lewd behaviour towards an undefended woman was not possible in reality. Now I realise it is.

Mumta is not in tears: she has probably exhausted all her tears by now, after all, this was not an experience that happened the day before. But we, her listeners, are left numb, silent, and actually nauseous.

She continues because that was the worst night of her life and there is so much she must have gone through. 'That night was a long night. I was sore all over and ached with the thrashing. That was not the end: after all they were all there to humiliate and torment me and the next day was a Sunday. I struggled to get up and pleaded to be allowed to go and drink water from the tap down the passage. I limped along and had some water and returned, and all of them laughed and shouted at me. They asked whether this was worse or complying with the CI's request to send her daughter-in-law to his house. "What is the worst that could have happened to her: that he would have had sex with her? So? Don't women have sex? What's the problem with you women? So much pretence and for what? You know, you all have and enjoy sex, then what is all this prudishness about?"'

I have myself often wondered how men view this subject: something similar was once said in front of me by a superintendent of a jail about a woman who had narrated her story about sexual molestation at the hands of her brother-in-law. In an aside he said, '*Arre naatak karti hai. Chaahe isko devar ka bartaav pasand hi aa raha ho! Ghar wala nahin to devar bhi chalega!*' [She is just being dramatic. How does one know — she may actually be enjoying the brother-in-law's advances. If not her husband then her brother-in-law — what's the difference? Sex is sex.]

What can she say in reply to these innuendos and taunts? They are the sort of comments many woman are subjected to — sometimes with more sophistication and finesse and sometimes in this raw and crude form. Harrowing experiences are made worse with the words that accompany them and then it becomes a matter that relates to the body *and* the soul. It was not difficult to visualise Mumta's pain, of both body and spirit, as she sat there nursing her sores and bruises after the perpetrators had clearly exhausted themselves and left her to suffer. For all of the next morning she just sat in that room in pain.

'The next day was a Sunday. My daughter-in-law brought some food for me which they did not allow her to give me. She saw my state and said she was going to report it. "To whom," I asked her. "This is the place that we usually report such things *beti*, so where were you thinking of going?" She started crying because the previous day she had already learnt of the way her husband had been beaten in his cell. It was too much for her and I told her to go back home and see if she could meet someone on Monday and tell them what was happening inside this police station.

'That night the CI came and took me back to his room. He looked at me and said, "come here". Dare I refuse? I moved closer and he unzipped his trousers and put his organ in my mouth and had oral sex with me. I spat out and he slapped me. Then he left. The others outside knew what was happening and the three (from the night before) came in. First R., then S. and then R.G. had intercourse with me. While each did this the others watched. When they were done, I slumped and my clothes were strewn all over the place. R.G. was sitting on the table, shirt all dishevelled, and smoking a cigarette, and said, "You have good thighs". Saying this he got up and put out his cigarette first on my thigh, then on my breast. He lit another cigarette and then pushed the burning cigarette into my anus!

'Then the other fellow lit a cigarette, and they all sat there after the orgy at my expense and I dare not look at them for fear of eliciting some other frightful response: but they didn't need any provocation. "Put out your cigarettes on her breasts guys!" said R.G. "Let's not miss the good parts!" So S. and R. got up and came towards me. I put my hands across my breasts but that didn't stop them. Both stubbed out their lit cigarettes on my breasts and I let out a scream that only got me a kick!'

I shudder and Mumta stops talking and there is a long silence. We all look at each other. What is there to say? It's all over and done and there is a terrible feeling of helplessness. When there was something that needed doing we weren't there, no one was. What about safeguards? It is preposterous to suggest that there have to be safeguards at a police station for protection from the police! I feel like hanging my head in shame. The words 'shame', 'degradation', 'humility' and even 'ruin' keep coming to mind and up against our sensibilities. One feels an acute sense of discomfiture at what happens to people and at one's powerlessness.

While we recoil at the sheer horror of it, Mumta goes on to tell us that there was more. 'I was then dragged out of the room and placed in a corner outside so that before the other people started coming into the police station I would not be found in the CI's room. I kept biting my lip to control the pain and also because I had been threatened with dire consequences if I made a sound', she says, recounting her agony.

And then we are really put to shame. For the rest of Mumta's narration is about how she herself did manage to do something for whatever it was worth. They did not let her go that day: she would be too sore and in pain, and likely to attract attention. The next day (in the evening) she was allowed to go after giving an (informal) undertaking that she would deliver ₹ 3,000 to the CI. Her son was not released: he was sent to 'K' Jail.

Mumta went to the Magistrate's house that evening. She narrated her experiences and showed him the marks all over the body. 'It was not a pleasant experience to meet someone unknown and have to describe and reveal the intense and intimate details of what one has been subjected to. To be honest I was afraid — after being assaulted and abused by state functionaries, how am I to feel assured that I will either get sympathy or be believed by yet another functionary. You can't blame me for being distrustful and sceptical, can you? But he listened, and while I have no idea about the feelings and thoughts that were going through his mind, he did help. He sent me to two advocates R. and S. to whom I had to narrate accurately all the events and happenings yet again. This was for the record. It was like living through it again and again and again: and each time you narrate it you feel ashamed for letting it happen and then get so desperate that you think you will become insane.

'I went home and cried a lot that day. The experience itself and the exposure again and again to convince people that it has happened were too much for me. Ever since my son got married and a daughter-in-law came to the house I looked upon myself as a middle-aged woman and certainly not the object of anyone's sexual transgressions. I was so shattered by running around seeking help that I hadn't realised the depth of my hurt (not just the physical hurt but also my bruised spirit). Only when I was finally in my own home and supposedly safe that I for the first time reflected on all that I had been through and then collapsed.

'Next morning I went to the 'K' Jail to see my son. I went to meet the jail superintendent to apprise him of the circumstances in which my son had been jailed. He saw my devastated physical state and my swollen body and asked what had happened to me. I had to recount all that had happened that weekend and he was aghast. He called his *'jamadar'* [attendant] and told him to get an auto-rickshaw and directed me to the Mahila Mandal (women's organisation) to meet Mrs 'S'. Whatever may or may not have come of my visit to 'K' jail for me, my son was released on bail later.'

Small mercies become such significant achievements and the source of so much light when there are dark clouds all around. Mumta was clearly relieved even in her pain that something positive had happened. She also took comfort from the outcome of her meeting with Mrs 'S' who assured her that there would be some immediate action on her behalf. For better or worse, the incident got publicity; a demonstration and a rally were held and Mumta was taken to the Superintendent of Police and to the local MLA (Member of the Legislative Assembly). After that she was sent to A.G. Hospital for treatment which she badly needed. Her body was singed, raw, sore and bruised, and just the rest and security of being in a safe place was a mercy.

The local MLA and R.R. (party leader) came to see her at the hospital. This attracted media attention and there was press and TV coverage of the incident. How she actually felt about this media focus we would never really know. While her reluctance to talk about the sordid parts of the story was evident, it also seemed that the number of times she had narrated her experience had helped to relieve her trauma somewhat. She talked confidently about her experiences and with bitterness when it came to references to the men in question.

It would be unfair to surmise that she had overcome the shock of being shamed, dishonoured and humiliated, and one probably had to accept her reason for making her experiences public: 'I went for all the media exposure of the gruesome events because I did not want all this to happen to anyone else — ever. After all, my daughter-in-law could have been subjected to it but I was able to safeguard her dignity. Once my *izzat* [honour] had gone I was not bothered about myself and decided to expose it all. People just have no idea what happens anywhere when doors are closed and someone somewhere has full authority not to open them.'

We sit there pondering her experience which seems almost to be made up of separate segments — first the ruthlessness and inhumanity at the hands of the men at the station, and following that, her (voluntary) encounters with the media, with social activists, political groups and many others in an attempt to make the incident as public as possible to get some relief.

It is the nature of this relief that perplexed us all. I wondered if I would have had the mettle and nerve to face repeated queries from an all too curious media about the gory details of the experiences that had left me physically and emotionally scarred. Would I would ever feel sure that those political figures who were so concernedly offering me solace and 'justice' were not in fact thinking something quite the contrary even as they played their politically correct card by giving succour at different levels. Was I succumbing to deep cynicism towards how men would react to such instances? Was I indulging my resentment that more often than not, people were fascinated with horror and that while they couldn't relate to it still felt the need to react in some way? Something bothered me, and I almost didn't know myself just what it was.

But I was not satisfied with the follow up. Mumta had filed cases against the perpetrators and when the Chief Minister of the state heard of the matter, he offered her ₹100,000 as compensation. As a result of the publicity, all those involved absconded and were found weeks later by official search teams and questioned thoroughly, after which they were sent to jail. A few months later they were released on bail and came back to 'K'.

Nothing stops the vindictive; needless to say, what Mumta said subsequently did not surprise any of us. Events like these never play themselves out to the satisfaction of the victim and nor do they slowly peter out. That was part of the discomfort I felt when Mumta narrated the role of the media and official interventions.

'The CI let some time pass and one day some constables came to fetch my son for questioning. It is easy for people to say "don't go, they have no reason to send for you", but in the light of our collective experiences we thought it better to submit. My son went with the cops and didn't come back. We waited for five days and wondered how to complain and to whom. No point going to the local station — they are the ones who took him away in the first place. So, we searched high and low and finally found him in a well — there was a smell and a body was floating. We reported the matter and there was a postmortem that suggested that he had been killed. My son had been given something to drink that made him unconscious and then he was thrown in a well. Of course, I knew who had done this — but do you think I could speak up? I have two other sons. How much could I put at risk?'

We understood that predicament: when so much is lost there comes a point when weariness and fatigue and disillusionment and disappointment take over, and there are two ways one can go: give up and let the worst happen, or fight and *then* let the worst happen. Either way there is a worst that has happened already. If more 'worst' is to come, how much 'worse' could it get. But the weariness and fatigue begins to set in because for some people the intensity of the incident has waned somewhat, and their attention is diverted in other directions. There are so many things that could be attended to that might fetch better gains, even if of an intangible nature.

Police personnel called Mumta again and said that since the state had given her ₹100,000 as compensation, they would offer her ₹200,000 if she made a statement to the authorities that at the police station that night she was unconscious and didn't really know what had happened to her and who had done what. Clearly, they were furious that she had gone to the Magistrate, the local legislator and the media and consequently made a mess of their lives when she had been expressly told not to say anything.

It was clear what they saw as a 'mess of their lives' — that their records had been tarnished. What was that mess compared to the mess in Mamta's life? Nothing that they had done to Mumta directly affected their lives — only the consequences of her actions on their jobs and future in the service. Tainted careers would pose a problem. Mumta's life was so full of mess that she was left clutching at straws and making things worse for herself.

The 'cops' sent her a message again a few days later that the Chief Minister was coming to 'A', the nearby district, and that she would be given treatment at a big hospital where she should reach at 4 pm. Vulnerable and without choices, she went.

'S.R. and four others accompanied me to "A". Just before arriving at the destination S.R. got off and instructed the others to take me safely onwards. The vehicle first stopped at the police station and we got off, and while I was reluctant to alight, they said, "This won't take a minute". So, we went in and they did some paperwork and in a few minutes we were on our way again. They took a very circuitous route around the city and I wondered what was happening: but then I didn't exactly know which hospital I was being taken to. Suddenly we were in front of a big building which they said was a hospital. It was stupid of me to not realise that something might be amiss: why would those responsible for ruining me take me to a hospital? But I thought that they might have been under strict instructions and dared not disobey. Two women in white sarees were at the gate and I thought, Well may be this *is* some kind of hospital!'

I didn't have to be told the rest. They had brought her to the jail under the pretence of taking her to a hospital. They had stopped off at the police station to do the paperwork required to keep her in custody and here she was, in jail. This was the last straw for us. Deep down we were all asking the same question: what is it about you Mumta that makes people take advantage of you?

That was her fifth vulnerability — ignorance and lack of education. She was ill-equipped to understand what she was signing at the police station and had no idea that she was sealing her own fate, as she admitted in her narrative.

'I have been here a while now and have not been allowed to meet anyone. I don't know what kind of papers they prepared at the police station that made my entry to this place so easy. Clearly, they had prepared a statement that related to the original offence of selling packets of liquor at the behest of the CI. After all the original arrest for that offence was still on the records: the CI had registered it and all that they needed to do was get that from the station and make it all legitimate. All the other things that had transpired in between and the horrible things that had happened to me physically and otherwise had no meaning for those admitting me to the jail. They went by the papers presented by the constables who brought me there. They did see the marks on my body even though they were not so fresh as before, and asked how I got them. I told them, but some believed me and some didn't.'

While I begin to feel a sense of frustration at the craftiness of one set of persons and the sheer naivete of the other, I realise what it is that is causing me to react with anger and annoyance. It is the absence of choices in lives that makes people not just desperate but also imprudent and unwise. And the perpetrators know this, and so the vicious cycle goes on and on.

This was a tale of rash behaviour and blunders on all sides; a wild, reckless and disastrous saga. The worst deeds in the drama (the repugnant happenings at the police station) were no longer the primary focus, and other incidents (the selling of illicit liquor almost under duress) had became the legitimate reason for her being in jail. Between that offence and this punishment so much that was abhorrent and repugnant had happened, but it was all wiped clean. We were back to the start, with the sale of illicit liquor becoming the crime with the accompanying procedures that must take their course. The DIG (prisons) was told about Mumta's case on one of his routine rounds of the jail and was apprised of the fact that she had been sent to the jail without being taken to court: He was surprised and said he would look into the matter and he did. There was a meeting of several officials — magisterial, police and jails (including the 'guilty' from the police station) — and the outcome was the decision that Mumta would remain in jail for a year for her original offence of selling illicit liquor.

Was this a cover up? Why was there no appearance before a court? Why this complicity? All of these questions engaged our thoughts. We decide to push for a writ of *habeus corpus* to be filed along with the detention orders and the grounds for detention. Finally, when she does appear before a judge and he hears her case, he orders an inquiry. Meanwhile she returns to jail because of the papers she signed which said that an offence had taken place. And so we get into the process — that never-ending trail of procedures observed more often than not in the 'letter', often at the cost of the spirit. Perhaps, justice is after all about the letter of the law and not the spirit. She violated a rule in the books, it is put down on paper somewhere, and she is an offender (even if yet to be proved guilty). All that is required now is for the procedure to be followed by a penalty and it is the end of the line: so much time in jail and after that one begins afresh. Or so the law thinks. And what about the incidents at station? Maybe the ₹100,000 took care of that.

As far as 'R.G.', 'S' and 'R' were concerned, they had simply had a sexual orgy. Nothing was recorded, so there was no 'process' or procedure, therefore no rule-book violation, and therefore no penalty. That's the way it works. The records won — they showed a legal offence on Mumta's part. The moral/ethical misconduct of the perpetrators was known, but there were no records, in the absence of which what passes for punishment is suspension of duty, transfer, perhaps some public humiliation, and then all is forgotten. So, my earlier discomfort had a cause and while it still prevailed we had a new set of issues to contend with. I was not able to go and see her myself and received this note from my colleague Veena who had been pursuing her case and following her through all her emotional trials and tribulations:

Mumta's condition has deteriorated and she is in acute depression. She was sleeping all the time and in the afternoon did not show any movement. Some of the prisoners informed us about her condition and we went to see her with the doctor. She was not eating and was not ready to drink milk either. She was throwing out each spoon of milk that was fed to her. She has stopped talking to anyone. After short spells of silence she suddenly starts laughing like a hysterical person. The doctor has given her anti-depressants but nothing has changed yet. I have come home and rang the prison in the evening to ask how she was: they said her condition was the same.

That was the last on Mumta: she had lost it — in every sense. She had offended, legally, the circumstances and the advances of the CI. But this is not an acceptable excuse; she was sexually victimised by her 'official' protectors, horrendously molested and barely survived her physical injuries. She fought back to vindicate herself but finally lost. She lost a son, she lost her dignity, she lost her self-respect and eventually lost herself.

Note

Mumta's story is not the only instance of the high-handedness of the police and the brazen disregard of the principles that underlie the role of the police in a democratic society. There are several instances of harrassment by the police towards women in their custody that are reported time and again by the media in different parts of the country. In some cases women have committed suicide as a result of the violence and brutality at the hands of the police.

Most people are familiar with the more publicised cases of police atrocity that created ripples for a long time: the Bhagalpur blindings in Bihar (see Shourie, 1983) and the Mathura Rape Case (*Tukaram and Another v/s State of Maharashtra*, 1978) fundamentally shook the country's faith in the police. The acrimonious coverage in the media seriously damaged the image of the police even as senior police officers tried to redeem that image at conferences and workshops for the next twenty years. Not everyone understood the significance of those events: something vital was missing in the police's guiding principles and the whole system needed a hard second look.

Mumta's was a double penalty — at the police station and the prison — and ironically may have got lost in the many instances of police misconduct had the victim not actually been imprisoned and come under the gaze of volunteer-workers. The horror of what Mamta went through and the sheer vulgarity of the behaviour of the uniformed protectors of society had been seen before. Its recurrence was disconcerting especially because a commission had been set up in the aftermath of the earlier instances to ask the right questions about just what was wrong with our police and police stations. What is our expectation of the police force and what is their expectation of themselves? Something is seriously wrong if these two sets of expectations are totally out of sync with each other; in short what drives our police force?

Do the answers sought then and now relate to the ethos or basic tenets of the police? The underpinnings of police culture still retain the ingredients of that all-pervasive colonial ethos that was the driving force of other areas of the criminal justice system from the middle of the nineteenth century to its present-day form. Like the Penal Code of 1860 and the Prisons Act of 1894, the Police Act V of 1861 is the definitive document for policing even today and represents objectives that serve the interests of rulers and are not about accountability to the citizenry. Like Macaulay's penal recommendations emphasising the instillation of fear as a primary function of punishment, the Police Act of 1861 recommends a police 'so shaped in personnel, powers and procedures as to be a terror to the law-abiding citizen'. The tenets for policing today still come from the same Act that was the mainstay of the colonial regime and was by design a force for establishing order and control in society by severe and ruthless handling where necessary in case of disorder. Protection of society demands severity in dealing with miscreants and maintaining order, which in turn means preventing disorder with firmness. All rhetoric notwithstanding, this is still the guiding principle of everyday policing.

Police reform seems to be an obvious choice in suggesting change when there is turmoil in society. Against the background of 1857 and the Torture Commission Report (Madras), the Madras District Police Act XXIV of 1859 was passed and extended to all of British India as the Indian Police Act of 1861. It recommended the complete removal of Indians from positions of responsibility and a strengthening of European supervision. The model for the new mode of policing was to be the Royal Irish Constabulary established by the British in the early 1800s to quash a series of Irish rebellions. Colonial Ireland had a centralised paramilitary police force while England and Wales had decentralised police systems. Colonial states, it was felt, needed a police answerable to itself and not to the people in a region. The Irish model was particularly popular among British officers in India because of their service and social links with Ireland. Sir Hugh Rose, who was Commander-in-Chief in the Indian army and had served in Ireland, said in 1861: 'no system of police has ever worked better for the suppression of political agitation or agrarian disorder than the Irish constabulary'. After being 'perfected' in India, this colonial policing system was implemented in several British colonies.

The London Metropolitan model set up in 1829, another possible choice for the Indian police, was considered inappropriate. The British developed a strikingly different system for themselves and the London Metropolitan Police was an unarmed police service accountable to the local population through the office of the Home Secretary and which focused on prevention of crime through cooperation with the local community. But in India the organisation was structured with the interlocking of supervision and control: control over the police department by the civil administration, and the supervision of Indian police persons by European supervisors, as also a rigid hierarchy with superintendency on top, inspectorate in the middle and constabulary at the bottom. Superiors did not engage in ordinary police work: they made sure everyone else did their tasks properly, i.e., firmly.

There was a review of the police force at the beginning of the 20th century at Lord Curzon's behest and a commission was set up in 1902 to address inefficient and corrupt performance. India became independent 45 years later, but the Police Act V of 1861 still forms the backbone of the police force. Democratic principles and constitutional safeguards notwithstanding, nothing in police functioning has changed so radically with independence.

Just as the 1857 mutiny acted as a spur for the colonial power in making its law and order policies more stringent, regardless of the emphasis on uniform codes and law, there have been some historical moments when independent India got an opportunity to revamp its obsolete police force. The promulgation of the democratic constitution was one such opportunity and the post-emergency period when a National Police Commission was set up was another. The National Police Commission of 1978 highlighted several aberrations that have plagued the performance of the police for a century and a half. Brutality, corruption, politicisation, inefficiency and lack of professionalism — these are only some of the words used to describe the police and the 1978 Commission believed the police force had to rid itself of these unflattering descriptions.

Commissions have pronounced on the shortcomings of the 1861 Act and on the failure of the force to meet the demands of modern policing in a democratic system: the buzz words are law and order, and as guiding principles for policing, are endorsed by both state and society and bracketed to suggest their interconnectedness. But maintaining order at all costs is asserted as the greater priority without which nothing would work. It is a lame excuse that we must *establish* order first before enforcing law. The former is invariably achieved by forcible means, the latter cannot be so achieved. The Act of 1861, following as it did a period of total disorder, was not designed to be democratic in spirit or in implementation.

How does all this impact the kind of cases discussed in this chapter? The role, goals and purposes set out as primary for policing still see the maintenance of order as an urgent objective. An understanding of the causes of disorder or disharmony are not part of the police's brief, and as a result they become social fire-fighters who bring order by any means. What ensues is the development of all the skills required for quelling rebellious behaviour, forcibly weeding out miscreants, ruthlessly ensuring that there are no repeat acts of hostility and belligerence, and instilling enough fear and awe to make them a dreaded force. If such an image is allowed to be nurtured for too long, there is no space for the real qualities of policing in a healthy democracy: accountability to citizens, respect for the judicial machinery, and prevention of crime and disorderly conduct through links of trust and cooperation with the people. The absence of these guiding principles and the public's lack of faith in the protectors of society is what probably prompted the force to adopt the kind of comforting rhetoric ('with you for you always') that some States have done.

All these failings exhibited themselves in the behaviour of the police personnel at this particular station where Mumta was held for all of that brief period. It is not that they did not know the boundaries of the law that determine their conduct and behaviour. How then do excesses occur? Some of the feedback from people suggested a few reasons. '*Yeh sochte hain khakhi pehan rakhi hai to roab jamana hai*' [they think the uniform helps to create awe which is meant to keep people in their places]. Others said police personnel feel they have been given power and it is meant to be used. Yet others said, '*Inko tehzeeb nahin sikhai gayee*' [they were never taught that they have to be cultured and civilised in the line of duty].

These comments are simple inferences from those who have been psychologically and emotionally injured by individual police personnel. A more insightful analysis would be one that looks at two features of police performance that seem to continually contradict each other: expectation and execution, or ends and means, and the inability to reconcile the dilemmas that follow. The cadres that interface with the public and those with supervisory roles have minimal interaction between them — almost as if they were from different planets. If the ordinary citizen has complaints about police performance at the interface level, whom would they complain to? Seniors who are out of reach for the simple folk?

Cases of excess multiply till a stage comes when change becomes imperative if society is to survive. The Police Act Drafting Committee was set up in 2005 to revamp the system. The prioritisation of the Terms of Reference (TOR) of the PADC is interesting. Its first task is the drafting of a new Police Act to meet the challenge of the 'growth and spread of insurgency/militancy/naxalism etc'. Then it must help to bring about attitudinal change in the police, including its working methodology, to elicit the cooperation of the community and to meet its expectations from the police in a modern, democratic society. Thirdly, it must provide for the use of scientific investigation methods to tackle 'futuristic trends and organised crime including cyber crime and technological additions in the hands of criminals etc'. Finally, 'the concern for human rights, weaker sections, women and the people belonging to Scheduled Castes/ Scheduled Tribes' must be addressed. When social justice, human rights and concern for weaker sections is the last in order of importance and combating insurgency and quelling rebellion are the primary anxieties, it is unlikely that police misdemeanours behind closed doors would be a major concern at any level.

It is regular day-to-day police work that contributes to the diffusion of conflicts and maintenance of order. Stern short-term measures for maintaining order rather than long-term objectives for looking into the underlying causes of problems can lead to a dangerous volatility. The strategies to deal with 'naxalism', political unrest and regional demands have generally used force to curb violence without creating any alternative ways of police involvement. Consequently, the police become the 'enemy' and a target for agitators, and are seen not as neutral agents of the law but as armed spokespersons of the entrenched establishment.

Police brutality and violation of a (normative) professional code is one aspect of Mumta's experience, i.e., the impunity with which the police can commit such heinous acts as they did. The other (more positive) aspect is Mumta's ability to do something of her own volition after all her suffering. That it was not a replay of the Mathura Rape Case (where the courts had difficulty convicting the police constable because there were no visible injury marks and therefore the intercourse was considered consensual) is probably attributable to some changes in the law relating to offences relating to women: the rape law was amended in 1983, cruelty against women was made a crime in 1984, dowry deaths became an offence in 1986, and domestic violence in 2005. While the

Mathura Rape Case brought a new offence relating to rape on the books — that relating to rape by a police officer within the premises of a police station — it also added that if there has been sexual intercourse and the woman says it was not consensual the court will presume that that was indeed so.

The absence or presence of the law, however, is not the whole problem. Rape by persons in a position of authority (police officers, jail wardens, hospital staff, etc.) has been addressed by the Rape Law of 1983 and changes recommended. Before that the Indian Penal Code (Sections 375 and 376) had little to offer for the burden of proof question always trumped the woman whoever she was and wherever she was. The 1983 Act changed the Code, and Clauses amending Section 376 made rape in custody punishable by imprisonment.

Clearly, much is still needed and need to be done. Apart from the law, the question of credibility and definitions still remain as stumbling blocks. In Sakshi v/s Union on India (1997), a host of issues were brought up including the question of definitions, the inadequacy of the law and the need for a fundamental changes in the law on rape and sexual assault. A change from the old to the new (if there is a new) however is not just about change in the law. Old habits die hard: the men in uniform were still on top and Mumta's courage could only get her that far.

This trajectory of the evolution of the police has a bearing on what people suffer 'inside'. While some states have gone to great lengths to present a better image to the public and seek community participation (Andhra Pradesh), others seem content with the old policing methods, justifying them with every new threat, real or potential, internal or external. If threat to security becomes a rationale for severe policing, the citizen as person is the first casualty.

Add to that the vulnerability of women in general and the defencelessness of women of particular groups and strata in Indian society, and we have the makings of a one-sided relationship between the police force and women. Men in uniform stand by each other if aberrations in performance are brought to the notice of any one section of their ilk. *Espirits de corps*, it is called, to suggest morale and belief in a common cause. That the common cause serves another larger cause increasingly gets lost and the results are there for all to see. Covering up aberrant behaviour cannot be condoned and if there is to be a review of police performance, this, above all, needs to be addressed among other things. Hopefully, the next attempt at police reform will take this on board.

4

Bina's Fourteen Years of *Jailvaas*

I never thought I would see her again. I have photos of her from almost fifteen years ago when she was a pre-trial prisoner in Naini Central Jail in UP — one of the first jails I researched at length (and breadth, and width, and all other dimensions that a jail purports to have). I spent hours and days on the records, on interviews, on examining and understanding the layout, on the activities and facilities and why they are what they are, on why the surroundings were so stark and bare, on why the prisoners in the carpentry and foundry sections were actually making handcuffs and leg irons as part of work, on why their wages were still calculated as '4 annas' when we had gone metric in the year 1956 and when daily wages had been revised so many times in the outside world. I also made several visits with the Chief Judicial Magistrate to understand the actual process of remand extension and the manner in which he conducted it within the jail precincts — the questions he asked and the replies that he got. I was impressed with the magistrate's agreeable manner while he conducted the sessions.

Since no jail is incident-free on any day, in the course of this activity a guard suddenly brought in a man bleeding profusely with a gash on his forehead and holding his hand over his face.

'Sir' said the superintendent to the magistrate, 'may I trouble you to please look into this matter. This is a recurring problem for us, and one that we are a little hesitant to tackle without expert advice. We have a Canadian prisoner who was arrested in Benaras for possessing and using drugs. He has been brought here and kept in Enclosure A (for special prisoners). Everyday he creates some problem and today this one has occurred. He asked a prisoner to sweep his barrack. While the fellow was sweeping he picked up the Canadian's bag and tried to put it aside in his own way. The Canadian accused him of stealing from his bag and gave him a hard blow on his face. The fellow knows he can call upon his embassy for support if we push him or say anything that he can misrepresent, so he takes advantage of that and takes out all his frustration on either the staff or prisoners'.

There we were faced with a crisis within an hour of arrival. I wondered how this was going to be tackled. But for them, this was almost a matter of routine.

I made several visits to this jail, a relatively large and high-profile one in this state. As far as I was concerned, I was researching and understanding a male prison (not the least of its features being the section where Jawaharlal Nehru lived when he was imprisoned several times during the national movement before independence in the 1930s). It also housed 'terrorists' from the Kashmir region detained under the Terrorism and Dangerous Activities Act (TADA, as it was popularly known). Studying them, their attitude, their behaviour and the facilities accorded them was an education for a novice like me. They were in a separate enclosure reading interesting books — one I vividly recall was *'Ek mianey mein do talwar'* [Two Swords in One Scabbard]. They were cooking their own food (that day it was mutton curry and rice and smelt wonderful from a distance), they wore good clothes and were getting along splendidly among themselves. On a subsequent visit a few weeks later, they were being taken away from Naini Jail and I met them and took a picture. They were in good spirits and I asked them to tell me how they had been looked after: they said a lot of positive things and then suddenly asked if I, as a researcher, would like them to write out their views about how they had been treated. I can't explain why they offered to, but they did, and I had all of them sign a written statement in which they had a lot of praise for the superintendent. Maybe an investment for the next time they came back to Naini!

While I continued with my exploration and investigations in Naini Central Jail, what I failed to realise was that the jail had a female enclosure adjoining the main building where pre-trial prisoners from the vicinity were kept till their sentencing, after which they were sent to the women's jail in Lucknow. I asked to be allowed to spend some time there with the women and also take photographs of the premises and the prisoners. 'There are very few women there,' I was told, 'but do visit by all means'. So I did.

A male warder took me inside the enclosure (a separate nondescript gate just down the lane from the main prison's quite large, typical and very ornate prison gate) and also accompanied me inside the jail. I was a bit surprised at that; I thought he would accompany me to the gate and hand me over to the staff in the women's section and then return to the men's prison. He seemed to be known and welcomed and he stayed for a few minutes before returning. As soon as I entered, the woman-in-charge welcomed me and asked what I would like to know. By then I was aware that the best way to start a fruitful prison visit is to talk to the person in charge congenially and respectfully and then move on to the 'real' difficulties and dilemmas surrounding the prison.

So we talked: I realised with amazement that she was most uninterested in the women. Her first words to me were: 'Don't be misled by their woebegone faces: most of them are here for really bizarre acts of criminality. They are cunning things these women and know how to spin yarns to get sympathy. We know just how they should be handled.'

Right I thought. So I know where I stand on this one. 'Oh I'm sure you know best,' I said. 'After all you have so many women come and go you know what they do and how they behave, and I am sure you know what their needs are.' My last statement was intended to be sarcastic but was taken at face value. And the warder responded with zeal.

'Oh yes', she said. 'We know their needs alright — some of them are really devious creatures. You see that rather fashionable-looking woman there. She is wearing a fancy blouse with her *saree*. She was admitted some days ago and was so rebellious you will not believe it. Because she didn't get her way in all things she did something really strange: she tore her blouse down the front, and then began shouting when the male warder came to leave a prisoner, saying that he had ripped her blouse and was misbehaving with her. You see these are the kinds of things we often face and then some people say, "Oh these are women don't be harsh with them." Now you tell me, Ma'am, how would you deal with a situation like that?'

I naturally have no answer (especially at this point since I had less experience of women prisoners, of prison staff and the relationship between them). At this point in time, 15 years later, I could answer her from a more than informed standpoint. But at that time she was in command and I just went along learning and observing and making notes and asking questions as lucidly as I could to elicit the most comprehensive answers that I could. In prison interviews, even my limited experience (just about two years then) told me that the nature of the question and how it was presented were crucial. Equally, the response would be tainted by the respondent's vested interests, attitudes, position, mindset and everything that goes with their individual and social make-up. But despite my limitations, I didn't feel too handicapped for some reason.

Then I saw her: a loner who was standing apart from the rest in a red and mustard coloured printed *saree*. She had a lost air about her, but a pleasant and sensitive face, young and very aloof. She had a child with her and just stood watching things around almost with disinterest.

'Who's she?' I asked. 'She stands apart from the rest and in the time I have been talking to you I have been watching her — she is not here, I mean in thought. She seems too lost and hasn't moved very much from where she's been standing.' I had even taken a picture of her almost without her knowing it and then she saw me and moved (an inch?).

'She's Bina,' the warder told me. 'She's something else. Not one of those dowry death women, or spouse killers. She is here for having killed two minor children. Rather a long story with a few strange twists — but it is tantamount to murder and she is dazed as a result of being brought to jail for what she did.'

'What?' I exclaimed . 'Killing two children? How and why on earth?'

'As I said, it's a long story, Ma'am. When you come again, why don't you ask her?'

I moved along the courtyard. Other women came forward and said, '*Namaste*, Ma'am', and I felt like squirming. I still do when I visit prisons because I have a feeling that the women are probably secretly thinking, 'What do you think we are: some kind of curiosity object or what? What on earth have you come for? You know you won't be doing much for us, so why bother to make the journey all the way across town to come and visit the jail'. Most of these women were from surrounding villages and less sharp than the urban women I encounter everyday who try and give me careless answers to questions.

Then a woman came up to me and said she was the teacher, whose job it was to make the women literate and teach them about living and life through stories — classic tales that were interesting and hopefully had a message too. She said she lived outside the premises and came each day to work with the women.

In a far corner, a woman was trying to light a fire in a brick *choolah* (makeshift fireplace, this one — just six bricks one on top of the other set out in a U-shape). She wasn't getting anywhere although she had been at it ever since I arrived. All she was creating was a lot of smoke and I had sneezed a couple of times as it tickled my nose and made my eyes water. I asked the teacher what was happening. Why was she lighting the fire, and why was the fire not starting, and why all that smoke. She walked two steps away from where we were, and I understood from her manner that she wanted to tell me something in confidence.

'The women cook their own food here: it doesn't come from the main kitchen in the men's prison. Why you might ask? Because someone would have to keep coming to deliver it — and if it is someone from a men's prison there is always that issue about letting too many men come for duties to women's prisons and so on. So it is decided that it is best that they cook themselves. They take turns and manage. This fire is being lit for lunch.'

'Lunch?' I ask, surprised. 'It's already 2 pm. And she hasn't even got the fire started.'

'That's the way it is here, Ma'am. And do you want to know why? Because the wood is damp and hence all that smoke. Why is it damp? Because the tender for the supply of wood was given to some crony known to the superintendent and the contract is ensured. The rate is fixed per quintal, so they wet the whole supply of wood so that it is heavy and they make more money.'

This was my first exposure to the corruption nexus inside prisons. Since then I have become so well informed about forms of prison corruption that I could write a book just on that. At the time I was furious at this relatively 'minor' instance of corrupt practices.

'What an unfair thing to do,' I exclaim. 'She could be at it for another hour and the fire won't light and they will not have had lunch. When on earth do they eat lunch? In the men's prison they are through by 12.30. And when will she cook dinner?'

'Don't ask. There probably won't be any dinner', is the reply.

The whole area is a barren and muddy bit of land. There are only two cottage-like structures — one constituting the living quarters and the other a room with a *verandah* where the teacher takes classes and where people meet with the women when required. The place where the women light the fire has a small shed-like structure behind it, presumably for the kitchen stuff and for storing other supplies. The women just wander about with nothing to do, and aside from cooking (and then eating and clearing up) and assembling for the teacher, they are idle and seem quite depressed.

'Would you like me to get the women together so that you can meet them all and get to know them', asks the teacher.

'Yes, and also ask them if they mind my taking pictures of them, and tell them they will not be published. They will be my personal pictures reminding me how sad faces are inside this place. I also want to record the ages of the children accompanying them.'

We go to the *verandah* and they sit around in a circle. The teacher sits in the centre facing them and tells them about me. She tells them I am not a *patrakar* [journalist], I am not from a charity, and I am not a lawyer. She has a problem herself in defining what I really am. I don't blame her; I hardly know myself. By then I have taken a few pictures and far from antagonising the women, it has made them smile shyly. They cover their heads with their *saree pallu*, or adjust their hair almost as if they were readying themselves in their Sunday best. I try to reassure myself that the ice has been broken.

I decide to start talking to them. I tell them that I have come to learn about their lives, to understand why they are here, and the circumstances that led to what they did, how they feel here, how they view their future and whether their families are helpful and sympathetic or not. I admit I know little about women in jails and have come not because I am curious, but because being a woman I want to understand what leads a woman to commit the offence that has brought her to this place.

Some women start talking together and I ask them to please speak one at a time. So, each one starts to tell her story, and of the nearly twenty, at least three-quarters 'did not do it'. All of them have things to say about how their families' lives would be ruined with them being away, and that they have left little children behind who will suffer in so many ways. What could I do to help that?

Good question, I think, but I don't have an answer. And while many of them continue talking I look at the woman in the red and mustard *saree:* she is silent and has not spoken a word and as I look at her, our eyes meet and she looks away. She sits cross-legged on the floor and the child is in her lap. I don't want to push her so I don't bully her into talking. I turn to the teacher and say, 'Why is she not saying anything, I wonder?'

'Bina why are you not saying something to Ma'am', the teacher asks.

No reply.

'Say something at least. Tell Ma'am your name then and your daughter's.'

No reply.

Bina does not talk and the more silent she is the more curious I get. I can't force the issue and realise I will have to wait till my next visit: she may say something then. Most of the women I talk to show concern about the lack of contact with their families, repeating again and again how they must be suffering because all the members depended on the women. Some of them start crying and wish that they had not let their families down and jeopardised their future. This is their prime worry: how is the family managing (or not).

I have spent about an hour with them and all the while also have an eye on the progress of that fire. It finally gets going just as I am leaving: with some new wood and vigorous blowing it takes off, still smoking. They must have had smoked *dal* and *chaval* for lunch.

As I make my way to the exit (of the women's section) the teacher suddenly comes running and hands me a tiny piece of paper with her phone number written on it. 'Just keep this Ma'am, I would like to meet you outside the prison whenever you can spare the time.' I take the number and realising she doesn't really want to make that request public, I slip it into my bag and say goodbye. I also give her my address in case she wants to get in touch herself.

I am escorted to the main jail and then am driven back after a relatively exhaustive visit to one of the large, historic and well-known central jails of the largest and most populous State in India.

As the magistrate drives me back, he says, 'Look at all the things that happened all on a day's visit: the visit, the remand extensions, the Kashmiri detenus, the incident caused by the Canadian prisoner, and of course your visit to the women's section. Quite a full day wouldn't you say?'

I agree and say I need to follow up the many strands and would really like to be able to make several trips freely and unreservedly, and is that possible. He says he would arrange it and vouch for my bona fides and send me a letter to that effect.

While I contemplate the focus of my next visit, it is not the TADA detenus, or the Canadian, or the other features of the visit that is occupying my mind. It is Bina. I have not got to know anything about her and I am a bit perturbed that a woman with a child and one so young has been accused of killing two children in her village. It keeps bothering me. I need to know why. And yet Bina is so incommunicative that I think I would never be able to get to the bottom of it.

I go back a few days later after my letter for unlimited access arrived. The superintendent gives me tea and biscuits and asks what I would like to do that day. 'Two things', I said. 'I want to look at some records and I want to spend time at the women's enclosure'. That is easily arranged in reverse order so that it doesn't clash with their lunch. Considering how long it takes them to light their fire this is a better arrangement anyway.

The teacher [*guruji*] is delighted to see me if no one else is. Staff usually has mixed feelings towards visitors: they are welcome for a change, but resented for their curiosity — too many questions, too many comments and too much criticism. But the teacher has little to lose; how much can one say to a teacher who is teaching illiterates the alphabet and basic words and telling stories with good messages.

I tell *guruji* that I want to talk at length with Bina without making either her or the others conscious of the fact that it is my prime objective for the day. She says she will find a way to work around that. She assembles them together again and starts telling stories. Half-way through she beckons to me that Bina is standing alone under the tree and would I like to try and talk to her. I slowly make my way in that direction and bend down to talk to her daughter. Fortunately, I have a biscuit in my bag and I ask the teacher if I can give it to the child. She takes it and smiles. Bina looks at me quizzically but says nothing. No words and no responsive expression either.

I ask her name. Silence. I ask the name of her village. Silence. What did you do that brought you here? Silence, of course. So, where does one begin? I've exhausted all the usual routine questions, so where do I go from here? *Guruji* comes to the rescue.

Arre Bina! Ma'am ko batao to ki tum kahan se aayee ho. Shayad who tumhare parivar ki khabar laa sakey! [Tell Ma'am where you've come from, maybe she can find out about your family].

Silence again. But now she starts moving her body a bit: there is a cemented platform at the tree where we have been standing and *guruji* has taken the initiative in sitting down and beckoning both of us to follow. So I do, and offer another biscuit to the child. Bina takes a step in our direction then stops. She holds her daughter's hand and comes and sits down with her on the cemented platform. It is hot and sunny and I am happy to sit under the tree.

Guruji tries again. '*Bina tum agar baat nahin karogi to kuchch nahin hoga. Chalo, kuchch to batao*' [If you don't talk nothing will happen. Come on, say something].

I chip in saying, 'Which village are you from? I belong to Allahabad town, but I know the surrounding areas well — so which part do you come from?'

'Dighi village in Tharwai,' she says.

First words, and very important at that. Where one hails from always means the most for people who *are* their village and their community. Village is the beginning and end of their existence and that is something one realises more and more as one goes deeper into the lives of those who have been brought to these neutered places.

'What does your husband do?' I am not sure if that is a good question, but I ask it anyway. I had given myself a choice between 'How old are you?' and 'What does your husband do?' and I felt the latter had more meaning: age means little to people who don't have to connect events in their lives with age and dates.

'He has a cycle rickshaw.'

'Does he earn enough from that?'

She stares at me again. 'What is enough?' she says.

Yes, you're right, I think. What is enough?

'Oh, what I mean is could you make ends meet and feed your children?'

'Of course, I could not. Which rickshaw puller's family can?'

I am not sure that I am going about this the right way and look at *guruji* who takes the cue.

'Bina. Look, let me explain. Don't hold back because you think this is a useless exercise and nothing will come of it. What have you got to lose anyway? May be something good might happen. So, why don't you open up and tell Ma'am some more about yourself. She is not from the jail department, but she is working towards jail reform and justice issues, so let's give it a try. After all she doesn't even know why you are here.'

We sit quietly, as she contemplates her next move.

'I lost my son, she says. 'I lost my five-year-old son. Everyone will want to know what I am here for. Hardly anyone has anything to say about the fact that I lost my only son.' She is devastated but does not cry.

'I had three children — an older daughter Anita, a son and an infant daughter (points to the two-year-old in her lap) who was six months old and whom I was still feeding myself when my son died. My five-year-old son was very sick for many months and we tried every treatment possible in the village. All the doctors, *hakims*, *vaids*, and faith healers could not save him. He was our only son.'

Even *guruji* admits she has not heard anything as cogent from Bina till then. I don't interrupt. Maybe she will talk some more, maybe she won't. I decide to take my chances.

Guruji says to her: 'So you must have been really saddened by the son's death.'

'I fell ill and even though I had a baby to feed I just could not get myself out of bed to attend to my infant daughter. I would feed her and then would just go back into a stupor and a state of unawareness [*sudh budh kho baithi thi*]. It was as if my legs just would not move. That was for me the worst time of my life. Now of course, so much more has happened.'

'We had even tried *jhar-phook* on my son. An *ojha* told us that we must perform *jharh-phook* and get the evil spirit away. "Someone is cursing him," he said, "and we needed to neutralise and counteract that". So we did. But nothing worked and he died. They all tell me I had become mentally unstable, but I don't even remember what had happened to me. Yes, I think I had become *bawari* [crazy].'

She is beginning to open up a little, but is still not ready to talk about the events of that fateful day in November later that year when two boys were drowned and she was arrested and accused of having killed them. We don't push. We continue to talk about her son.

'You know how much a son means in our lives in villages: everyone blesses a mother who gives birth to a son. And then he fell ill. Someone clearly cursed him. God does not do such merciless things. He is kind. Some mean human being cursed him.'

'Why do you feel that?'

'Because we had a neighbour [Santram] who was not at all kind to us and the *ojha* said may be this is Santram's curse on the child. Who knows. Why should Santram curse my child even if he does not like us? But I think he probably did. I am sure he said at some time, "Let her son die, what do I care", and he died. Can you imagine losing your only son?'

'I am sorry that such a thing happened to you and now you are in this place with two little daughters?'

'They say that the older one will be taken away from me because she will soon be too old to be kept in the prison. Her father will take her because they don't allow ....' and she trailed off because she didn't want to go into technicalities that she might not have understood.

'Does your husband come to visit?'

'Very rarely. Right at the beginning he did. But now it is already a year since I came here and now no one comes. What would they come for? To hear depressing things and look at my depressing face? So, I have no news of them.'

I wonder what the rickshaw-puller husband would be doing about now? Has he 'moved on' to other things? Who will take care of the older daughter when she turns seven? And why is Bina not weeping? She looks composed even in her grief and desolation. Or is it a numbness that I am interpreting as composure? It is a little unreal, but no one else thinks it unusual. Gradually I do get answers (spoken and unspoken) to many of these perplexing questions, but it takes time.

In the meanwhile the questions come flooding to my mind, and I figure then that I need to systematise them and then approach her. What exactly happened that day? Maybe, I should see the records. Maybe, I should see the police reports.

'I will come again' I tell her, as if I am assuring her. Actually I am assuring myself I suppose, keeping the path open for our future interaction.

The fire routine has now started. The place is once again filled with smoke and I wonder when the meal will actually be ready.

❋❋❋

Guruji contacts me and we meet outside the jail, actually at the teashop of a woman prisoner who, along with her husband, had been sent 'in' for a 'dowry death' and they were out on bail and running their shop again. I talk with them too, and as with everyone I meet, I hear a long-winded story about how they 'didn't do it, weren't even there on that fateful day', and so on. I take pictures of the couple doing brisk business at the kiosk. The woman makes me a cup of tea, milky and very sweet. It is certainly not something I enjoy, but large amounts of milk and sugar in the tea is a sign of generosity and one cannot refuse it. What is interesting for me is the stark contrast between an acutely depressed Bina 'inside', fresh with her wounds, and this couple out on bail, running their shop normally, and vigorously protesting their innocence. In both cases there are offences, there are victims, and guilt still not proved: but one set of offenders has been able to use the legitimate procedural path to temporary freedom and are for all practical purposes living normal lives 'until further notice', while the other is 'rotting' inside and hardly likely to get a taste of freedom any time soon from what I can make out of her circumstances and wherewithal. And yet, when this woman at the tea shop was inside the prison, I have no doubt she must have looked as woebegone as Bina and to the cursory eye the two would have been grouped into that large and all-inclusive category of 'women prisoners'.

Guruji and I talk at length over tea at the shop: that jails are strange and unreal places for human beings. If I was envisaging change of any kind, I was fooling myself. "Why would they want to change anything, Ma'am? Think about it. There are vested interests at every twist and turn of prison management and oddly enough even prisoners are so set in the whole system that you would have to wake them from their stupor to advocate change.'

I can tell she is all worked up and uptight about things 'there'. Being somewhat on the fringes of the real system and clearly not in the inner circle, she has a kind of cynical objectivity about the goings-on inside. That has its disadvantages. Not treated as an insider obviously irritates her, but it also means that she is able to distance herself somewhat from the arrangements of the system, even if from her own standpoint. I listen, carefully aware that she has her own agenda.

'The female in charge in the women's section is a real terror,' she says. 'You know the story she told you about the woman who tore her own blouse and blamed it on the male escort? Well, the real thing is, it was she who ripped the woman's blouse because she was irritated by what she called the woman's *adaayen* [airs and graces].'

I realise that *guruji* was not happy working there: 'No one really likes working in a jail. But a job is a job. When people first come to a prison, whether it is staff or prisoners, they are different from what they become as time goes on. Everyone gets a twist in their personalities,' and adds quickly, 'I am sure I have too!'

'You cannot imagine the small and big things that go on inside and by all accounts these "things" are one or another kind of corruption. You seemed perturbed by the racket relating to the wet firewood at the jail. Well let me tell you every person in the staff avails him or herself of the rations that come for prisoners. *Dal* [lentils], *chaval* [rice], *ata* [flour], vegetables, edible oil, even cooked food, it is all pilfered and everyone knows it. So, whom will you report it to?'

I have a smile on my face and she understands. 'Why am I telling you all this? Just in case you think that your pleas or suggestions or recommendation will move someone to act, I feel I should tell you that there is nothing but disillusionment waiting at the other end.'

My smile vanishes and she can see that too. 'I don't want you to think I am a pessimist. I also had some hopes of enabling the women to learn something even if I am not the greatest educationist. They are so ill-equipped that even if a little bit of what I say trickles down into their behaviour and conduct it will be an achievement. But you know what? The staff don't really want the prisoners to be better equipped. So, I am not about to make any dent in that direction.'

What we have here, I think, as she speaks, is an attempt to both vent her own disillusionment and to address, vicariously, my dreams and visions of reform and change. I will still carry on but it helps to know how she feels.

Then she talks about Bina. Clearly, she has noticed that I am concerned about her. 'Bina is a mess,' she says. 'Because the offence involves the death of children she is not likely to get any compassion at any stage. Of course, she has not been tried yet. There seems to be a complicated story here, but no one will hear it and in any case she does not talk. So, I don't see her getting anything positive coming her way. While it is true that as a teacher I can only do that much, I must tell you with honesty that in any case so many women come and go that I can't begin to get involved in their stories. But this woman needs to be investigated independently, and if you can I am sure it will help.'

Both of us then need to move on. I thank her for coming to see me and for giving me tips. Nothing is different. I am not any wiser about how we can work towards alleviating what I believe is a difficult situation. And while she has defined the problem, she hasn't offered any solutions. Yet there is a ray of hope: she still thinks I should keep at it. So, I am a little less despondent than I might otherwise have been — I don't feel completely deflated because even if I can't do, even if I can't help much, some small thing somewhere will help someone.

❋❋❋

I don't get anywhere with Bina's own narration. And I have other jails to visit. I leave the town, and when I return many months later, several of the women are still there. Bina certainly is: after all she was charged with murder under Section 302, so she wouldn't have gone through any conclusive process for justice *so* fast (given the track record for trials and sentencing). *Guruji* is still there and apparently happy to see me. Bina gives a curious smile of recognition and we sit down to talking '*haal chaal*' (greetings of well-being). Her daughter is a little more settled (I usually dislike the use of that word for prisoners — it suggests that they have actually become comfortable in a place as wretched as a jail). She looks more self-possessed and less disturbed and does not cling to her mother.

I am told that Bina has a hearing in court at the end of the week, and I take down the details. I have already decided to go through the records at the lower court in the meantime to acquaint myself with the official version before I get Bina's, if at all. I tell Bina I will meet her in court and meet the lawyer too. I make my way to the District Court on the appointed day and meet with Bina in the Court 'lockup'. She is elated to see me because prisoners are bullied while they wait for hearings and my presence is a message to the police escorts accompanying the *bandis* [prisoners] that they had better not step out of line. She is visibly relieved. I go to the cell where prisoners wait before they are called to have a chat with her and tell her I will meet her next time at the jail. There is no sign of her husband at the court. Her daughter is singing quietly in the corner. I take a picture of her and she giggles.

Now for the records. By the time I next meet Bina a hearing and a judgement have already taken place. A few legal contacts in the lower court and I am able to get some of the records. The story is fully narrated in the details of the First Information Report, the case of the prosecution and the Judgement. Bina herself was not really able to tell me anything with clarity: it was just too traumatic for her. This story is therefore pieced together from many strands.

Bina lives in Dighi village in Tharwai (in Allahabad district) with her husband, who is a rickshaw-puller, and three children. Santram and his family are their neighbours. Early in 1993, Bina's only son died of an undiagnosed illness preceded by a high fever for many weeks. The family believed he was possessed and doctors, 'medicine men', faith healers, herbal cures and even 'exorcists' were summoned to drive away evil spirits and cure the boy. Nothing helped. Various rites and rituals were performed and even human sacrifice was recommended. Unfortunately the five-year-old boy died, and the family was devastated with grief. Bina was wrought with guilt that they had not done enough to save the child. A local *ojha* even told her that someone had cursed the boy and that had she repelled the curse with appropriate rituals her son may still have been alive. Over the next few months she allowed herself to be persuaded that her neighbour Santram had cursed her son.

Bina became ill and took a long time coming to terms with the son's death. Together with this, she had two other children — Anita, a daughter, and a six-month-old baby she was still feeding. She was distraught and dysfunctional. There is little that we glean from either the records, or Bina's own narrative about how her husband had reacted either to the son's illness, death or Bina's subsequent despondency. Bina's near collapse seemed to have been common knowledge in the village.

Some months after the passing away of Bina's son, the unfortunate event relating to Santram's sons occurred. It was around

Diwali in 1993 and the village was busy with festivities and religious ceremonies. Bina says she was in no mood for celebrations and stayed indoors. She didn't even perform *pooja* (formal prayers) to Ganesh and Lakshmi because she was angry with God. In an atmosphere of lights, fire crackers, feasting and music there was enough happening in the village for all.

This was the night (13 November) that Santram's son Raju (eight years old) disappeared and there was a further commotion. Santram went to look for him, as did many of the village folk. About 7 am the next morning, the boy's body was found in Ram Bharose's well. The younger son, Ramu (one year old), had also gone missing the previous evening while everyone was looking for the older son Raju.

On the morning of 14 November, Santram allegedly reported the matter to the police that his younger son, Ramu, who had also been missing since the previous evening, had still not been found, and as he was an infant it was a cause for grave concern. A constable prepared the First Information Report (dated 14 November 1993: 7.30 am) and a search was organised. At the police station that morning, someone reported seeing Bina on the 'airport road' and a search party was sent to look for her and interrogate her. Later the same day, Ramu's body was recovered from another well about 500 metres outside the immediate village premises.

Bina was arrested because statements taken from several people alleged that she was seen roaming around on the outskirts of the village. The main evidence on which she was arrested was the statement Santram's (minor) daughter Suman made, alleging that Bina had come to the house (on the evening of 13 November) and asked for water, and when she went to get it, Bina ran off with the little boy. Suman also deposed that she asked Bina why she was carrying her little brother away, and she said, 'Your mother asked me to bring him to her as your parents are busy looking for their older son.'

According to the prosecution, when Bina was confronted by the police that afternoon she was told that she had been seen taking away the boy, and that she had also been seen returning from a place some distance away from the village. She allegedly confessed that she had thrown the boy into the well. However, in her defence it was stated that she denied having either thrown any child into a well, or made a statement indicating the direction of the well. The First Information Report that I read had a phrase that intrigued me for a long time: It said, 'Bina first denied having committed the act but when she was pushed — *'baar baar puchhne par aur zor dalne par'* [after repeated interrogation and pressure] — she said she had done so'. I pondered over the phrase for a long time and wondered what kind of exchange the interrogating officer might have had with her. She also said that witnesses were giving their statements under pressure from the police, and that Santram's charges were made in collusion with the police. She said further that the *daroga* came to her home and she was beaten into confessing that she had committed the crimes. She had not given any information about the bodies being in a well, nor any assistance to recover bodies, as the police alleged she did.

This was the basic minimum information that was derived from the records and files. It was not really an open-and-shut case; there was a crime, there was perhaps some enmity between neighbours, two children from the same family being drowned was too much of a coincidence to be an accident, and there was evidence given by a minor (family member of the victims) about the accused being seen carrying off the younger of the boys.

But the records also have many statements and lacunae that do not form a substantial part of the deliberations. The defence case at the lower courts was that there was a discrepancy about where they found and then arrested Bina. In one account it was stated that she was arrested in the vicinity of the well where the infant's body was discovered. In another *bayan*, it was stated that she was arrested from her house. The judge, however, seemed to feel that this was a minor discrepancy. Similarly, there was no independent witness who actually saw Bina with either of the boys, and certainly no one saw her throw them into a well. As a minor, Suman could well have been coached to say what she did the next day: the first record of her statement was revealed in Santram's statement at the *thana* the morning after the alleged event when he reported that his older son was found in a nearby well and the younger was missing.

Bina was charged under Sections 363 and 364 of the Penal Code — which relate to kidnapping in order to murder — and was then sentenced to life imprisonment by the District and Sessions Judges. The case went into appeal. While browsing through the files at the High Court where the appeal was pending, I once again read all the statements made from the time of the FIR. The incident was mystifying in many ways and several features made one uncomfortable. While a serious view had to be taken of the fact that two innocent children were found dead in two separate wells, it was also a fact that while Bina was supposedly convincingly implicated, no one in the village was able to say that there might be some flaws in the case due to the fact that no one had actually seen her throw the children in, nor seen her with them in the vicinity of the wells. Only Suman, the minor sister of the children, said that Bina took the younger child away from the house that evening. The defence lawyer stated that there are several houses around where both Santram and Bina live, but no one else seems to have said that they saw her or the boy with her.

The transcript of the statements and records of the case including the judgement seem to be heavily weighted by the seriousness of the incident and the consequent need and expectation to sentence a probable offender as soon as possible. The judge states in the judgement that the defendant's plea that there was no apparent motive and that there was no conclusive proof were not serious considerations. 'The paucity of statements on Bina's behalf is conspicuous,' he said.

An appeal was filed for Bina on 24 February 1997 on the following grounds:

1. because the conviction of the appellant is against the weight of evidence on record;
2. because the conviction of the appellant is bad in law;
3. because the sentence is too severe.

A plea was made to the effect that the court allow the appeal to set aside the order of the court and acquit the appellant, and that the appellant may be released on bail while the appeal is pending.

Nothing positive happened in Bina's case: neither was her conviction set aside nor bail granted. She has been in prison all this time. She was sent to Nari Bandi Niketan in Lucknow in 1997 after the appellate court confirmed the sentence. While she was in Naini jail, her husband came to see her a couple of times. By the time of her conviction in 1997, her older daughter was almost seven and taken away to be reared by her husband because she was too old to accompany her mother to the Lucknow jail. So, first Bina loses her five-year-old son in 1993 to a fatal illness, then in 1997 her seven-year-old daughter (who was three at the time of the incident) is taken away from her. And then the husband's visits stop once she is taken away to Lucknow (not that he visited regularly at all when she was in Naini Jail). She came to Lucknow with the younger daughter (who was a babe in arms at the time of the event) now aged four. Then, as time went on, this child also reached the age when she could no longer remain in the jail. Bina had clung to this, the only dear thing left in her life, but it was thought necessary that the child's interests and future take precedence over anything else and she was put into care.

It was evident that nothing was the same for Bina since that fateful Diwali night. She did not appear to be very sociable to begin with, and her husband does not seem to have played a substantial part in her experiences in the narratives and reports surrounding this saga. She was mentally ill-equipped to face the trials and tribulations that ensued and that too alone and without support from *anyone*. Nothing helped. She had acute problems with adjustment, and it was difficult for her without any personal guidance to survive the traumatic experience of the trial and detention.

She once said about the incident that she was so sick she had no idea what she was going through. She remembers nothing at all, and adds, 'If I had had my wits about me, do you think I would have committed a wrong?' It did strike me that she may have been delirious enough to do something. But the point is that none of this came up for consideration at any point during hearings at any level because no one was really there to vouch for Bina.

Although not discussed in the pleadings or discussions, some supplementary features of the case did strike us as odd: I found it strange right from the start that Bina had no support from any corner at any level. She now said (in her 13th year of imprisonment) that it was because Santram was the *patidar* of the village. Odd that this fact never came up in the records; the influence of a *patidar* was likely to far outweigh the protests of a rickshaw-puller's wife. And where, in all this, is the husband, we keep asking ourselves.

Given all these extraordinary circumstances surrounding an uneducated, totally rustic and inexperienced woman, it becomes difficult to understand how, even as Bina is found guilty on the basis of these facts and features of her case, the sentence is as severe as it is. Life imprisonment is indeed the punishment for such an offence in the books: after all two children died unnaturally, with the possibility of foul play, and the family is bereft of their children as Bina was of her son. But a woman with two little children to take care of should have given the sentencing judges something to think about. With all due respect to the fact that the law and legal procedures have to be given supremacy in all matters, the facts showed that it was not a water-tight case. Here, we have a legitimate need to punish for a shocking offence — but who got punished, and how, received relatively little attention.

What we are left with is a problematic that defies solution if we look at the big picture. While the judges did their jobs and the offender was punished 'justly', the question of what was solved or resolved does arise. Hopefully, Santram and his wife felt somewhat vindicated, even though their children were gone forever and that hurt could not be healed by any vindication. Bina lost her son to begin with and then her family fell apart. We had no idea of how her older daughter fared once she left jail and returned to her father.

So, what happens to Bina, the person Bina. We resume the story through her eyes. Bina has now been in jail for 14 years. She recalls her time in Naini Jail (three-and-a-half years) as frustrating years spent in the false hope that she would be out soon. Her husband stopped coming to see her while she was there (even though her village was close enough). She hardly expected him to make a trip to Lucknow! It was her fears and worries for the older daughter that made life unbearable for her. She dreaded that the worst would happen to her daughter and there was no way she would know. Clearly, she had no faith in her husband.

Living in fear and anxiety day in and day out made her very ill. She lost her mental balance and equilibrium and needed treatment. This was arranged, but only with the limited facilities available in the jail. She was so unstable that she could not take care of her younger daughter any more. A 'caretaker' (woman prisoner) was appointed who took good care of the child. Bina was put in the (jail) hospital, but her condition did not change. On one occasion, she was found taking water from the septic tank to drink. She would often sit on the dusty and muddy ground, picking up mud in handfuls and rubbing it on her head. Somehow she seemed attracted to filth and had to be forcefully kept away from such places.

Other prisoners recall how she once went near a lit fire and deliberately spread her *saree* over it and did not move even when the edge of her *saree* was in flames. The other women ran to save her and put out the fire, but then she had severe burns that had to be attended to. As the list of such incidents increased, she was examined and labelled mentally ill.

In March 2000, her younger daughter (now aged seven) was sent into 'care'. This was the last straw and Bina was not able to cope with so many negatives. She completely lost her mental equilibrium and was examined by experts from King George's Medical College. Their opinion was that she was in need of prolonged medical care and treatment and needed to be sent to the mental institution in Varanasi to be professionally treated. She was sent to Varanasi in July 2001 and returned in January 2002 with the report that she was not really mentally 'sick' and could be treated with medication.

Coping with anxiety and fear still remained a problem, and Bina was as unstable and shaky as ever. Because she showed signs of 'abnormal' behaviour, she was re-examined by the King George's team again, and this time they said she was *schizophrenic*. She was sent to Varanasi again because there was no provision for her security (she being a prisoner) in Lucknow. She was in Varanasi from June 2002 to March 2004. Her medication continued for six months after she returned. The drugs helped to 'normalise' her behaviour and it was said, *'Ab yeh theek ho gayee hai'* [She is fine now.]

Bina has scarcely any recollection of the Varanasi hospital. She says she assumes she was unwell and sent there for treatment. 'It may have been a fever or something, I really have no idea.'

'So, do you feel alright now?' we venture to ask.

'I suppose I do,' she says. 'I am constantly worried and anxious. Perhaps, the older daughter [who would be about 17 now] will soon get married. We marry our girls early and ideally she should have been married by now. But my little daughter in 'care' — what will happen to her? When I am released, can I take her home?'

The idea of her release fills us with trepidation. What home is she talking about? Does she still have one? Again and again, the same question looms ahead of us.

In April 2006, an application was made on Bina's behalf to the District Magistrate, Allahabad, to consider her premature release on several grounds. In a reply from the District Magistrate, it was stated that this was not possible as the residents of the village where she came from were apprehensive about her return and not confident of her behaviour were she to return. The consideration relating to the gross damage that was being done to Bina with each progressive day was not of any consequence in this matter.

She is still in the women's jail, just 35 years old with really nothing to live for. She will not be easily considered for release in the 'clemency list': the response is usually, 'Two innocent children were killed'. Circumstantial evidence inflated by statements of witnesses that wear thin against the gravity of the incident and its consequences, and the almost total lack of support of any kind for the rickshaw-puller's wife throw up many unanswered questions. Something awful happened that did not seem accidental because it was a double fatality in two different locations.

We are once again faced with the dilemma that recurs in our work: There is a thumb rule in criminal justice that if there is an offence and a 'likely suspect' who is then dubbed an offender, there has to be a punishment/penalty. There is a certainty that relates to the offence but no foolproof certainty relating to the particular offender. The judge may have pronounced, but if his judgement and its premises are anything to go by, there are apparent loopholes. Our dilemmas and quandaries in Bina's case relate neither to a capricious sympathy-factor for a distraught woman, nor a lack of faith in the principles of the legal/judicial system. There are features about the case that are not tidy enough either at the legal or human level for us to just let it be.

And yet when nearly 14 of her 35 years have been lost to a prison in order that legal and other requirements are met, the serious question now is, how desperately should one seek Bina's release, given the realities surrounding the future of incarcerated women generally and this woman specifically. Where would we send her when she is released — we don't have the answer. When asked, she always says, 'I would go home, and marry off my daughter'. Again, what home is she talking about? The village that was hostile to her to the last man? The home where we don't even know the whereabouts of the husband? She realises, the future is bleak and full of insecurities and she wouldn't know where to begin. We don't either. We ruined her life and that of her daughters even as she *might* have ruined that of Santram and his family.

Returning after 14 years of *jailvaas* is quite different from returning after 14 years of *banvaas* — the latter is a hero's welcome, the former results in ostracism. In the one, life may begin again without acrimony; in the other, there is nothing but animosity and antipathy awaiting the return.

What should we do? What should she do? Is there an answer? The questions keep coming, and while it is not intended to suggest that there is a totally flawed system at work here that needs to be changed, it does strike one as bizarre that a whole range of questions that are legitimate and unsettling cannot be answered to any one's satisfaction while the legal system delivers the 'goods', i.e., legitimate punishment. She will be released when her term is over. She will be 'deposited' in the village from where she came. The system will have done its job. What happens then is not really their concern. Someone somewhere needs to make it a concern. But how will they if they are not acquainted with the Binas of the world.

Charged under Sections 363 and 364 of the Indian Penal Code that relate to kidnapping and intent to kill, Bina was given life imprisonment. Section 363 states: 'Whoever kidnaps any person from lawful guardianship shall be punished with imprisonment of either description for a term which may extend to seven years, and shall also be liable to fine'.

More importantly, Bina's offence fell squarely within Section 364: 'Whoever kidnaps or abducts any person in order that such person may be murdered or may be so disposed of as to be put in danger of being murdered shall be punished with imprisonment for life or rigorous imprisonment for a term which may extend to ten years and shall also be liable to fine'.

Three children related to the incident died in Dighi village that year: Bina's son died of a prolonged illness, and Santram's sons because Bina took the *ojha's* advice and allegedly threw them into two separate wells. For a Eurocentric readership, the details of this case would smack of primitive tribalism and be categorised as the result of archaic practices of a custom-ridden society that the 'rational' West left behind centuries ago. Dismissing them as antiquated and therefore inconsequential for the larger and more rational debate about crime and punishment would be an error. The living realities of people and the issues they throw up, no matter how difficult to handle, constitute *their* realities and need to be addressed.

Such cases occur from time to time in non-urban environs, and while they are often diabolical and deplored by one and all, they still need to be evaluated. They range from curing by such practices as smoking out spirits by *jhaar-phook* (burning concoctions in dried vegetation and waving the smoking *jhaar* over the possessed), driving out curses by sacrifices, vanquishing *bhoot-pret* [demons] through nocturnal rituals, and human sacrifice. In 2004, Poaltore village (near the Bangladesh border) found itself in the grip of a spate of illnesses that had taken the lives of many, including infants. A village *sabha* (meeting) was called and the local *ojha* said a curse that had been put on the village had to be removed. He identified the 'witches' and prevailed on the villagers to kill a village man Bhola (name changed) and his two sons. Fate was on their side and the police, who had been tipped off, rescued the men and patrolled the village for some time to prevent similar occurrences. But a middle-aged woman was not so lucky. The local medicine man had pronounced that she must die if the calamities (including recurring illnesses) befalling the village were to be averted. A nail was hammered into her skull and as she screamed she was bound in a sack and dumped into the Murti river. The police recovered her body two days later. That the villages in these cases were remote and surrounded by swamps and thick jungles, creepers and banana plantations, and infested with poisonous snakes, giant spiders and rats, were not considered a part of a remedial plan to ward off death from diseases: the *ojha* had pronounced the cause of the calamities and he was obeyed.

Dhigi village was not Poaltore, inhabited mostly by hill tribes who had their own rituals. But it still had an *ojha* in whom people believed to the exclusion of regular doctors who may have been few and far between but were certainly there. Bina, however, was so hopelessly inadequate in handling problems that she took recourse to the only path she knew, having faith in the *ojha*. Where parallel systems of survival still exist, they cannot just be swept aside with the rational legal broom. The challenge is how to persuade and encourage people to choose. Cases bordering on exorcism do take place and need to be tackled.

Of all the cases one came across which revealed the complete ignorance of the legal machinery on the part of the accused, Bina's was the most unsettling. She was from a rural background, uneducated, but more than that she was hopelessly inept at comprehending or discerning choices in the face of adversity and had no guidance in how to deal with misfortune. I once asked her about her parents and why they did not help at any juncture. Her answer in the dialect of her region was, '*Hamaar mayeka ghar to chhoot gava, ab oo sab ka karihen?*' [I left the maternal home, so what can they do for me]. The customs and traditions taught from childhood are the survival kit for millions and life's answers, for better or worse, come from that kit. When disaster strikes, there is a desperate attempt to run for cover which in this case is the shelter of known remedies. But they lead to further disasters, and so life goes on.

It is a situation that needs action. One State has sought to pass 'the Black Magic Bill'. Maharashtra's Bill No. LXXXIX of 2005 states its goal in the Preamble:

> To bring social awakening and awareness in society and to create a healthy and safe social environment with a view to protect common people in the society against the evil and sinister practices and customs thriving on ignorance and to combat and eradicate the evil, sinister and *aghori* [see note at the end of the chapter] practices born out of beliefs propagated in the name of so called divine and supernatural or magical powers or evil spirits commonly known as Black magic by quacks and conmen with sinister motive of exploiting and harming the common people in the society mentally, physically and financially, thereby destroying the very social fibre of the society.

That this has been regarded as a problem worth addressing with gravity and concern is praiseworthy. Tantric priests, *babas* and *gurus* of the *aghori* sect practice their 'black magic' in urban areas of Maharashtra and more importantly, in semi-urban areas around Mumbai (Nallaspora, Mira Road, Vasai, Virar and Malad). Young girls are abducted and sexually abused, children are killed for sacrifice and bizarre rituals are performed in ashrams and in the vicinity of temples to drive out spirits and curses. Complaints come in from the community around the areas and the police (law and order) conduct raids, but on their own admission are unable to do much. 'Whenever we receive complaints we go to their quarters, conduct raids and prosecute them for cheating. But they are difficult to nail.' The general lament is the absence of a law against practising black magic.

Two features highlighted as goals in the Preamble to Maharashtra's Bill are relevant in almost every Sate where similar practices exist:

1. To bring social awakening and awareness in society, and
2. To create a healthy and safe social environment with a view to protect common people in the society against the evil practices and customs thriving on ignorance.

Such practices would be made into offences under the Act, and as a deterrent, stringent penal provisions would be provided for such offences including making them cognisable and non-bailable. A vigilance officer would detect and prevent contravention of the provisions of the Act and the rules, and collect evidence for effective prosecution of the persons contravening the provisions of this law.

The Bill recognises just how many of our negative practices thrive on *ignorance*; it realises the importance of creating *social awareness* and sees the Act as contributing to a healthy and safe social environment. The questions that arise again and again are: (*i*) is enactment adequate to end such practices?, and (*ii*) will penal provisions as deterrents create the *social awakening and awareness* that is the aim of the Act? This is being discussed in the light of the uphill task faced by the members of the Maharashtra Superstitions Eradication Committee that has been fighting for the passage of the Bill since 2005: 'The government is not able to push the Bill for fear of annoying religious sentiments which may cost them precious votes', said the founder of the Eradication Committee (*The Sunday Express*, 24 October 2010).

Bina's story exemplifies this problem: the law is able to punish Bina for a heinous act because kidnapping and murder are part of the Penal Code. The *tantrics* and *ojhas*, who propagate rituals that lead to these 'crimes', are beyond the reach of the law (for there is no law, only sections dealing with 'cheating', etc.). The passage or non-passage of a law of this nature (and other laws for that matter) is so steeped in vested interests that one cannot help but wonder at the law's intent and extent. Colonialists are not the only ones suspect when laws are promulgated.

The inevitable conclusion: if the passage of a law is so interest-ridden, how effective is it likely to be in its achievements. And a corollary to that: how would the law address the ignorance, blind faith and lack of awareness of the 'believer' without whom the magic would be redundant.

These are concerns that we voiced repeatedly in this case. Bina's *ignorance* in day-to-day life (the lack of awareness mentioned in the Black Magic Act) was a source of intense discomfort and ire for us. The other concern related to Bina's *helplessness* in prison (penal provision as deterrent) where she languished and then for all practical purposes perished in so many ways.

Ignorance was not something new to us. More than half the women in prison in the States of Bihar, Uttar Pradesh, Madhya

Pradesh and Rajasthan fit the ignorant category not just for lack of formal education but also a lack of awareness about the environs they live in. But that did not stop them from holding their own as individuals and being able to speak for themselves when required. Ignorance of the law and procedures did not prevent them from making their voices heard when required. Bina's ignorance on the other hand was about life's basic choices and that was her downfall. While she paid the price for her *individual failing* (and if punishment is about paying a price, Bina certainly did), who would pay the price for *society's failing* in enabling her to deal with the environment she lived in? Who was responsible for the fact that she (like so many in our stories) was married as a child, lived in poverty and ignorance in a small village, never went to school, had no guidance or assistance in her hour of need, and knew nothing about child care? She turned to the *ojha* and she was on her way down a slippery slope. It is not enough to make the Bina's of the world a statistic in our demographic classifications: their lives are catastrophes waiting to happen. What we are able to do about it? Is there a law for this?

Her rickshaw-puller husband was the only bread-earner. Relatives were conspicuous by their absence. The neighbourhood was hostile. Her child falls ill and she runs from pillar to post to no avail. She goes to village medicine men who prescribe all manner of concoctions and even suggest the need for human sacrifice to ward off the evil spirit. Finally, she is faced with the death of her five-year-old son. All she knows thereafter is panic and devastation. She herself gets sick and makes desperate moves. For months she is almost bed-ridden and beside herself with grief. She is still in touch with the *ojha* of the village who had tried to cure her son but failed. He gives her what she needs — a reason for his death and an inducement to remedy that. Her son was cursed and human sacrifice was needed which she had failed to offer. He even goes to the extent of telling her whose curse was upon her son.

The procedural and punitive machinery is not just helpless in this case, but also hopeless. By its own measuring gauge, the legal machinery presented too many loopholes: evidence, investigation, interrogation and witnesses. Bina makes the situation worse by being the loner she is: no one to speak for her and no one to ask why. Something was terribly wrong and the law could help only that far. She gets her *amicus curie* and after that she is on her own. Her period as an under-trial in Naini Jail had a negative impact, and it makes one wonder if she might have been better off in a State with a superior record of detention than UP, for instance, Andhra Pradesh. But that would beg the question: had she been in Andhra, would she have been less ignorant and less desolate?

Bina was baffled by legal mechanisms and betrayed by the social environment. What she had needed all along was an enabling environment built by the community, the society, the law and the state. Three lives may have been saved and Bina herself may not have been lost.

回

Note

The *Aghoris* willingly transgress all ascetic (and Hindu) taboos, and are convinced that by 'reversing all values' they will speed up enlightenment. They prefer to live on cremation and burial grounds and surround themselves with artefacts of death, like human skulls, out of which they drink and with which they perform magical rituals. Human sacrifice, incestuous sex and bizarre physical interventions form part of their remedial cures.

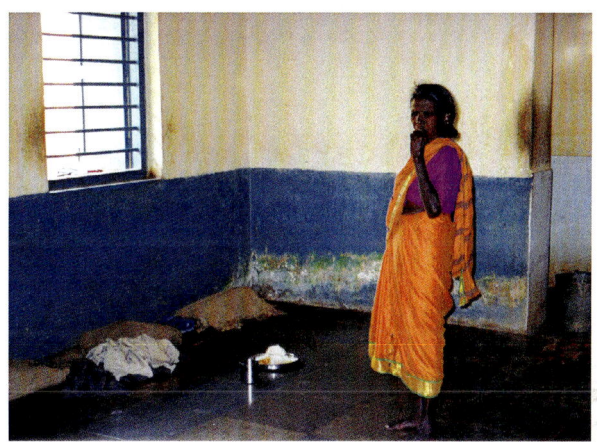

Elderly women: Too old to stay locked up
Jaipur, Hyderabad and Bhopal

Younger women: What of their futures?
Hyderabad Women's Prison

Pensive faces that never smile

Lucknow and Rajahmundry women's prisons

Only the dress defines them
Pre-trials and convicts in Hyderabad

Gates and corridors define their lives
Rajahmundry, Andhra Pradesh

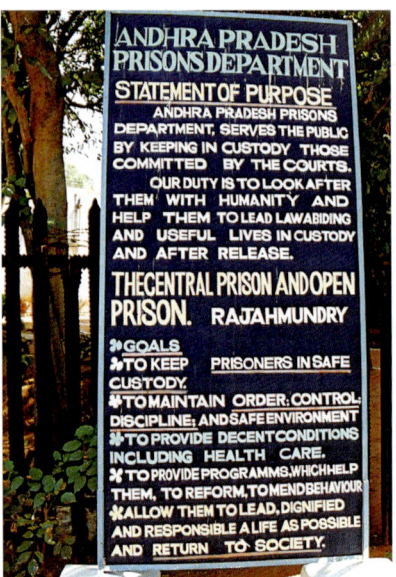

Prison facades and mission statements
Jaipur Central and Rajahmundry Women's Jail

More gates and more barracks
Hyderabad Women's Prison

Activity time: Stitching inside and Rangoli outside

Jaipur and Hyderabad

Tackling illiteracy
Tihar and Jaipur style

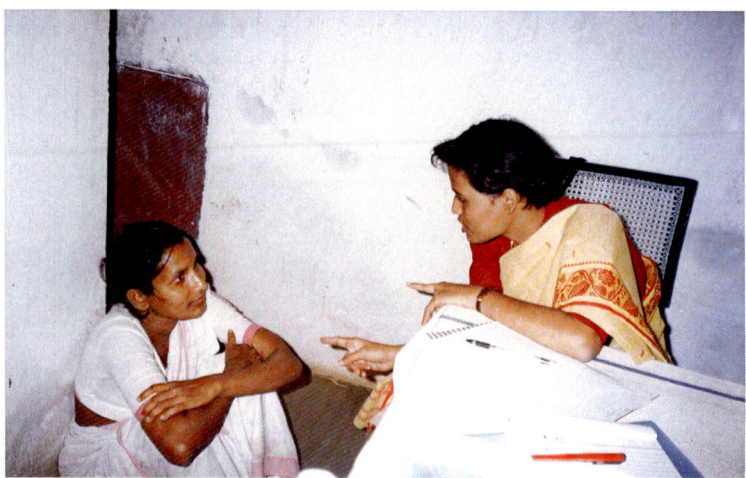

Counsellors at hand to help whenever needed
Hyderabad

Being addressed in group sessions

Rajahmundry

Meals — a time to relax?

Jaipur and Hyderabad

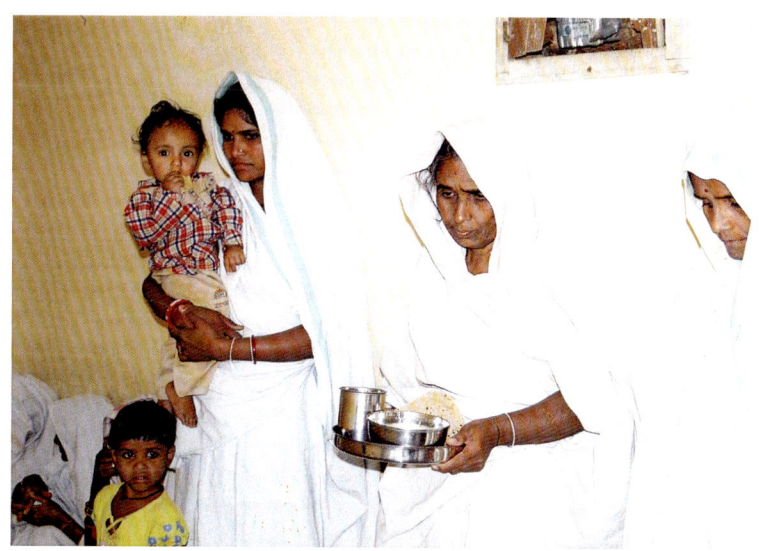

Not for everyone

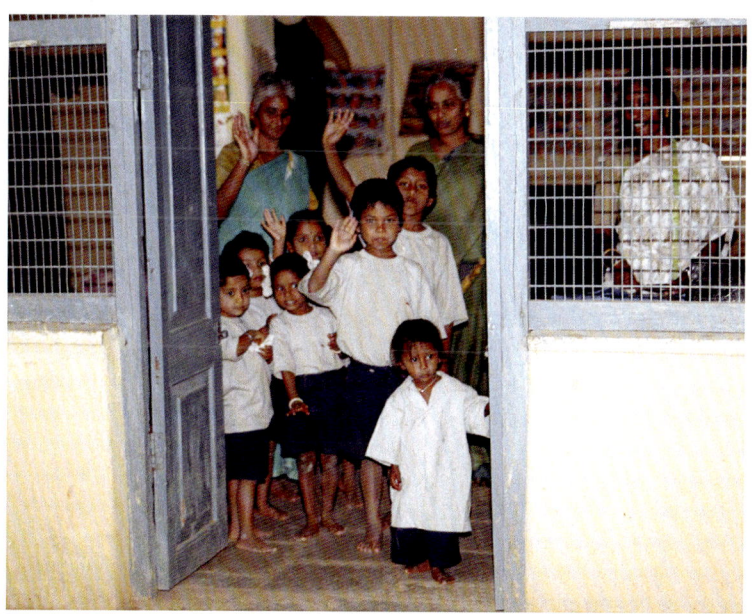

How happy can anyone be 'inside'?
Children in Hyderabad Women's Prison

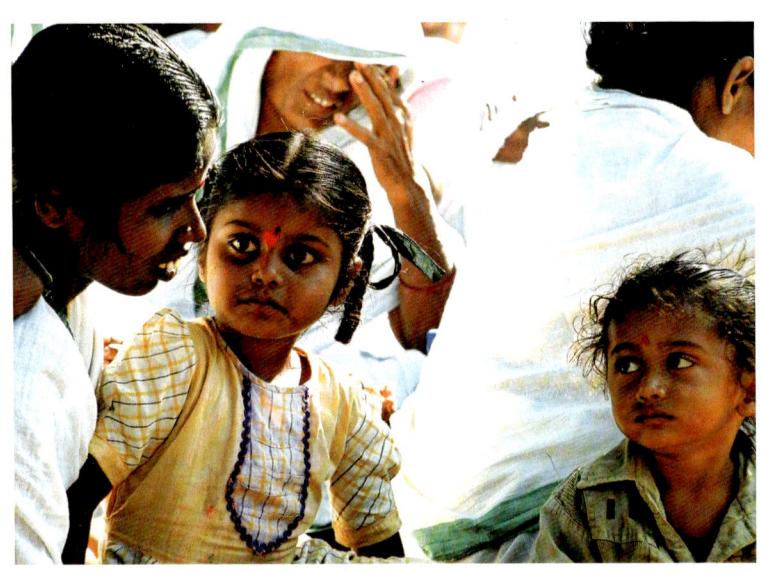

Children don't belong 'inside'

Rajahmundry and Lucknow

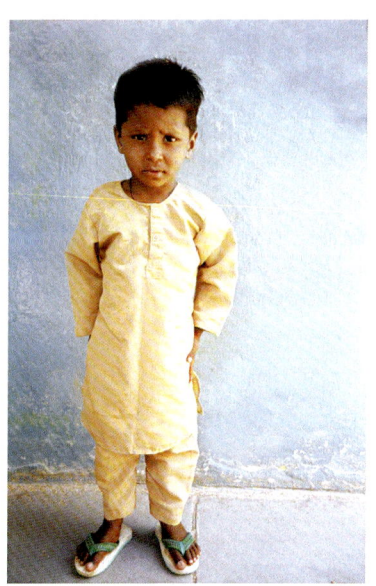
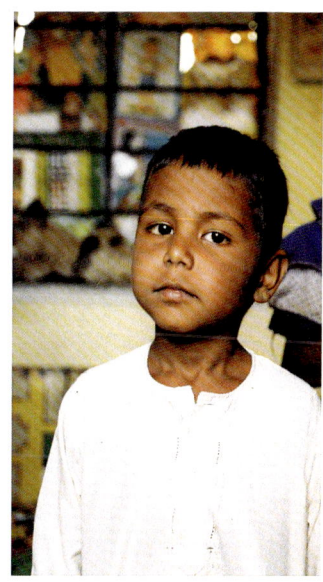

Children don't belong 'inside' — ever
Hyderabad and Jaipur

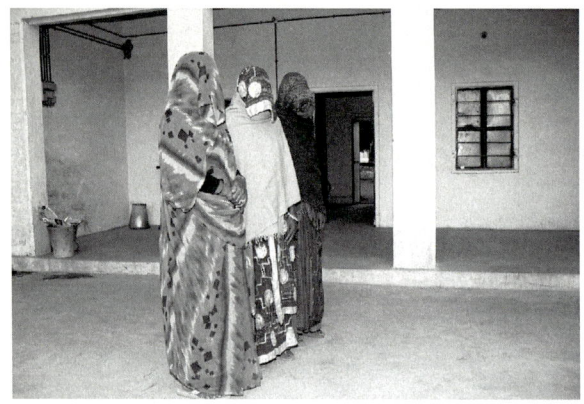

And then there are open prisons where families can live as families

Sanganer Open Camp, Rajasthan

5

Hasina, the Husband Slayer

There is no greater offence than a woman killing her husband. Maybe that applies in other societies as well, but in India it is a sin of the worst kind and unforgivable, apart from being a (legal) crime and therefore unpardonable. Hasina is guilty of just such an offence (and *sin*), and even if she is released after serving her legal punishment, she is unlikely to find any release from the stigma that will pursue her and form part of her moral punishment for the rest of her life.

In a land where role models for women comprise mythical characters that are blemish-free in terms of service, humility and obeisance, anything that falls short of these ideals is inevitably reprehensible and unacceptable. A woman's primary role is of service — from being a good daughter, to being a good wife and mother, and so on, and each role is set out carefully in mores, customs and traditions that are handed down in oral, or written time-honoured conventions. Any deviation can have dire consequences. That is the bottomline in social behaviour for women, and most women (and men) are acutely aware of what is involved if one strays from this path.

'Perhaps, I didn't follow the code set out for women — do your husband's bidding regardless of what he does,' Hasina admits, as we sit with her in the barrack in her corner. She had been ill for a few days after her first visit to us, so we ask if she would be happier in her own space. She is saying she would come to our room when she is better.

'I am 28 years old now and I was married when I was 15. I had my first child when I turned 16. I conceived seven children out of who four died during pregnancy or just after birth.

Now, I have three children — two sons and a daughter, the youngest child being 11 months old. She was born after I came into the jail.

'I really don't have much to say about my family: what does family really mean I don't even know. Everyone talks about "my family", "my family"; well, I am not so sure about this concept — maybe there is such a thing, maybe there isn't really. I can't say. So, what shall I tell you?'

Most of the time we hear women lament that they miss family when they are in prison, and here is a woman striking a different note. She must have a reason.

'I have no parental home; my parents died when I was very young. I don't even have any visual memories of parents, except very dim ones of a mother who braided my hair as a child. My two brothers, my sister and I — we were all brought up by our paternal grandparents. The brothers and sister are all married and settled in their own homes and have no time for me or for my life. So, what can one say when asked about home and background?'

Her life is virtually a blank. Not having memories of childhood is still better than ugly memories, I thought, but in this particular case, a complete dearth of memories can make the present seem even more unpalatable. Women locked up in prisons lean on old memories to survive: their smiles (and tears) are all about memories. Memories are the relief-providers that prisoners can fall back on when the going gets rough, rather like the song from the famous Bimal Roy film *Bandini*: '*Ab ke baras bhej bhaiya ko babul, savan me leejo bulay re*' [this year, dear father, please send my brother to fetch me during the monsoon season]. The powerful imagery of a childhood spent on swings, toys, mango trees and sugarcane fields, festivals and playmates is the sustenance for the most wretched of situations: Hasina clearly has none of that.

So, naturally we move on to why she is in prison.

'Well, you know I am here under Section 302 for killing my husband. Everyone knows that. You should see the way the male prison staff view me when they come to take the rounds of the prison. The superintendent never stops to comment on my offence even when he is on a routine inspection. Sometimes he introduces me to people as a "spouse killer". I wonder if he exhibits a similar indelicacy when he takes rounds of the men's prisons and comes across a man who has killed his wife.'

Good question, I think to myself, and before unfolding the details of Hasina's trials and tribulation, a brief interjection about how people like her are viewed by those in charge of the prison may not be out of order. The incident (and my subjective musing) is being recounted because it relates directly to the discussion about how particular categories of prisoners are viewed by those in charge. Spouse killers are likely to get a particularly harsh deal at the hands of the male section of the administration and my exposure to this attitude during one of the superintendent's rounds of this prison only confirmed what Hasina believed and I feared.

'Oh, I know Hasina, she's been here for years. I know her well', the male superintendent said to us with confidence and a smugness of which we would learn later. 'Do you?', I thought. 'Do you *really* know Hasina? That's what you all think, you who are in charge of this place: just because someone's been in this place for years and years, you know her/him ever so well. Do you know anything more than the fact that Hasina killed her husband? Yes, she committed a legal offence and, of course, the law prescribes punishments for such acts, so she is legitimately imprisoned. You have repeatedly shown scorn and disdain at Hasina's brazenness and called her "*besharam*" [shameless] for committing the crime of all crimes — killing a husband. However, there are more particulars in the case than are dreamed of in your beliefs, Mr superintendent. Did you also learn what the skirmish was about? That the husband was brutally molesting her — something he was regularly prone to do each time he came home dead drunk (which was at least five times in the week). Do you also know that on this particular occasion he threatened to rip open her vagina (with a knife no less) if she did not consent to having sex with him? Do you know that he picked up the knife to demonstrate to her just how he would rip her apart; but while he was about to actually bring the knife to her body after pinning her down on the floor the knife fell from his hands, and while Hasina picked it up *intending* to strike back if he moved any closer something else happened that killed the husband. Not Hasina. Not the kitchen knife, but another player in the drama of life. No, of course, you wouldn't know that. All you know is that she is a spouse killer, a murderer charged under Section 302 of the 160-year-old Indian Penal Code and therefore should be locked up for life. If you had your way you would taunt her each day for her *crime*, and in your eyes her *sin*'. All this is an imaginary conversation I have with the superintendent with whom I am doing the rounds when he does his weekly inspection of the prison.

His remark was significant because I had been on a round with the same superintendent in the adjoining men's prison in Rajasthan. A pre-trial prisoner was working at a painting and showed it proudly to all of us. 'Look how talented he is', said the superintendent. I looked at the painting and said, 'Yes, it is a good painting'. But I was curious to know more about the prisoner. 'What is he here for?' I asked. 'Oh, it is alleged that he raped a woman', the superintendent replied. *Alleged*, I thought. I have never heard the superintendent say that about any pre-trial woman prisoner that she is *alleged* to have killed her husband or harassed her daughter-in-law for dowry. It's always 'She has killed her husband' even when she has not yet been sentenced.

Attitudes, mindsets, conditioning, preconceived notions, gender constructs, power-positions — there are so many ways to describe what many male superintendents and jailors in Rajasthan (and any other State) think about women's crimes and women criminals. A woman prisoner like Hasina is a criminal first and foremost. No one bothers to paint a picture of any kind of Hasina's life before prison. The assumption is that she had no childhood, or a youth with desires and aspirations. It seems futile to paint pictures of normal lives for those whom we have consigned first to the dustbins of society, and then if they did not conform to our social and legal frameworks, to those other places of confinement that are worse than dustbins.

The question is for whom would we be painting pictures of normality anyway? Not for Hasina. Not for the superintendents and jailors who are busy reminding themselves about the terrible things Hasina did that deservedly got her this punishment, and who have condemned her altogether. And not even for ourselves to enable us to ease our phlegmatic consciences. So, why bother with the Hasinas of the world, wherever they are and whatever their fate may be.

This difference in approach is not likely to change for a long time and is directly related to the images of women that are actively promoted in any patriarchal society. 'She is not so virtuous.' 'She is not a good woman.' 'She was not a good wife.'

Hasina is an easy target, the butt of many crude statements made by male officers who have their own ideas of womanhood, and in Hasina's case they know there is no family support: this always makes a difference for a woman in prison, as was the case with Bina. Can anything be done about it? While I feel unsure, I still believe one can.

The husband was a drunk and, as she says, that means he really drank hard. 'There wasn't a day he didn't come back totally inebriated and falling all over the place, and if you crossed his path when he was in that condition all hell was let loose. But then, there is no law about thrashing your wife, is there?'

There is actually — the law on domestic violence — but it is not for the Hasinas of the world. We hear stories about drunken husbands often enough to know that it is an ugly scenario, but Hasina is trying to tell us not to regard it as yet another tale of a drunk man merely creating mayhem in his home. 'The children hid in nooks and corners because they were petrified, but I had to face him. After all, when he asked for his meal I would have to produce it. When I did produce his food, woe betide if there was anything wrong either with the meal, or with the way I set it out or served it. Throwing *thalis* and *lotas* was a commonplace occurrence. Often, the utensil that he threw would strike me and cause a wound on my head or face, and it was a lucky day if I wasn't injured or abused. If I got provoked and questioned his behaviour, it was hell, and if I chose to be quiet and hope that it will pass, it was hell. Either way I was in for it.'

'I think people don't really know just how violent a drunken man gets and especially with his own family and more particularly with his wife. The degree of violence is unimaginable and the foulness of the language is even worse. It is a very pathetic sight to watch your children watching you being beaten by whatever comes into the hands of your spouse. I would not wish that for anyone, and that too, day in and day out. I always had bruises and cuts on some or other part of my body. It does not change, and at some point or other even your child asks, "Why do you take it?" Your children wonder why you don't have what it takes to stop it all.'

The part of the children's reaction stops me. I haven't thought too hard about what happens to children when they witness the ugly humiliation of their mother. Do they pity her and does that dilute their respect for her? Or are they embarrassed and wish the situation away? These questions are so intense that I almost tune off from her narrative of her own experience. I am not really treating this as a typical case even though Hasina keeps adding every now and then, 'Yes, I know you have heard this before', or 'This is probably a stale scenario for you'. I am hard pressed to convince her otherwise. I want her to know that each person's personal sorrow is as intense as another's, and I would not be dismissive of the distress and damage she has gone through just because it comes into a category of 'drunken (violent) husbands'. I want her to know that I do not view problems and situations in broad categories, that every detail she is telling me is a vital part of her life and that I wish to understand all of it. She clearly needs reassurance at every juncture that she is being acknowledged as an individual in her own right and not as a typical woman prisoner.

The discussion has to stop: Sometimes, paying too much attention to one prisoner upsets others and one has to terminate a conversation abruptly to turn to others who might want to talk. We tell her we will come back the next day and move on to sit with Chandni who has been waiting to talk to us. She is only 22 years old and the previous day she had made a comment that got us thinking: 'I have even stopped praying to God,' she said, 'I have no faith in Him: look at me, no one comes to visit. When I was arrested my husband said to me that if the police arrest you I will kill myself. I wonder what happened after that. It was a family property dispute at her paternal home, and in the skirmish a person died. Initially nine persons (her father, his brothers and their sons) were arrested and people reassured me that I would not be arrested: I was two months' pregnant. But here I am. Many of the male members got bail. But I didn't. I wonder why.'

I wonder too. It is so frustrating when one has no answers to so many of their questions. One just listens and gropes for reasons and possibilities. Who can answer all the questions that come out of a prison? Even when we leave the gates, we try to find answers, but they don't come easily. Even the law and justice system fails to give answers and is a silent spectator like us.

The following day, Hasina is pensive. Seeing her like that makes it hard to resume the conservation from where we left of. Sometimes, we just sit with the prisoner and start a general conversation about something, anything, that might also interest the prisoner. I ask someone in the barrack why there is no TV set these days. 'It went for repairs, Ma'am, and never came back,' says one woman. 'Don't these people realise that this is the only distraction in our otherwise drab lives? What does it take to get a TV repaired? But then it is for prisoners, so why bother.' I make a mental note so that we can bring it to the attention of the DIG who we know will take immediate action.

We turn to Hasina and ask, *'tum theek ho'* [are you alright]? 'Yes', she says, and gives a sigh: 'It always happens that one particular day has to change the course of someone's entire life. For some that day might be a harbinger of good things; for some it is the final catastrophe that spells doom. My husband made sure that my doom had come and his own as well, I suppose. He came home heavily drunk late one evening and began pushing me around. He pushed me down and started to lift my saree to have sex. I pushed him away and he picked up the kitchen knife and said, "Will you or shall I tear it open with this?" I told him to stop but he kept threatening me with the knife and warning me that he would tear up my vagina if I didn't agree. I kept screaming because he was hurting me, and finally managed to push him away and being as drunk as he was, he fell back. By that time the children were all near the door, and screaming too and telling their father to stop.'

How much worse can it get? I often wonder when I hear these personal stories why we regard Indian films as exaggerated and removed from reality. What Hasina is telling me sounds like a scene from an Indian film, but it isn't — this is reality. Difficult to decide who takes the cue from whom — films from reality or the other way round.

'He started to get up with the knife in his hand and made his way towards me and I moved backwards. As soon as he came close enough to me to strike me suddenly almost out of nowhere a pressure cooker was hurled at his head: he fell and hit his head against the wall and bled. It was my son from behind me: he had come in when he heard the screams (as he did on so many other nights). Only this night he could not take it anymore and picked up the first thing he saw and threw it at his father out of fear and disgust. My husband was still alive and I said we should call the police or a doctor or the hospital, but he refused. I called my husband's younger brother who lived nearby and he in turn called the police.'

'The police came and so did a doctor who attended to the wound and gave medicines. My husband's drunken brawl happened at about 8 pm and despite the doctor and medicines he died at three in the morning.'

'Neighbours had heard the noises and shouting, and because they were used to the drunken brawls and the ugly scenes that followed, they stayed away. When his brother came with the doctor, and then the police came, they gathered around. My son kept telling the neighbour's wife that he hit his father hard with the cooker because he went on beating his mother. Clearly, the neighbours believed him and told me to tell the police exactly what happened. They said that the boy was a minor and would not be sentenced, given all the circumstances.'

There is always a fly in the ointment: this was too easy I thought. Something very unfortunate had happened, someone had died, and *that* someone is a husband and father of three. The true story would not hold. It was inevitable that she would be accused on the grounds of wife abuse and I was curious to see who would engineer this.

'My brother-in-law had already given a story to the police. He accused me of killing his brother and said that I had a hot temper and that there were arguments frequently, but that his brother was a reasonable man, he had a government job and that

I was a difficult wife. He lodged a complaint against me and I was taken to the police station and questioned.'

What must it have been like, I thought: imagine the state of the children and the boy who chose to take a stand on an issue that at the best of times is delicate for a child — one parent abusing another violently as the children watch helplessly even as they are enraged. I kept thinking of the boy picking up the pressure cooker in a fit of desperation and striking the father. If that is what happened, it must have left a deep wound on his mind too.

'In any case I would not have liked my son to be dragged in courts and at police stations — minor or no minor. I am almost glad they put me in and didn't touch my son. But look at me: paying a price again. As if I have not paid enough of a price being beaten for all of these years. You have no idea about the nature of the thrashings I used to get. It is embarrassing to recount and the hurts are always as fresh as they were then.'

I close my eyes for a minute and think how it really must be for her and for her children to go through such experiences almost as a routine. It happens the world over, they say, but in such patriarchal cultures where time has stood still for women and the disadvantaged, the sores and wounds left by the abuse of power by men remain raw in mind and spirit, even if the physical bruises heal.

She shows me the scar of a deep cut on her back: it has filled up somewhat because it is not fresh, but the depth of the cut and how it must have bled and hurt for weeks is not difficult to imagine.

'This was made one night when I fell asleep after waiting for hours for his return. It was past midnight and he still had not come home and I fell asleep right next to the stove. Usually I hear him when he comes and start warming the food for him before he begins his abusive language and his rough handling; but that night I dozed off and didn't hear him come. He entered and saw me, and I have no doubt was filled with rage and fury. The next thing I knew was a hard swift blow across my back and I thought I was dying from the shock more than the hurt. He had picked up the heavy round *tava* [griddle] on which I make *rotis* that had been lying on the stove and swung it across my back with all the

force in his hand, and because he struck it sideways the edge cut
into the back and split the flesh where it struck. My head started
reeling and I saw he still held the *tava* and I screamed. Our son
came running: he had already heard the beginnings of a fracas
and knew he had to stay away. But when this happened and he
heard my scream he ran in and stood in front of me'.

'The sight of the son at such incidents evidently always infuri-
ated the father more: and that he should come to his mother's defence was something almost immoral in his eyes. When he next
lifted the *tava* I thought he would strike the son, but I pushed the
boy away and stood there. He lifted his hand with the *tava* — like
you know those things at the games they show…'

'Discus,' I volunteer.

'Yes. Yes. Discus. And he just swung it and struck me again, this
time sideways, and it hit my head and I fell. I have no idea what
happened after that. I lay there, I suppose, till I came to my senses
a few hours later and saw my son sprinkling water drops on my
face. He wiped the blood off my face and back. He then put some
rags on my wound on the back to soak the blood, and told me
to go to sleep. I said to him, "What about his food?" And my son
said, "That *harami* [bastard]! Let him go hungry. It's almost
morning anyway and he has fallen asleep. Can't you hear him
snoring?" That was the first time I heard my son use foul language for his father. I couldn't believe my ears. I wanted to say
something but the words wouldn't form and my eyes just closed
and I fell asleep with the gash unattended to and still bleeding.
I was in pain but so exhausted that I fell asleep in due course.'

She was silent for the next few minutes and so was I. What a
nightmare. But no, it was not one nightmare: she said there were
many such experiences she could go on narrating.

'You will get tired of hearing the things that happened each
night. They are brutal and merciless and it is unthinkable that
it should happen in people's homes behind closed doors, but it
does. And the trouble with closed doors is that such doors are
legitimately closed and no one can claim a right to enter. It is one
and the same in a house and in a jail, isn't it?'

'Yes,' I said. 'The home is private and often one hears people
say, "This is a personal matter we can't interfere". Even the police
say the same thing. So, who will help?'

'But you see, Ma'am, even I am not sure just how much I want people to enter my personal domain. After all, as they say in our language, *"Apna hi pait nanga karne vali baat hai!"* [One is baring one's own body to the outside world.]'

She is so right, I think. I know just what she means. Within the home, the perpetrators of cruelty and brutality live comfortably behind closed doors. But those who are the victims are uncertain about how they view transparency. Transparency might save them from brutality; on the other hand, the world can see the humiliation, and that too cuts both ways: in a joyful and happy situation it doesn't matter who sees you. But who will open their doors for you if there is humiliation, dishonour and indignity.

She voices my thoughts: 'It is a strange experience to want to be saved from cruelty and shame but not to want the world to see how you are being dishonoured. That is how it was.'

Yes, I can see that. All those cases of women who hide their bruises and will never let on that the husband was responsible for them. During a field survey I was doing for advocating human rights for women, a teacher of the village told me that I would be horrified if a woman lifted her *saree* at the waist and showed me her back or midriff: for every five women at least three would have blue marks and bruises at some place or another. Hasina is only confirming what I hear elsewhere. .

Safeguarding her *'laaj'* [dignity] by shutting out the world and resenting transparency in her daily life, Hasina has landed herself in yet another opaque environment. Prison has its own oppressions and here too you have to bear it in silence. It doesn't help to complain. The only difference is that most of the others are also in the same boat: they all go through one or other form of bullying and collectively hate the perpetrators.

'Now, it is all over. There is nothing to hide and nothing to live for. At least then I had the children and I put up with everything for their sake. Now the brother-in-law has taken away the children. I have no idea what is happening to them.'

'But why did he take away the children? It doesn't appear like he loved them and would care for them as an uncle.'

'Oh no,' she says. 'He had no use for them. He didn't like my children; he resented the fact that I had children at all because he had no children of his own and had separated from his wife years ago. He didn't have much of a job either. My husband had a government job albeit small, but as you know, government jobs always have some benefits like pensions and things. So, my brother-in-law thought he could lay a claim to my husband's pension on the grounds that the children were being taken care of by him and my in-laws. The children were taken away by them almost immediately after my arrest.'

She has the infant with her and she clings to the girl like she is the last thing she has that is hers: not even her own life is so precious now.

'The trouble is that I am illiterate and unable to fend for myself. I never did a job. It never occurs to our kind of people — and that includes our parents and other family members — that we might need education and self-dependence one day. I wonder why they think that way. Probably, because traditionally we are daughters and then wives and then mothers, what would we do with education? But here I am — I was a daughter almost without parents, a wife almost without a husband, so where did all that tradition get me? To this?' And she lifts her *saree* again to show the gashes on her back and sides.

My colleagues and I look at each other. They have been playing with her child while Hasina and I talked so she feels at ease without an audience. We all experience a sense of helplessness. So many questions, so few answers. The questions overwhelm us more often than not, and we sometimes pretend that we understand them but do we really? What are the answers? Are there answers or more questions? Often, it becomes too much for us to assimilate, and yet that is what we are here for — to make some sense out of the lives of those who are trapped within these walls for terrible experiences that have formed the backdrop for the greater part of their years.

Acutely aware that we all subscribe to and believe in the justice system that we expect will bring equilibrium in our society, we make no attempt to soft-peddle issues that are grave. When offences are committed, there is a process that has to take its course and that is as it should be. Someone lost his life here and that is serious. Each time we talk with offending women, the queries we are faced with are suggestive of something that none of us is seeking to do. 'Do you want these women to walk away scot-free'? 'No' is the realistic response. But do we want them to end up with a future that is equally traumatic? There was a life before they came here, there is a life here, and we hope a life after they leave. Are all three components of their lives not equally vital?

For the superintendent, however, Hasina is a spouse-killer — nothing more, nothing less. He politely tells us, 'Hame iss se kya matlab ki woh kahan se aayee aur kahan jaayegi?' [How does it concern us where she is coming from and where she ends up?] And then he looks at me and says, 'Madam, do you know my background and my past life? It is probably irrelevant for you and rightly so too. So, why should the past life of these women be of any concern to us? They are offenders, they committed crimes and they have to be punished. Whether it is one year, two years, four years, or 14 years — that is not my problem. The judge decided that and sent them here. We keep them here and then when they have served their sentences, we let them go. The rest is not of any concern for us.'

With that mouthful he dismisses our concerns as trivial and inconsequential. It may not be a concern of the punitive machinery, we keep telling ourselves, but it is a cause for reflection for us. I had several altercations with the superintendent on several issues: put another way, we just didn't see eye to eye on anything, especially not on gender issues. The clash of mindsets is hard at all times, but when someone's life and future is at stake, it feels as if a collision is waiting to happen corner.

Our altercations with the superintendent were headed for just such a collision. He was smarter than us all along. He had instructed his deputy to keep a vigilant eye on our team for the slightest of misdemeanours. And that is what transpired. One of our researchers was accused of taking mail back and forth for a prisoner; another was accused of providing money for a prisoner's family outside; and yet another of taking her mobile phone into the prison.

The researcher was called to the office and questioned. She apologised and offered an explanation to the deputy. But this was just the slip-up the deputy was waiting for and it cost us all dear. It gave the superintendent ammunition to take the matter to his superiors to try and get our researcher suspended.

A 'hearing' was arranged before the head of the prison administration to resolve the issue. One could call it a figurative coming to blows, but once done it set the record straight. Officers have a head start on all fronts: not just in relation to subordinate staff and prisoners, but even visitors, activists, and project and programme workers. I should have seen it coming when I took issue with him on his portrayal and descriptions of women inside. I should have realised that as the longest functioning non-governmental organisation in that prison, we now had a special presence here — our workers had the freedom to go where they wished, could stay with prisoners, talk to them, delve into their lives and problems, and assist in any way possible (within the prescribed rules and regulations). It would only take one irate jailor to gather together some minor complaints to persuade his seniors to clip our wings and halt our project. Unfortunately for him, it did not quite happen that way.

The 'hearing' in the office of the head of prisons was not pleasant. I decided to accompany my associate to add some weight to her pleadings. The superintendent was so excited at firing shots at my colleague that he had to be disciplined a few times by his boss. We stood our ground that it was the easiest thing for any staff member to accuse project workers of just about anything and get prisoners and staff to support the accusation. I pointed out to the Director General that my associate had apologised to the deputy for inadvertently taking in her mobile phone on one occasion and also for taking the address of a prisoner to be able to contact her family and assure them that she was alright. But there were no *mala fide* intentions. We insisted we had very little to gain and much to lose from stepping out of line, and that in fact we were being victimised for our strong views and perhaps our reformative zeal for which we were being constantly derided by the superintendent. As a last punch on behalf of the organisation, I offered that we were happy to close 'shop' and go home if our presence irked some officers and staff. That probably clinched the issue.

Jail administrations have unwillingly and grudgingly had to accept that volunteer organisations work in prisons: the presence of well-informed human rights groups in all fields has pressured prison systems into showing (or showing off) how readily they enable non-government organisations to enter and work with substantial freedom. We were lucky that the senior officer had been in charge for all of the years we had worked in the prisons. We had actually heard him boast about our work at his speeches and we could sense it brought him credit too. We did have much to show for our presence. He concluded the informal 'enquiry' at his office within an hour. We left and no greetings were exchanged with the superintendent thereafter. 'He is sulking', I was informed. A few weeks later, when promotions and transfers were due in that State, we learnt that the superintendent had been sent to another prison without a promotion because this was not the first time he had engineered such situations.

So, rule number one: Never take on prison staff even in academic or ideological debates. We did pay a price. For a while we were being watched by guard staff and we in turn were also on our guard as we interacted with the prisoners.

Hasina was glad to see the superintendent go. She had had enough of his scornful taunts even though he came to the women's prison only once a week. If he so much as heard that she was complaining of constant headaches and wanted the doctor to prescribe medication he would give her a mouthful about her past, about her crime, and add, 'this is not your *mayeka ghar* [parental home] where you will be pampered, this is a prison where you are serving a punishment'. She wondered if he ever thought about the prisoner as a person even for one brief moment, or were all the women just defined by their offences.

The Hasinas of the world are incapable of standing up to the system, any system. They are circumscribed by so many layers of social tradition and tutored for so long in their prescribed roles that there is little by way of negotiation or manoeuvre in their lives. They carry a heavy social load accompanied by an inherent inability to discard it. They are conditioned to believe that if they tread this prescribed path without stumbling, life will be smooth and easy. And then the jolt — nothing in the prescribed tenets is really meant for their personal well-being. The advantages all lie on the other side — the side of those who have prescribed them. It is always about losing; there are no gains in their lives, just losses.

Perhaps, we all carry baggage from our past: customs, traditions, rites, habits, and all the conditioned responses that are
handed down and strongly affect our future and our interactions
with others. But at some point, with encouragement from some
quarters, we do manage to fight some of that baggage and say
'enough'. Those without that encouragement have neither the
means nor the methods.

'I was provided a lawyer who kept making me put my thumb
impression on papers and I hadn't a clue what he was doing.
He never considered it necessary to inform me about what he
was up to. He just said, "You are unable to read this, so I can only
assure you that I am doing the best I can". Each time I said to
him, "I know my husband was killed in that incident, but I have
told you the story, so what exactly are you going to do so that I
don't rot in jail and my children suffer?" But clearly, the lawyer
on the other side [my brother-in-law's] was working against any
relief that was even possible for me. I cursed my upbringing, I
cursed my illiteracy, I cursed my gutlessness that had landed me
here and I cursed all of society for not helping me when I was
being molested and battered. Do you know I even cursed God?
And that I know is a sin, isn't it?'

'I don't know, Hasina. Maybe, it is [morality is so subjective
I thought, who am I to tell her what is a sin and what isn't?]. I
know, you believe your God has let you down. This has to be
worked out somehow.' Again false hope and empty promise!

Hasina stopped smiling ages ago: You could try every trick
in the book but you couldn't get her to smile. 'What is there to
smile about?' she would say.

Each day we witness her decline: of the mind and soul not
just the body. Bodily decline makes itself apparent soon enough
and the doctor is called to prescribe medicine for fever, or weight
loss, or aches, pains and so on. But the mind just keeps declining. When you have lost everything that is life for you, there is
very little left to lose and it can do one of several things to a person. One person keeps staring at the sky all day, another con-
tinuously 'draws' imaginary lines on the floor, someone keeps
looking at her hands as if there should be something there that
isn't, another woman just cries and can't stop. There are many

who shout, scream, rave and rant, and are finally labelled and a new place is found for them — a home for mental patients.

I have already been involved with Niru's case in a jail in another State; she is in prison for killing her husband. There are so many similarities in the events and circumstances. There is no hope in this case either. Some details differ but she too is labelled a spouse-killer. She too was married at sixteen and had a drunk for a husband who beat her each time he was drunk and harassed her for more money (she was the breadearner in that house). The difference is that she is 50 years old and has grown-up children. Here too the son intervened each time to save his mother, but succumbed to his injuries when on one occasion his father hit out at him in a fury. Why was the husband not arrested? Because he threatened the wife that she should call it accidental death otherwise he would kill her and sell their daughters to the 'flesh trade'. Niru was petrified and kept quiet for the sake of her daughters even after she lost her only son.

Not that the incident changed her husband's behaviour in any way. He was back to his old ways, to drunkenness and wife-beating. The violence increased and each day someone was at risk. One night he came stoned on dope and picked up a heavy wooden implement to attack Niru. Her sister and her children were present at the time and her sister's son came to save his aunt. Fearing that her husband would either strike the boy or her, she pulled the stick out of her husband's hand and struck him a blow on the head and he fell. 'I don't know if he was dead or not, but I thought if he gets up he will certainly kill me so I struck him again.' He died and Niru was taken away for questioning by the police.

'I have admitted more than once that I killed him, so there is little you can do by way of getting me relief; release, of course, is out of the question. Once I have said, "I killed him", no one wants to know anything else. And it is therefore irrelevant too that so much happened to me at his hands all of my married life! It is not an issue. They are not interested in what it was that brought things to a head.'

It's the same with Hasina — once she acknowledges that she killed him there is nothing much to be said. For form's sake, we get them lawyers and legal aid and inform them of their rights. But we know and they know that the outcome for them is — many, many years 'inside'. Is there a point then to get them to talk about their lives and torments? Is it wise to take them through their anguish again? We would like to believe there is a point until the sufferer herself says otherwise. For those who believe that the only path is the legal path, they are not always on the right track. There are others who know that these women don't have a chance at the hands of the legal system: there was a legal wrong and the judicial machinery decided the price. But how did the machinery decide what they did? This seems fair as long as it is fairly determined. Sometimes it is, sometimes it isn't.

To question the system may be self-defeating because there is no other relief-provider. But every once in a while the system needs to be interrogated: either when it is faulty, or when the accused is so ill-equipped that some consideration has to be made for his/her benefit. Leaving such offenders devoid of any support is itself a grave injustice and one that rights' groups make it their business to address.

Life does not stop once the legal system has delivered the goods: released or convicted, the accused still has a life. For those who are sent to prison, it may be a difficult life, but it is still a life. The prisoners still have needs because they have a life. Who will remind the state about that if it forgets? This is a reality the handling officers would rather forget: jail functionaries are so used to believing the worst about those in their charge that the last thing they want to be concerned with is providing for them. Members of the staff believe they too have difficult lives and question what they see as the fuss we make over prisoners. If we tell them that prisoners have been deprived of their liberty and choices by being locked up the retort is sharp: *'To inhone jurm bhi to kiya hai!'* [Well, they have committed a crime!]. Rule books, guiding principles, international standards, constitutional provisions, human rights training — all these fade into insignificance once the gates are shut, and order has to be maintained. Regardless of offences, of socio-economic background, race, colour, caste, gender, religion, character or personalities, the needs of those inside have to be intelligently determined and then administered, taking cognisance of differences. Part of our brief is just that.

We could not really make any legal intervention for Hasina. There was a death, she took the blame, the witnesses (partial or not) testified and she was tried. She was paying a heavy price for the act. In a sense, she said, he too paid the price for his act, so they were even. The Protection of Women from Domestic Violence Bill (2005) acquired the status of an Act of Parliament only after Hasina had been convicted. And in any case, she was not the real killer and was not about to let her son be convicted. There were too many twists in her story.

She endured the thrashings and there was really no intervention then that would have had the force to enable her to fight what she was enduring. She repeatedly questioned the law's silence on what happens to so many women behind the closed doors of their own homes. Not that there was any doubt about the evidence: there are cases narrated by battered wives the world over about how they were beaten so much and so severely that they thought they would surely die. Elsewhere too, it is regarded as a domestic matter but finally the law did step in and some women gathered the courage to put a stop to it. In India, we have only just got the provision of the law, and it will be a long time before simple, ordinary women brutalised within their domestic spheres feel empowered enough to act. Life would have to offer adequate alternatives for them to turn to without prejudice and bigotry if their mammoth efforts (and mammoth they certainly would be) were to be worth the fight. The society and the state clearly need to work together and in synchrony.

For Hasina, the 'relief' (law relating to domestic violence) has come too late. But there were no prospects even if we had pushed her to fight. And then there was her minor son, who took the fatal step to protect her. She would shield him at all costs, and she did. That he was a minor and would have been treated with less severity and with leniency was of no significance to her. In any event, she would have gone to any lengths to protect her son and preferred being imprisoned herself.

We feel a sense of frustration when faced with the real-life situations of women like Hasina. These are their lives, lived each day in pain and with no sign of a better future. They are worse each day for wear and tear, living lives through the experiences of others for their own experiences are worth nothing.

There are so many different questions that each story poses that we often find ourselves out of our depth and wonder whose domain this really is: law-makers? lawyers? judges? activists? campaigners? feminists? educationists? All of these. Perhaps, one purpose of relating these cases for the general public is to seek responses to these questions and perhaps some solutions.

▣

Note

Domestic violence is not just a regrettable reality in Indian society, it is almost an accepted part of the lives of women and more specifically of women in dependent positions in many societies the world over. Gender arguments that place such violence squarely within the patriarchal set-up view the occurrence of domestic violence as a feature of the continued stereotyping of women's roles relating to the distribution of power in a society. Locating this stereotyping in biological (sexual) and physiological terms, its proponents continue to elaborate the gendered roles set out for societies down the ages for the effective functioning of society. Women are expected to be responsible for child bearing, child rearing, house keeping including domestic chores and men for earning livelihoods, defending the hearth and home, fighting off adversaries all of which tasks require physical labour, and all of which are the domain of men. Physical prowess is the hallmark of this division and a concomitant of this prowess is both the use of force and a right to physical space. At the centre of it all is the idea of control.

Portrayals of women in historical and religious texts in most societies are as home-makers conforming to the customs of the community and, above all, deferring to the men who provide the livelihood and support for family and community. The important feature of all this is the acceptance by women of this role for lack of choices and for all fear of chastisement should they disobey. This simplistic portrayal lies at the root of many of the ordeals and sufferings women are subjected to and helplessly accept as part of the cross they have to bear. One of the most common things we hear is, 'have you stopped beating your wife'. Such objectionable and odious phrases reveal something uncanny about the place of women in society and more so of women who are, or have been made economically dependent on the men in their lives. But the most important of all is what happens should a woman decide to change it all: she has no support from family and friends.

Wife-beating has been condoned throughout most of history. British law gave husbands the right to beat their wives for what was called 'lawful correction' until the nineteenth century. Blackstone summarised this tradition in the late eighteenth century: 'The husband also might give his wife moderate correction. For as he is to answer for her misbehaviour the law thought it reasonable to entrust him with this power of restraining her, by domestic chastisement in the same moderation that a man is allowed to correct his servant or children' (Blackstone, 1996, vol 1, 432, cited in Pahl 1985). The *right* of a husband to beat his wife was abolished in 1891.

It is interesting that even in the West with all the trappings of a rights-oriented environment, domestic violence is not that easy to tackle as an offence. It is under-reported even though it is said to account for 16 per cent of all violent crime, and affects one in four women and one in six men; 77 per cent of victims of domestic violence are women. It has more repeat victims than any other crime (on average, it is estimated that there will have been 35 assaults before a victim calls the police). On average, two women are killed every week by a current or former male partner and allegedly one incident of domestic violence is reported to the police every minute (Crime in England and Wales, 2006/07 Report).

Analysed logically, domestic violence is not a subject of a specific law. It is a label that has been placed on other existing crimes such as battery, or assault, or other forms of violence punishable according to existing statutes. Several other criminal laws can also be labelled as those on domestic violence if they occur in the defined circumstances. The label of domestic violence does not increase the statutory penalties for the offence. However, the domestic violence label does require additional conditions to be placed on the defendant who has been found guilty, and protective measures for the victims. Logic aside, clearly, the creation of a law for domestic violence is a consequence of a long history of violence within the home/family. Historically, in its modern incarnation in most parts of the world, the law dates from around the time of the women's movements of the 1970s. Logically too, while the traditional perspective is that victims of domestic violence are predominately women, this is not always the case; men, children and the elderly are also vulnerable to domestic violence.

This said, there is an abundance of evidence to show that it is mainly women and children who are the victims. Children, who themselves suffer violence at the hands of a parent, are in the main protected by the state though child protection procedures. The remedies provided by the civil law are therefore generally used for protection for an adult victim. Various individuals and groups have defined domestic violence to include everything from saying unkind or demeaning words, to grabbing a person's arm, to hitting, kicking, choking, or even murdering. Although for our purposes, domestic violence refers to married or cohabiting couples, it has been pointed out even in relation to the law passed in India that it is not gender-neutral. This will be analysed after discussing the Act.

The enactment of the Protection of Women from Domestic Violence Act, 2005, is theoretically designed to protect women from violence in the home, a location hitherto regarded as a private domain and beyond the purview of the law. Admittedly, women could earlier approach the courts under the Indian Penal Code (IPC) in cases of domestic violence. However, the kinds of domestic violence contemplated by this (PWDV) Act and the victims recognised by it, make it more expansive in scope than the sections of the IPC. The IPC never used the term 'domestic violence' to refer to this objectionable practice, perhaps because it is a *practice*. In fact, the only similar class of offences addressed by the IPC dealt with cruelty to married women. All other instances of domestic violence within the household had to be dealt with under the offences that the respective acts of violence constituted under the IPC without any regard to the gender of the victim (assault, battery, etc.) This posed a problem, especially where the victims were children, or women who were dependant on the assailant. In fact, even where the victim was the wife of the assailant and could approach the courts under Section 498A of the IPC, she would presumably have to move out of her matrimonial home to ensure her safety, or face further violence as retaliation. There was no measure in place to allow her to continue staying in her matrimonial home and yet raise her voice against the violence perpetrated against her. This, together with many other problems faced by women in the household, prompted the enactment of this law. This commentary focuses on the constitutional perspectives of this progressive legislation.

The salient features of the Protection from Domestic Violence Act, 2005 are as follows:

- The Act seeks to cover those women who are, or have been in a relationship with the abuser wherein both parties have lived together in a shared household and are related by consanguinity, marriage, or a relationship in the nature of marriage, or adoption; in addition, relationship with family members living together as a joint family are also included. Even those women who are sisters, widows, mothers, single women, or living with the abuser are entitled to get legal protection under the proposed Act.

- 'Domestic violence' includes actual abuse, or the threat of abuse that is physical, sexual, verbal, emotional and economic. Harassment by way of unlawful dowry demands to the woman, or her relatives would also be covered under this definition.
- An important feature of the Act is the woman's right to secure housing. The Act provides for the woman's right to reside in the matrimonial, or shared household, whether or not she has any title or rights in the household. This right is secured by a residence order, which is passed by the court.
- Another relief is that of the power of the court to pass protection orders that prevent the abuser from aiding or committing an act of domestic violence, or any other specified act, entering a workplace or any other place frequented by the abused, attempting to communicate with the abused, isolating any assets used by both the parties and causing violence to the abused, her relatives and others who provide her assistance from the domestic violence.
- The Act provides for appointment of Protection Officers and NGOs to provide assistance to the woman with regard to medical examination, legal aid, safe shelter, etc.

The Act recognises the breach of a protection order or interim protection order by the respondent as a cognisable and non-bailable offence punishable with imprisonment for a term which may extend to one year, or with a fine which may extend to ₹20,000 or with both. Similarly, non-compliance, or discharge of duties by the Protection Officer is also sought to be made an offence under the Act with a similar punishment.

The PWDV Act thus gives a more expansive definition to the term 'domestic violence', a term hitherto not even used in legal parlance, by including in Section 3 physical, mental, verbal, emotional, sexual and economic abuse, harassment for dowry, acts of threatening to abuse the victim, or any other person related to her. Primarily meant to provide protection to the wife or female partner from domestic violence at the hands of the husband or male live-in partner, or his relatives, the law also extends its protection to women who are sisters, widows, or mothers. Domestic violence under the Act includes actual abuse or the threat of abuse, whether physical, sexual, verbal, emotional or economic. Harassment by way of unlawful dowry demands made to the woman, or her relatives would also be covered under this definition.

Lauded by many and criticised by others, the PWDV Act, like so many that deal with acts that are regarded as 'practices', lends itself to abuse as well. While the totally ignorant would not have the wherewithal to use it, those who wish to settle scores can also misuse it (against spouses as well as the female members of their families whose 'rule of thumb' they abhor). While that is not a reason for faulting the Act, it is a reality check suggesing that the ignorant (Hasina) who are the real sufferers would still be left in the lurch. They would not report the violence unless they had assistance from the community whose writ and jurisdiction have been the mainstay of their lives. The law would have to have supplementary aid closer to home for the likes of Hasina. In their mundane day-to-day lives, the concept of the law is about as remote as *pardes* [a geopraphically distant land].

6

'Vimla to Pagal Hai!':
[Vimla is a Lunatic!]

◙

And then there is the mind — that invisible unknown or less-known part of us, the state and status of which often makes or breaks our lives, but which still continues to occupy only the margins and periphery of our attention and concerns. A small physical injury on a finger gets more attention and care from us than something that happens inside our heads, that shows no physical aberration on the outside, but shows plenty of behavioural symptoms that suggest something is fundamentally wrong. All kinds of events and incidents occur in a person's life, affecting the mind in different ways, some effects being acutely damaging and debilitating, but then it is assumed that the person will be able to 'get over it', 'overcome it', 'put it behind him/her and move on' and so on. Unfortunately, our own experiences and the observation of the experiences of others indicate sufficiently that this is not how it works and that some remedial measures are needed to address any wound in the mind too. And no other place demonstrates this fact more than the opaque, mysterious structure surrounded by stone walls, studded on top with pieces of glass, sometimes with electrically charged barbed wires running around the perimeters, and iron grills and enormous big gates — all aptly referred to as 'bricks of shame'. The structure seems meticulously designed to overawe, intimidate, frighten and almost terrorise all those imprisoned within it.

Vimla was an inmate too — she looked fifty, but her biographical notes told us she was thirty-six years old. Her hair was unkempt, in fact, exceptionally dry, scruffy and messy, her face was dirty, she was barefoot and on the whole, looked really grubby. She had clearly been made as presentable as possible for the 'parade' and kept fidgeting with her garments as if they were alien to her body. She looked blankly at the bleak and dusty surroundings, but while she was expressionless, almost helpless and certainly powerless, she still had the kind of appearance that made you wonder whether it was a good idea to go too close to her. The jailor had lined up the prisoners of 'Barrack 4' as if they were in a parade when I went to meet them after several days of interacting with the women in the other 'barracks' (dormitories are called barracks in Indian prisons, in the military terminology of the colonial days, matching the ethos that underlies the running of the institution).

I have always found this 'parade' introduction distasteful, but there is no other solution to the problem of how I might first view and then later be introduced to the women in each barrack. The staff members actually think they are being 'open' and 'transparent' by arranging this 'public' production. So, we have the introductions in the parade style, each inmate pointed to as her turn comes. This is Seeta, she is charged with 'dowry death', and sentenced to seven years. This is Paro, she is still on remand and was arrested under the Narcotics Drugs and Psychotropic Substances Prevention Act (NDPS); she has already been here three years, but the trial hasn't taken place yet. And so we go down the line till we come to Vimla, who clearly stands out as the odd one physically as she stands sideways with her back almost turned to us. Before there is a formal introduction to Vimla and her reason for being here, a yell resounds in the room, startling me.

It is the jailor who shouts at Vimla, 'Stand straight!' Vimla looks shocked and her body goes into a convulsion. The woman next to her gently catches her arm and straightens her in the line, saying softly, 'Vimla, *seedhi khari ho nahin to pata hai na kya hoga?* [Vimla, stand straight otherwise you know what will happen, don't you?]'. But Vimla is in a reverie, quite oblivious to what she is being told. She reverts to her old position, and does not stand straight as ordered to, clearly upsetting the jailor and warder.

The jailor is clearly agitated — and this is not going to help me much in talking about or to Vimla — saying, 'Why do you people bring her out when she can very well be locked in the *kothri* (store room used for disciplinary lock-up)? We can do without the adverse publicity that Vimla's case brings us'.

This jail for women is not really overcrowded (overcrowding can be such a relative aspect of a prison that it needs some discussion; the study of a mentally disturbed prisoner might be the most appropriate place to do that, later). Generally, women's prisons look and are less overcrowded than men's prisons. Women have a way of using their space in a manner that makes the prison look relatively bare and unfilled and almost tidy and clean. A closer look and more interactions with the women tell another story, to which we shall return as we see where the institution falls far short of women's needs than a men's prison does.

But back to Vimla — as I watch her, she scratches her dishevelled hair, confirming my suspicion that she has lice in her hair, a not uncommon occurrence when women live together and do not have high standards of hygiene as in this part of the world, worsened by the acute shortage of water in this desert State. She then moves on to scratching other parts of her body and as she pulls up her shirt sleeve to do so, I notice the bruises: they are red and blue and the arm is swollen. Perhaps I wince because the jailor promptly offers an explanation: 'I believe she fell down the stairs the other day and hurt herself. Warder! Has the doctor given her the medicine?' Before the warder could answer, the jailor says: 'Good! See that she attends the infirmary regularly.' Great show, I thought. I must look gullible, or maybe no one told her I had worked on projects in women's prisons for more than 15 years now. And what stairs is she talking about — the one little step that leads into the yard? There are no stairs in this prison.

The 'show' over, my colleague Neena, who has been working on some of the women's case studies, takes me to the room assigned to us for our project. We clearly need to talk about the experience of this last 'parade'.

'How on earth are we going to get to Vimla?', I ask, worried and perplexed at the whole phenomenon of coming face to face with a person who is so 'not there'. 'How will we get to understand the mind of Vimla?'

'It will take some time,' my associates say, half-reassuringly and half-apprehensively. 'It will be an uphill job and even more uphill will be finding a solution to Vimla's problem. Clearly, this is an intricate problem that needs particular attention and one that the "authorities" seem unable to address. And because she is an embarrassment, it's certain that we will be looked at with some suspicion and even hostility by the jailor.'

'So, how shall we do this?', I again ask. 'Facing hostility is not new for us; we know that behind the sweet smiles of the jailor, the underlying attitude, as we plod from woman to woman, is not one of acceptance. The supervisory staff feel we intend to show them up, no matter how much we try to convince them that we are here to lend a hand — where there are too few hands — and that we really could be on the same side. The worrying bit is that we are not likely to get much information about Vimla's background from her directly as we have been able to do with other women. What should we be doing to know about her, and also to see what can be done about her problem?'

Vimla is not the only 'mentally ill' person we have come across in a prison, but certainly the most acutely and visibly mentally disturbed person we have encountered so far. Basic conversations with her yield little about her past but plenty about her present condition. She talks very little and while she is generally meek except when provoked, her replies to our questions are always sharp and cryptic. She is able to tell us her name sometimes; at other times she would say, 'How should I know?' She has no idea where she came from, but from her records we get some details of her village and background.

Vimla belongs to a not too small village in the State and some-times refers to her childhood when reprimanded. 'If my parents were here they would not tolerate what all of you are doing,' she would say. If one asks her why she wears a particular garment (an ill-fitting, worn-out and torn frock) for days together, she would say, 'Why? Don't you like it? My mother made it especially for me,' (which was not quite true, of course, since she had had no contact with her home for ages). Clearly, she goes back and forth in time and in her life depending on her mental state. Her short incoherent statements about her life are the nearest we get to her past, especially her parental home. Her barrack mates, however, are able to fill us in on some of her background.

'When she first came here she was not in such a bad shape,' one of them volunteers. 'She was dazed but not behaving as she does here and now, doing things which clearly indicate just how acutely mentally ill she really is. She doesn't belong here and should have been handled with care right from the start. Throwing her at the deep end on arrival has made things really bad for her. She was already dazed, and she is now so traumatised, she's like a blank wall sometimes.'

It soon becomes clear to all three of us (my associates Neena, Kiran and I) that the object of our exploration and investigation here is going to be a bit different. My associates rightly point out that there are two definite reasons why we are working here: simply put, we have to understand who the women in the prison are, and why they are here (that is, their backgrounds and offences) and then to observe and address the nature of their experiences in prison. Seeking answers that would minimise their agony and maximise their ability to live somewhat decent and dignified lives now (while in the prison) and when they leave (healing and rehabilitation) has been always the underlying reason for much that we do. Faced with the kind of person Vimla is (or has become), it is clear she could not just be a *case* for us. She portrays one of the most important reasons for our work among women prisoners and epitomises the most drastic effects that locking up can have on those who are on the verge of cracking up because of what they had done and what had been done to them. It has been our submission for cases not as severe as Vimla's that each woman needs a different kind of handling if she is to be prevented from going over the edge. With Vimla we are already seeing the worst effects of the lack of 'special handling'.

'Why are you here?' we ask her. Foolish question perhaps, for she looks dazed, her face blank, and then answers slowly, 'You should know — you brought me here. I didn't come of my own accord. Someone brought me here.'

We observed her while we worked with her for almost two years and it was evident she needed special medical attention apart from the 'special handling' we kept recommending as we went along. We suggested several times that she needed to be in a hospital, and it was with some effort that our intervention got the attention it deserved. By then, of course, we believed Vimla was almost 'beyond repair'.

Gradually, a sketchy picture of Vimla's story emerges. She was married to a drunkard who took a sadistic pleasure in thrashing her for the smallest thing. That wasn't all — he took a perverse delight in thrashing her naked. So, each time he was drunk, he first ripped off her clothes and then beat her with any object that came his way. The staff had gathered this from her case records when her hearing was held, and had shared this information with some of the 'old' hands at the prison. It took a while for us to gather this information, but then the reasons for a lot of Vimla's actions became clearer to us. She had none of the shyness relating to her body that other inmates showed. Other women complained that there was no 'body privacy' in the prison: for dressing, for using the toilet, for a bath, for attending to other personal needs — everything was so public. But for Vimla, bodily exposure did not seem to be a problem. Some in the prison called her *besharam* [shameless], but it was evident that she had no sense of the 'shame' they were talking about and thanks to her husband's manipulations, nakedness for her was associated with being punished. She had no awareness, or comprehension about many of the things that others complained about, and she was punished for the behaviour she manifested as a result of this, as if she was being deliberately mischievous. No one bothered to go deep enough into her behaviour to see that Vimla was mentally challenged and needed treatment that was different and special.

'She has been put in the barrack at the end of the passage so that she is near the toilet and bathing area, but she takes off all her clothes at any time, any place,' one of the women said. 'Each time she is reprimanded, there is a moment when she is almost expecting to be told that she should take her clothes off — and then she waits to see what will happen next. Earlier, people used to actually treat this as a *tamasha* and made fun of her, laughing at and mocking her as she did this. Some would even provoke her and say '*Vimla, kapre utaro* [Vimla, take off your clothes] and she would start doing just that. Gradually, the novelty wore off and they began treating it as a serious and disturbing problem, and a few of them would hurry across to tell her gently that she should not take off her clothes.'

We were told that when she first entered the prison, she looked shell-shocked. Over time, her behaviour deteriorated because she just couldn't cope with the endless instructions — 'do this', 'don't do that', 'sit here', 'finish your food', 'wash your plate', 'wake up', 'go to sleep' — and no one assisted this traumatised being who had come with some rather sordid experiences as part of her baggage. When she went in for meals, people moved away from her because there was no telling what she might do with the food. Sometimes she just spat it out at the table, sometimes she would go and throw it in the toilet, often she would just not eat and if coaxed, would run away from the kitchen after throwing her *thali* on the floor. This caused resentment because then the other inmates had to clean up the mess.

Vimla found relief in smoking every now and then if some obliging person gave her the *bidi*s she wanted. She would retreat to a corner of the prison and sit quietly to smoke and actually looked as if she was at peace. If the convict officer (CO) caught her smoking, it was 'discipline time' again — the stick. No amount of pleading from anyone that it was really a harmless act that gave her some solace, helped. 'Rules are rules', the CO would say. It was strange how she was treated as if she were 'normal' when banal rules were violated, and as quite abnormal at other times when she did bizarre things.

She was never aggressive towards people, but her whole demeanour, even when she was doing weird things to herself, was something other women could not take in their stride so they just stayed away from her. Most women knew the penalties for not obeying the staff (no matter what the staff said), but Vimla had no logic to draw upon to see her through her daily life, no indicators that told her that she should refrain from doing something that would be frowned upon, and this was clearly a running sore for the establishment.

'One morning,' Neena says, 'there was a cultural programme organised by a group of women from outside, and there was singing and dancing that day. We were all asked to participate, so Kiran and I also went along. Suddenly, out of nowhere, Vimla emerged — she lifted her dress right up and started dancing. She was not wearing underwear and it was really very embarrassing for everyone. But she had no clue about what she was doing. Everyone was really upset. A CO grabbed her forcefully, took her inside the barrack and gave her a hiding. As if that was the answer!'

There is a phenomenon in Indian prisons that we have been questioning and battling with for years: convict officers or COs. Senior prisoners who have clocked in the years and shown 'good conduct and responsible behaviour' over the years become COs and are entrusted with the task of managing prisoners if and when required. The CO in charge of the prisoners in Vimla's barrack couldn't have made things worse for Vimla. Impatient, bossy and constantly on the lookout to gather 'brownie points' from the staff she spared nothing to discipline Vimla. Each morning, Vimla had a problem waking up, mostly because she had been given sedatives by doctors if she had 'misbehaved' the previous day. The 'wake-up routine' for Vimla bordered on crude brutality: the CO would first shout out Vimla's name, and if she didn't stir, the CO would return with a stick and first poke Vimla with it, and then if she still didn't respond, she would beat her, taunting her all the while, saying that this was not a hotel where she could sleep as long as she liked. Vimla's reaction may only have been bewilderment for she hadn't a clue what a hotel was.

Fellow prisoner Radha told us about an occurrence. 'After seeing this happen day after day,' she said, 'I intervened one morning and told the CO that what she was doing was absurd: "Vimla is not normal," I said, "and even though she is a prisoner it does not mean she is not a human being. How can you start beating her like that?" But the CO paid no attention. That day I decided I would do something about it. So, I went to the deputy jailor and asked to be put in charge of Vimla's care. I volunteered to help Vimla so that we did not have the kind of distasteful scenes that were becoming frequent and were too damaging for Vimla. Fortunately, she agreed and from that day on I have been trying to assist Vimla in whatever way I can. I try to make others see her less as an object of ridicule and more as a human being with problems that need urgent solutions. It has been absurd how we have all treated her as things got worse,' Radha said. We noticed over time that Radha had decided to take charge of helping Vimla when things got out of hand for her.

After a few instances of the kind that happened on the day of the cultural event, Vimla was kept locked up, particularly when there were visitors. No one, even then, took the initiative of ensuring that it was time Vimla was given 'special handling' of a psychological and medical nature.

Her plight was unimaginable — she seemed to have lost track of the simplest things that she clearly must have known about at some point in her adult life. She was at a loss when her monthly periods started. She would just go on as if nothing was amiss until someone would notice her stained clothes and pass a rude comment. '*Arre pagli dekh to kitna khoon laga hai!*' [You mad-hatter, can't you see your clothes are all stained with blood!]. The taunts and locking up only made matters worse: she often just sat in the open courtyard and used it as her toilet. Once she was actually seen handling her faeces and was prevented from putting it in her mouth by a fellow prisoner. That was when it was decided that there was a need for urgent and dramatic intervention.

Neena and Kiran, who had been following Vimla's case closely, believed that was the last straw and there was no room for any dilly-dallying anymore. Off they went to the authorities who sat in the corridors of power down the road, and placed the note they had prepared on Vimla's case and condition before them. By then they had gathered some details, albeit sketchy, about her background. The story of Vimla's drunken husband was nothing unusual; there were many women who had the same story. But that she was severely beaten by him and in rather crude circumstances was something that shocked everyone. It now dawned on people why she was not really aggressive, but did strange things quietly and submissively, why she was not terrified of undressing in public, why she almost waited to be thrashed when she did something wrong, why she didn't care about her appearance and cleanliness ('it didn't matter to anyone, so why bother?', is how her mates looked at it).

The day of the dramatic events that resulted in her husband's death were only sketchily available for us. But by then we had figured out that the minutiae of the 'event' was not really that important. Our mission was different in this case. While it may have been possible for us to go and look up the details of the case in the district court we had made the decision that there wasn't time for all that if we were to get Vimla on to the 'repair' programme. What we had pieced together was that one fateful day when her husband thrashed her (after stripping her of all her clothes) in the inebriated state he was in, she pushed him really hard as part of her resistance and he fell to the floor, hitting his head against the stone floor. He was hurt but became more enraged because she had had the gall to retaliate, something that had never happened before — so he got up, pulled her by the hair and dragged her to the ante-room, a store-room. She struggled, pulled herself away and then picked up an axe that lay in the corner and struck him with it. There was blood everywhere and she was absolutely petrified. She has no recollection of the event — she blanked out and from what we gathered, she stayed in a blacked-out state for a while.

One has little information about how her court hearings went and how she pleaded or who got her the lawyer, but here she is — in prison for life under Sections 302, 307 and 324 of the Indian Penal Code. The details of the Sections are given at the end of this book but it might be stated that Section 302 is 'for committing murder', Section 307 is for 'committing an act having the intention and knowledge that such an act will result in death', and Section 324 is 'for voluntarily causing hurt by an instrument for shooting, stabbing or cutting or any instrument which, used as a weapon of offence is likely to cause death'. The latter Section also covers poisons, corrosive and explosive substances used for the above purpose. This Section excludes those covered by Section 334 and it might not be irrelevant to quote it here:

> Whoever voluntarily causes hurt on grave and sudden provocation, if he neither intends nor knows himself to be likely to cause hurt to any person other than the person who gave the provocation, shall be punished with imprisonment of either description for a term which may extend to one month or with fine or both.

There wasn't much that could be done now with her sentence and its validity: the problem here was far more pressing and related to a person's survival (body and mind) and the urgency made itself evident with each passing day. The machinery was put into gear for Vimla's 'treatment', a word that had so many implications and connotations when it pertained to someone's mental state.

Finally, she was seen by the doctor with a view to preparing a case that she needed psychiatric care and treatment. The hospital was contacted and Vimla was to be taken everyday to be examined first and then treated and, if required, be admitted so that the treatment was continuous and professional. That sounds easy enough but in a prison setting (especially this prison setting) the hitches and glitches are unending. There was the problem of 'escorts': prisoners have to be escorted by a constable when they are taken either for court hearings or treatment. Evidently, the doctors in question were on duty for such out-patients till 11 a.m. and the escorts were not able to get their act together to get her there on time. Each day they would return saying, 'She was not seen by the doctor' and it was accepted as a hospital slip-up. It was time to make a move and once again, Neena stepped into action. She decided to visit the hospital and have a chat with the doctors.

When Neena spoke to the doctor, he asked, 'Are the constables in the prison asleep in the mornings? Is that the reason why they can't bring Vimla in during the out-patient hours? How can we treat Vimla when she is never brought here on time?'

The penny dropped. The constables were clearly not interested in getting Vimla treated. For them it was a visit that had to be clocked in and that is what they did. The trip to the hospital was a chore they resented because it affected their duty hours. 'The constables don't want to do anything beyond the routine duties assigned to them,' Neena told the Inspector General of Prisons (IG Prisons). 'The result is that no tests have been done and therefore there has been no diagnosis.' It was time for action again. Neena volunteered to go with the constable if the IG Prisons permitted her to (which he did). That is how she made sure the timings were adhered to and some semblance of treatment commenced.

Vimla was examined and tested and then diagnosed with Post Traumatic Stress Disorder (PTSD) and related problems (such as symptoms of psychosis, which we shall discuss in due course). It was interesting to observe the reactions of the staff and management to the diagnosis. The moment they heard the word *'stress disorder'* associated with the diagnostic label they had various comments, and I paraphrase: 'Oh, what is the big deal here? We all have "stress". In fact, you people (us the project workers, that is) said so to us earlier that we were working under great stress and we were "stressed". So, what is all the fuss about? We should all be taken to the hospital and treated. Why so much fuss if all that emerges is a stress problem.' They had clearly forgotten the behavioural symptoms Vimla had demonstrated and the terminology and the label ("stress") put them off enough to view our concerns with suspicion.

We couldn't be dismissive of their attitude either: working in a prison is not the easiest job. Day in and day out, doing the head count of prisoners, locking them up, putting up with their idiosyncrasies and quirks, disciplining them, and still retaining some sanity to carry on with their own personal lives was surely not a comfortable life. The staff had become prisoners in more ways than could be described — they felt it and we knew it. They showed signs of 'burning out' and their personalities got affected in adverse ways. 'When we first came in,' they often told us, 'we, too, had some good in us. We didn't come in to brutalise people. We started out believing that we would do our jobs the best way we could and perhaps make a difference, a positive difference. But the institution took over: our ways and methods took shapes and turns that were determined by this wretched place. Yes, it is a wretched place that makes many of us careless and sometimes ugly things happen.' Imperceptibly, and often unknowingly, a few of them turned into little monsters or big ogres; some retained a semblance of humanity that came to the fore at times of crisis. But they were swimming against the tide: the norm was a matter-of-fact approach according to rules without any deference to different personalities or their needs.

Their reactions certainly make all of us pause to think about the environment we are working in. This is far from an ideal institution: in fact it is deplorable that society has ever come up with such an abhorrent idea, locking up people in cages and believing that it was going to make people better. It made everyone worse and that included the staff members, especially those who spent all of their time with these people from all kinds of backgrounds, who were condemned to this dumping ground by the system — and the dumping ground was the staff's work place, where they spent hours each day. Many told us they didn't even tell people outside they worked in a prison. 'Let's face it, the world outside looks at this place as the dustbin of society where criminals are sent as a punishment, and criminals are regarded as the scum of the earth, are they not? Why would we go around saying we work in such a place?'

This is not a new quandary for us: that one set of problems should throw up a new set of convoluted difficulties that need as urgent attention as those we are already facing. The staff members are very much on our schema and the plans we have made for change, but for much later. The original plan had been drawn up with the prisoners in mind, but now we felt we needed to revisit our own agenda. We had to view this set of workers in the institution as ends in themselves, which was a tall order since we have already gone far down the road, holding them responsible for so much that was wrong inside the prison.

'See what happens,' Kiran said, 'we scratch the surface and more and more crawls out of the woodwork. What a monumental task this would be if we went into everything that is wrong around here. Impossible!'

Very true, I thought. What Kiran was saying was that our 'agenda' had come crumbling down. We were working with a one-point programme — restoring dignity to one set of persons, and all the while there were others that were silently screaming for help. This was a predicament that couldn't be self-righteously dismissed.

'All right,' I asserted. 'First things first — it's Vimla for the moment. Each day is making life worse for her. Let's address this tricky puzzle and then move on to the next plan of action that will be devoted to staff on whose shoulders we are expecting the burdens of care to fall. They are resentful because we have been riveted to the issue of the prisoners' problems. This whole issue of Vimla and her PTSD has brought this to the fore. Vimla's problem hasn't gone away, and we need to explain to the staff the relationship between the prisoners' problems and their own. After all, it was the word 'stress' that had got this discussion going and so it shall be: we shall address 'stress' and bring in staff issues as well. This is the opportunity perhaps, to wrestle with some conceptual education for one and all — for us, for staff and for the outside world.'

Vimla was not getting better because the treatment was erratic, hospitalisation of prisoners was a problem (security and other factors came in the way) and perhaps the prolonged neglect of the problem had exacerbated the whole matter. There could be other Vimlas coming this way — pre-empting future problems of a similar nature was also part of our problem. There was a way to begin — by actively involving the staff in some of the courses of action.

'Okay, the staff is a bit upset because we made Vimla's malady a high priority, and the diagnosis labelled it as a 'stress disorder'. Let's explain what this is about to all of them. Let's not have everyone trivialise this malady by throwing it out because we are talking about words like 'stress'. There is something in all of us that wants to make words like *anxiety*, *stress* and *depression* sound like some common-place ailments that are all in the mind and unworthy of the attention that they deserve. We need an education here, so let's get our act together. Research and deliver.'

Apart from consulting doctors (psychiatrists) we went as deep as we could into the two well-known documents that had information on mental illnesses and disorders: the American Psychiatric Association's *Diagnostic and Statistical Manual of Mental Disorders* and the World Health Organisation's *International Classification of Diseases*. We studied as best as we could the whole phenomenon of PTSD, which we discovered is an anxiety disorder of serious magnitude. It can develop after a person has been exposed to one or more terrifying events in which some serious physical harm occurred or was threatened. It is a severe and ongoing emotional reaction to an extreme and acute psychological trauma. This stress may involve a threat to the patient's life or perhaps the death of another person, a serious physical injury or threat to physical and/or psychological integrity, to a degree that psychological defences are incapable of coping. In some cases it can also occur due to profound psychological and emotional trauma, apart from any actual physical harm — often the two are combined. The result is an extremely debilitating condition that is not only psychological but also physiological in nature.

So while the staff found it difficult to understand what all the fuss was about, with the stress angle we had established that stress was known to contribute to and trigger psychotic states. Any history of psychologically traumatic events and any recent experience of a stressful nature can contribute to the development of psychosis. Short-lived psychosis triggered by stress, we gathered, is referred to as 'brief reactive psychosis' and patients can spontaneously regain normal functioning within two weeks. In rare cases, individuals can remain in a state of full-blown psychosis for many years, or perhaps have attenuated psychotic symptoms (such as low-intensity hallucinations) present at most times.

So, while many people around us were reacting to Vimla's diagnostic results by trivialising the disorder because it was called a 'stress' disorder, we realised it was really time to explain to everyone what mental illness or disorder was really all about, and above all, that people reacted differently to traumatic events. One person may experience a horrific event as traumatic while another would not suffer trauma as a result of the same event: such is the stuff that makes up a human being and her personality and psyche.

We had a large poster labelled 'The Human Body' in our counselling room that had formed an important part of the health education programme: now we needed it to show the links between mind and body (in particular, the brain) and while this was not going to be an easy task, we felt the staff above all needed this instruction. It wasn't easy since we weren't really psychiatrists in the medical field; but that had to be turned into an asset since we were now required to use lay language to a lay audience. We explained the anatomy and physiology of the brain (to the best of our ability). Moving on to PTSD, we demonstrated with the help of the diagram that PTSD displays biochemical changes in the brain and that these are different in every mental disorder — so what happens in the brain when there is depression, for instance, differs from what happens when a person is going through

PTSD. Although we were reluctant to deliver such a lecture we knew it needed to be done, given the cynicism of the people around us (especially those who were going to be in charge of cases like Vimla's).

What this did for us was more than educational. It brought home to us that there is a dire need for in-depth work here in this environment. We can't expect the guarding staff to do it because they have the barest minimum educational requirements (school-leavers at best) to qualify for the jobs they are doing, such as filling forms, making lists of daily needs, locking up and doing the head count each day. The senior staff (a little better qualified) do not have the time. They are busy impressing the management that they are doing a good job running the prison. So, who would go into the details of the 'special needs' of prisoners?

'How does one say the following,' said Neena, 'that *in addition to biochemical changes PTSD also involves changes in brain morphology*? I scarcely know what morphology is myself. And then to say it all in Hindi?'

'Sorry, I can't help you,' I had to admit, 'but let's do some more research and carry on as best we can. We will ask a doctor to assist us.'

We also gathered simple information about mental disorders and illnesses from sources and made diagrams and charts to acquaint staff and prisoners with the maladies of the mind. One that was very keenly followed was a diagrammatic presentation that set out the extent and intensity of ailments. We had adapted from a book we had been consulting about mental health among Indian women (Davar, 1999). We had to explain as simply as possible that there is no progression in the disorders and that someone suffering from depression and anxieties, which can be addressed through psychological interventions, does not necessarily move on to a more acute mental disorder categorised with illnesses that needes medical intervention. Equally, a person with acute schizophrenia needs medical intervention and cannot be left in the hands of unqualified people who are not equipped to offer medical treatment.

It was a wake-up call for the prison staff, who had simply resorted to the convenient method of locking up prisoners with

Figure 6.1

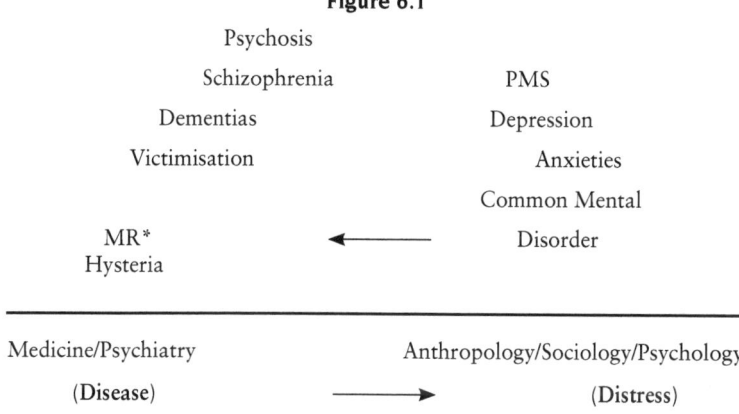

Psychosis

Schizophrenia   PMS

Dementias   Depression

Victimisation   Anxieties

                                 Common Mental

MR*   ←————   Disorder
Hysteria

Medicine/Psychiatry   Anthropology/Sociology/Psychology

(Disease)   ————→   (Distress)

Note: * 'Mental retardation' being unacceptable terminology in professional psychiatry and psychology is now replaced with 'mentally challenged or disadvantaged'.

acute disorders when they got out of hand or administering sedatives when visitors came to the prison. With the example of Vimla, we decided to highlight the seriousness of the problem, knowing all the while that it would probably all slump back to the old ways after our vigilance ceased. We would move on to other prisons, so the question was: would someone carry on the task in this prison? We had no idea and little hope, a sad admission for us on all accounts. But that is not enough. Blaming the system, the infrastructure or indeed, other people, is not what bringing in changes is all about. There was Vimla staring us in the face each day. Sometimes, someone would point out that she was but one in this collective of almost 400 persons, a collective whose complexion changed each day as some went out and others came in. But for us, it was not about statistics and even if figures mattered, we knew that thousands went through that prison gate each year, they came sometimes for days, sometimes months and more often, for years. Each one came for a reason (the law decided that reason) but went out worse than before. That was our major worry.

Vimla meanwhile was under medication and while it made her less erratic in terms of behavioural symptoms it was clear that the mellowing was the result of medication. The CO of her barrack was given the duty to administer her medicine twice a day: the infirmary doctor gave injections as advised by the hospital. They all followed the routine mechanically, hoping and expecting this would turn out to be an answer in itself. With all that medication, she was groggy most of the time. She slept for hours at a time, anywhere, any time, so her aberrant behaviour was at a minimum. This was neither an answer nor a solution. It was really a conundrum: she was medicated and therefore groggy; and while she was in that state it was hardly possible to say that she was recovering. But it was considered a solution for some of the staff as she was less likely to be 'weird'. The issue was, how could change be observed in her activity, or behaviour, or any observation made of her 'normal' activity, if she was half asleep most of the time?

How long was this to continue? More importantly, while she was being 'treated', was this environment, unnatural and uncongenial as it was, helping her recovery, if there was any? Would she be able to have another set of tests to ascertain where she was on the road to recovery?

When we asked the jailor, she told us, 'No, Vimla can't be sent to the hospital for observation or tests. It is actually quite a disruption for all concerned and we are poorly staffed anyway. The arrangements that have to be made for transport to and security at the hospital are just not possible and the staff is just not able to manage.' So that was that.

The pointers were in the direction of getting her away from these surroundings. For everyone around, Vimla was still a *pagli*, no matter what. It was almost as if they were waiting for her to do the next absurd thing so that their beliefs would be reinforced. It was a label for life: once a *pagli* always a *pagli*. Nothing more was going to be done for her here and yet some action was needed. Leaving her in the prison was a problem, but so was sending her out.

'She needs to be removed to a better environment,' Neena said. But where; and who would ensure her care? The discussion began, with those manning the prison moving towards her 'release', rather than continued treatment. It was their way out of a tricky situation, but was it right for Vimla? When she was told that she would be released and taken back to her village, far from being pleased, she was actually distressed and apprehensive. She said she didn't want to go. But the rulebook has no provision for a prisoner to remain in jail if the courts ruled (following a recommendation from the prison officials) that she could be released.

Vimla's release papers came in the evening. The practice is that family/guardians have to be contacted so that they can take her home. Alternatively, they need to be informed of her release and the prisoner escorted to them after they confirmed that someone would be there to receive her. Neither of these steps had been taken, or if they had, no response came that could enable Vimla's departure to her village. The local Mahila Ashram (Women's Home) had always told the prison staff that if a woman was released in the evening and there was a problem with her being taken to the village straightaway, she could be accommodated with them till other arrangements had been made. But when it came to the crunch, they refused to take Vimla: they knew her history and did not want a new problem on their hands. Even the local branch of Mother Teresa's Home was unwilling to let Vimla stay for a short while. Two grounds seemed to emerge as reasons for their non-acceptance: first, Vimla was a 'criminal' from a prison and second, she was 'insane'.

That was the end of Vimla: we knew what would happen next. The prison arranged for two persons to escort Vimla directly to her village. They took her to her in-laws' house. There was no father-in-law any more; and which father-in-law would have taken in a daughter-in-law who had murdered his son? But there was a 'kaka-sasur' (father-in-law's brother) — and he refused to let her stay. The two escorts from the prison reprimanded him for not accepting his family member back in the family and, no doubt after a few pressure tactics were used, they left Vimla there.

There was no follow-up, no feedback, and no further communication about Vimla. The system said it had done its best, but had it really? And whose best were they talking about?

This was indeed the end of Vimla.

Note

About one-tenth of the world's adults are afflicted by some form of mental illness at any point of time. There is a burden of disability ensuing from mental illness that has not even been measured for the most part, leave alone treated. With international pressure, some attention is being given to 'neuropsychiatric' conditions, but all in all, mental illness has just not been considered serious enough to produce effective mental health programmes. It is stigmatised but not addressed seriously.

India enacted a Mental Health Act in 1987 (to repeal the Indian Lunacy Act of 1912). It may have been a laudable exercise as a policy measure: legally, it provided a tool to invoke the law if care was not forthcoming for those who had mental illnesses/disorders. But the significant thing about being mentally ill is not entirely how the law views it: it is about the relationship between the society's attitude to it and the law's position on it. Being *pagal* (insane) has a stigma attached to it that many serious physical diseases do not have. And if that *pagal* is lodged inside a prison, it's a non-starter. The stigma and disinterestedness relating to mental illness/disorder stem from difficulties of understanding it and ignorance of it as well as the temptation of many societies to take it off their radar.

Some disorders are inherent, some develop over time and some are almost thrust on people. For imprisoned women, the one glaring reality is that prison affects women more adversely than it does men: this is not unrelated to the simple fact that the experiences of men and women outside, in their day-to-day lives and the expectations we have of them, all our rhetoric of equality notwithstanding, are vastly different and unequal. When women enter the prison gates they *all* enter with more fear and trepidation than men (considerable time was spent by us in men's prisons simply to ascertain this fact). Some are more petrified than others; some are able to put on an act and pretend they are not bothered (our revolutionary Naxalites *seem* better able to hold themselves together and to bear even the manhandling at the time of admission or thereafter; but while they may be in denial, even they have psychological problems). Some women crumble and break up from the time of arrest, and by the time the prison gates slam behind them, they have almost fallen to pieces.

No one in the prison pays much attention to the symptoms and manifestations of what might be called the slow 'cracking up' of a woman following her arrest. It is assumed that if she committed a serious offence, she must be in full control of her mind and senses. The facts, however, tell another story. The very act ('heinous offence') traumatises her tremendously. She can hardly believe that the event actually happened.

And because she has been wrenched from familiar surroundings (her life-line) into totally unfamiliar and near hostile environs, her journey from home to custody is long, arduous, relentless and bitter; for some women, it is more harsh and painful than for others — not just physically but more importantly and conclusively, mentally and psychologically. Sometimes that journey ends in disaster. The scale of incapacity resulting from the frictions and fractures within social relations that accompany the experiences of women at the hands of the criminal justice machinery has neither been observed nor measured by any agency. There is, consequently, a general apathy about issues that pertain to the area of mental soundness as it relates to a woman: the symptoms relating to anxiety, depression, melancholia, trauma, terror, hysteria or dementia among imprisoned women are all dismissed as 'barmy' or 'loopy' behaviour on their part. They are disciplined by officials-in-charge to behave in conformity with rules. This seems an easier route, with fewer complexities than the one that seeks an appropriate handling of their maladies and an attempt to make life both in the prison and outside, when they leave, less traumatising.

How societies down the ages have treated the mentally ill is an interesting commentary on their understanding of the subject. Much of our early institutional thinking on these subjects goes back to what we inherited from British ideas. Judged by their overt behaviour, mentally ill people were 'treated' without anyone really knowing what they were suffering from. The treatment ranged from physically driving out a demon (flogging, or torturing) to drowning and burning. These practices are well recorded in the literature of fifteenth- and sixteenth-century Europe.

In the West, the move to (institutionally) lock up the 'insane' goes back to about the eighteenth century when 'madhouses' increased. Before then, people with mental maladies had lived in the community and had been cared for or tolerated within their communities. Gradually, the idea of segregation of the insane from the sane gathered momentum. The treatment of unwanted persons in England is interesting. For those in abject poverty there were the poor laws; for being homeless and roaming aimlessly, there were vagrancy laws (the Vagrancy Law of 1744); and then, of course, there were common criminals for whom various punishments existed. The aim was to 'warehouse' people who showed deviant behaviour and overlapping abnormality with crime was an easy way to achieve that end. The concept of warehousing, including concealing and screening, is an interesting one that also relates to poverty, slums, stray animals, or anything unsightly and undesirable, 'criminal lunatics' being an ideal category.

The history of psychiatry over the last 100 years has brought the goings-on inside the mind to the forefront of our concerns. From earlier views of abnormal, aberrant, or abhorrent behaviour as the work of the devil or due to the presence of evil spirits, there was a change in the scientific period to the realisation that the mind defined human beings and it was possible to study it with scientific methods. This is not the place to dwell on the history of psychology or psychiatry, except to say that increasing knowledge about the mind has helped in better understandings of behaviour and actions and enabled methods and techniques that are able to address mental disorders and/or illnesses in a more wholesome manner than was possible before. The removal of the word 'lunatic' from common usage and then from the vocabulary of prison documents is a major step in our understanding of mental disorders/illnesses. In nineteenth-century Britain, criminal lunatics were considered dangerous and were segregated from other prisoners in separate dismal facilities. Many of the old prison-related documents, including the Prisons Act of 1894 (still the valid document for prison administration in India unless superseded by new Acts), even now have a category called 'criminal lunatics' although in practice it is unacceptable and in disuse.

The Mental Health Act XIV of 1987 has replaced and repealed the Indian Lunacy Act IV of 1912. The statement of objects and reasons of the 1987 Act emphasise a change in approach and points out that with a fundamental change in the attitude of society towards persons afflicted with mental illness, no stigma should be attached to such illness as it is curable, particularly when diagnosed at an early stage. The mentally ill, it further states, are to be treated like any other sick persons and the environment around them should be made as normal as possible. In the wake of advances in medical science and better understandings of the nature of this malady, it is evident that the Indian Lunacy Act 1912 (4 of 1912) has proved in its workings to be outmoded and obsolete, and fresh legislation with adequate provisions for the treatment of mentally ill persons is in accordance with the new approach.

The 1987 Act elaborates the necessary steps that would be ensured to make these objects feasible:

- To regulate admission to psychiatric hospitals or psychiatric nursing homes of mentally ill persons who do not have sufficient understanding to seek treatment on a voluntary basis, and to protect the rights of such persons while being detained;
- To protect society from the presence of mentally ill persons who have become or might become a danger or nuisance to others;

- To protect citizens from being detained in psychiatric hospitals or psychiatric nursing homes without sufficient cause;
- To regulate responsibility for maintenance charges of mentally ill persons who are admitted to psychiatric hospitals or psychiatric nursing homes;
- To provide facilities for establishing guardianship or custody of mentally ill persons who are incapable of managing their own affairs;
- To provide for the establishment of Central Authority and State Authorities for Mental Health Services;
- To regulate the powers of the Government for establishing, licensing and controlling psychiatric hospitals and psychiatric nursing homes for mentally ill persons.

Section 27 of the Act sets out the various Acts under which an order can be given, directing the reception of a mentally ill prisoner into any psychiatric hospital, making such an order the sufficient authority for the admission of such a person in a hospital or facility to which such a person may be lawfully transferred for detention.

Legislation has not, however, eliminated the ordinary people's discomfort with symptoms of mental illnesses. In a prison where mental disorders of one nature or another abound, there is no move towards an understanding of either mental illness or the Mental Health Act. The former would require a brief lesson in maladies of the mind and the latter in the details of the Act's provisions. Neither of these are components of the training that prison staff members receive either at induction or reorientation.

An additional need is that of focusing on how to employ scientific methods to investigate behaviour. Uninformed and cursory observation of abnormal, uncharacteristic and idiosyncratic behaviour often results in the worsening of the condition of the sufferer, producing yet another category that is consigned to the dustbins of society. Vimla had no genetic disorder: she had traumatic experiences that resulted in abnormal behaviour, which then became reason enough for society to dump her — not because she was responsible for what happened to her, but because we are inept.

The question of mental health has been through many twists and turns all over the world. When people were less well informed, the temptation was to drastically slot aberrant behaviour into a few categories, and then devise equally drastic remedial measures to address the aberrations. With time, knowledge about the mind has increased in lcaps and bounds. More serious disorders needing medical interven tion find a place in the formal system, but there are other types too and in any event, attitudes towards mental disorder have changed relatively little, making interventions a problem.

Reputable organisations have systematically classified lists of distinct disorders to provide a reference point for researchers and practitioners. The two acclaimed and most widely used manuals are the *International Classification of Diseases (ICD-10)* prepared by the World Health Organisation and the *Diagnostic and Statistical Manual of Mental Disorders (DSM–IV)* produced by the American Psychiatric Association (APA). The classifications have been set out with some precision, albeit with differing emphases and give lay persons a sense of what mental ill-health can be. Some questions still arise: whether this is a definitive list, or whether there are some indefinable, in-between and unexplored spaces where one may need to place persons who are not 'slottable'. A diagrammatic classification prepared from the two manuals appears in Chapter 2 of *In conflict and Custody: Therapeutic counselling of Women* (Shankardass, 2012).

Some of our encounters with women 'inside' revealed areas of disorientation that could only be gleaned from the confusion and anxieties writ large on their faces and expressed in their voices. Despite the fact that interventions were urgently needed, we could not find a label for their plight from professional lists of disorders.

7

Shobhavati: Married at Ten, Thirteen Children, Three Survived

◙

It didn't take me long to get Shobhavati to talk. Clearly she is relatively new to the institution and hasn't become, what we in our jargon call 'institutionalised'. She had been a pre-trial prisoner in another prison for about nine months before being brought to this one after being convicted of killing her husband. '*Dhara* 302' is what she answers when I ask her what she is here for (Section 302 of the Indian Penal Code).

She is neatly dressed and although uneducated, quite informed about many things, as I gathered in my conversations with her. She has opinions and is able to speak articulately on the issues that I wish to discuss with her.

Shobhavati was born in a village where her father sold vegetables. The family was poor and each day's sale of vegetables gave them just enough to eat. There was no question of sending the children to school because even if the tuition fee was waived, school meant money had to be spent on clothes and books and above all, that there would be no one to help the parents at home. They were three sisters and clearly, for the parents that meant three weddings had to be arranged, which was not just a burdensome worry, but also involved expenses. From the day each daughter was born, the parents had probably fretted about forthcoming expenditure.

'Our father worked very hard to make both ends meet and much as we would have liked to have gone to school, it would have been almost unjust to have suggested as much to him. I would have loved to go to school. If it had been possible, our father would have sent us, but clearly it wasn't. Mind you, he was not at all authoritarian, or overbearing: we had pretty free lives and he didn't stop us from being playful and having fun. We almost had a good time despite being so poor. That is why I wonder why I was packed off so early to go to another family.'

'My mother kept indifferent health and what with the lack of good, nourishing food and medicines when she needed them, she wasn't able to do too much work, either by way of helping our father, or even housework. So we did a lot of housework from a very early age. That was the case with many of the families in the village, so we didn't feel like we were abnormal. But every now and then, when family members from other villages visited, we found they were better off (or at least appeared to be) and then we felt demoralised. Life was tough and I don't know how we managed, but we did. Because we had no brother, we were all that the parents had to help them and to give them comfort — so we pitched in even if we often missed out on the fun.'

'I was married off when I was ten years old. Of course, my *'gauna'* was when I was thirteen, but once I was betrothed at ten, things changed — I was seen as belonging to another family and had restrictions put on me. No more that carefree childhood where I could come and go as I pleased. "What will people say?", my mother used to say. So, everything changed at ten.' (*Gauna* is a ceremony performed after several years of all child marriage ritual. Chiefly prevalent in the north of India, it signifies the sanction for consummations, and until it is carried out the bride stays in her parental home.)

'So how did you react to your parents' idea of getting you married when you were ten? Do you actually remember what happened? Was there an event? Did you dress up for it and were you excited about it?', I ask her, trying to remember what I was doing when I was ten — having fun with family, neighbours, friends, cousins, going for picnics, going to school, cycling, learning to swim, and (since I had only brothers) playing 'boys' games such as cricket and *gulli danda*, or with marbles.

'I don't have very vivid memories of the event. Yes, there was an event — I got fine clothes to wear and there was good food cooked that day for guests. There were some rituals and that's all I remember. But what followed was not much fun — because everyone behaved differently from that day onwards. All I heard from my parents was, "don't go there, don't do this, don't be childish, be mature". But I was only a child. Of course, some of these thoughts only occur to me now that I look back. At that time I just did as I was told.'

'Sometimes, I do ask myself now, why on earth did my father get me married then, when I was so small. Now that I have my own children and have had an experience of married life, I keep questioning the fact that I was sent away from my parental home so early. Was I a big burden? Did they not love me enough? I know it is a custom to marry off girls early in this part of the world — and these are questions that I ask now that I am 40 years old and have had so many experiences that I should not have had.'

Sounding quite dramatic, I say, 'Do you know that it is against the law to marry off children when they are minors? The law has been in existence for more than 75 years, from the British times. It was called the Child Marriage Prevention Act, 1929, and then in 1978, around the time you were married off, this Act was revised and was called the Child Marriage Restraint Act. The government is now revising it further in a new Bill. So, strictly speaking, your parents were doing something for which they could have been arrested'. Sometimes, we (my team associates and I) make these profound declarations, knowing that they are irrelevant in those parts of the country where it is not the *law* that comes into play in day-to-day life, but the *traditions, customs and mores* that people have lived with before 'laws' and 'legality' became the prime movers of society.

The State Shobhavati belongs to is one of the three states of India (Rajasthan, Uttar Pradesh and Madhya Pradesh) that have the highest incidence of child marriages. These are also the three States that have some of the worst indicators so far as women are concerned: low female literacy, high rates of female infant deaths, child marriages, dowry (and dowry harassment) and violence, within and outside the home. In Rajasthan alone, 56 per cent of women are married before they turn 15, and 82 per cent are married before they are 18. While these are mere statistics for the rest of the world, they are the harsh reality for those who live in these parts of the country. It is easy for me to wax eloquent about these matters, and suggest that someone should put a stop to practices that affect women so adversely, but for Shobhavati, child marriage was a sacrosanct custom that she was not equipped to fight. It is only now that she realises what being married off at ten did to her — but it is too late.

'Who do you think will remedy these things?', she asks us. 'Usually, if a law is violated, isn't it the police that steps in to say "this is against the law"? But the police are themselves part of the trad-itional society. They also come from our part of the world. How can we expect them to go against the trend? There was a *thanedar* [constable] in our village whose daughter was also married off at ten. Nowadays, social workers come to the villages to teach women to know their rights. But what does any knowledge of rights do where the practice is so deeply entrenched? Our village-folk say this is all "big people's talk, we have to protect our daughters from so much harm that can befall them. You can't go against the grain of the social set-up where you live and retain your soul," they say.'

Her words reminded me of the incident involving a social worker in Bhangarh village in Madhya Pradesh, who was trying desperately to enlighten women about their rights and to oppose child marriages. She was visited by an 'elder' of the village in her temporary home there and after a discussion that became an altercation, she suffered brutal violence — both her hands were chopped off as a warning that she should not interfere with the social customs of the people in the village.

Clearly, it is an uphill social task to convince people to stand up for their rights and justice, which are perceived differently by people from different parts of the society. The perceptions are criss-crossed by innumerable factors: regional traditions, the class divide, the caste divide, the educational chasm and gender considerations. Shobhavati is right: it is all 'big talk' to proclaim opinions on what is wrong and what is right — it reflects middle-class morality coloured by the smugness of those who have never lived in the abyss like she and her family did. Lofty ideals are so misplaced when reality unfolds itself in narratives of women like

Shobhavati. More often than not, I am almost embarrassed by what I regard as my credentials. It is an uncomfortable feeling at the best of times.

'The next thing I tell you', Shobhavati declares confidently, 'will probably also elicit a negative response from you — it's about dowry. We belonged to the *'phool-mali' jaat*, which does give dowry, but it is supposedly not demanded. (*Phool-mali jaat* is a traditional gardener caste among the Hindu, and in some regions [Rajasthan] accorded a high status compared to other manual occupational castes.) Parents give what they can and it is gracefully accepted and the custom is that no one should squabble and quarrel over what is given or not given. I was given cooking utensils for the most part: that was the practice in our caste. I don't remember that there was much complaining on the part of my in-laws, at least not when I was married off. If there was, I didn't hear about it. But then I was so young. There were other traumas that I had to adjust to.'

She was quiet for a few moments and then abruptly sprang a question at me. 'Ma'am,' she asks, 'when were you married, did your father give a dowry? After all, these practices are followed among the *bare log* [upper class people] as well; so what happened with you?'

I could see her mind ticking as I was taking her through experiences that she had not really questioned, or thought about, not to mention the fact that her isolated, secluded life has not really exposed her to the likes of me.

'I was married when I was 25,' I tell her. 'By then I had been adequately educated and had travelled to distant lands on my own. It is an experience that made a lot of difference to my life. And no, dowry was not and never had been a part of our family vocabulary. That was the case when my brothers married too. Dowry was a non-issue — parents gifted what they wished to their children at the time of a wedding. They would gift almost the same to the sons, which is what my parents did.'

'You are lucky, ma'am. There are women here from fairly well-off families who have harassed their daughters-in-law for dowry and made their married lives a living hell. That lady you were talking to earlier before I came in, the fat one, she is not exactly destitute and she is here for a dowry death. She cries from the rooftops that the daughter-in-law committed suicide because she had all kinds of personal problems, including liaisons with a paramour from her pre-marital days. She hardly expresses remorse that her daughter-in-law is dead; keeps calling her a witch who was driving her son away from her, the son who would be her support in her old age. When the jailor is around, she keeps protesting that she is innocent, but when we are there (just prisoners in the barrack) we often hear her say to her close mates, '*accha hua mar gayi, churel*' [good thing she is dead, that witch].

At this point, we had to stop: Shobhavati was clearly availing herself of the opportunity of a leisurely chat, something she had not been able to do for a long time, and we were not about to grudge her that — but there was someone else waiting outside the door. We asked her to visit us again the next day, or any time that she saw we were free and she departed with a polite *namaste*.

Of course, we hadn't yet arrived at the events surrounding the day of the disaster that had struck her and brought her here. But all in good time, we think. It is always an education to hear the remarkably cogent views of persons who, if we met them on the street, we might dismiss as undeserving of even a greeting, let alone a prolonged conversation. After each session with a prisoner, there is always a follow-up discussion amongst us. Our research associates are so seasoned by now, it is uncanny. Sometimes, they say quite unreservedly afterwards, 'That was a lie.' When I ask why they think so, they say with confidence, 'Oh, we can tell. The twitches, the body language, the silences when they wait to see the effect on us, and the eye-contact or lack of it.' My advantage in years is hardly an asset in the face of their interactions at so many levels with these women, day after day.

The next morning, Shobhavati enters our room in tears. We ask her with concern if something had happened — was there a fight? Had she been ticked off by the staff for some lapse or oversight on her part? What was it? She sits down, wipes her tears with her saree *pallu* and composes herself. 'Today is Janamashtmi,' she says. 'We celebrated the festival with such ceremony back in the village. And look at me now: one day merges into another without distinction. The worst is that now no one comes to meet me.

I have children, you know. I wonder how anyone in the establishment would like it if they didn't see their children for months on end. Does anyone ever put themselves in another's shoes in this place, or anywhere for that matter? Can you not intervene and tell them that they should pay more attention to our emotional problems?'

'Yes, we have every intention of highlighting some features about personal problems and difficulties, Shobhavati — that is what we are here for!' Kiran exclaims promptly before I make a tactless comment. 'When some of your mates are cynical about us and question our presence here, we struggle to tell them that there are aspects about being locked up that sink in only after they have been here a while: lack of visits, separation from families, not being present at festivals, being torn away from homes, sometimes unjustifiably. This is high on our agenda: to make your survival here somewhat bearable. We are aware that there are features about your lives that go unnoticed because the staff here is busy with routine activities and forget that you all have families, homes, past memories that all get soured in this barren environment. So, keep calm and let's see what can be done.'

'I am fasting today,' she says. 'And so are other women. We always fasted for Janamashtmi. At home we used to make a *jhanki* [tableau] of Lord Krishna's birth and life and it took hours but everyone joined in and we, family and neighbours, had some good moments together. At the end of the day, we cooked delicacies and all of us shared them. My mother did it all when I was a child and then I did the same when I had children. We sang and danced and it was a day we looked forward to each year — as much as Diwali.'

A song from Bimal Roy's *Bandini* rang in my ears, reminding me that at the end of the day, life is really all about memories, and I firmly believe that when one is low and downcast, a reservoir of happy memories sees one through. But for Shobhavati, it is a mixed bag, with unpleasant memories sometimes overtaking the pleasant. And soon enough that becomes apparent.

'If only so many things had not happened, I would have been at home with children and been somewhat normal. But look at me — I'm in a jail. I never in my wildest imagination dreamt I would ever be in a jail, never!'

'You know, the highlight of a woman's life and for which everything else is a preparation, is her marriage. Maybe not for people like you from good places, but in the village when a girl is born, there are mixed feelings. The first thought that enters a parent's mind is *"Iski shaadi karni hogi"* [she will have to be married off'].

'I went to live in my in-laws' home at the age of thirteen. I hadn't even begun my menstrual cycle by then. And, of course, my mother had told me nothing about it either. My sisters-in-law told me all about "making babies", that my husband would want to "bed" me and I should be prepared for it. It took me a while to come to terms with what was supposed to be "adult behaviour".

'You will not believe me when I tell you that I started my menstrual cycle five months after I had had sex with my husband. Can you imagine my embarrassment when one day my clothes were all stained? I was working in the field with my sisters-in-law and they saw that I was in a mess. They immediately took charge and told me what I should do. They cleaned me up and told me that each month I would be bleeding and needed to have a supply of cloth at hand to tackle this problem. They also gave me instructions that for three days I may not enter the kitchen, nor participate in *pooja* (prayers) and that I had to sleep on the floor for the duration of my periods. It was strange because I didn't really recall my mother doing all this. But then she kept indifferent health anyway, so I probably didn't notice the changing patterns in her daily routine.

'And then when I became pregnant, I only realised it when I was three months gone. I began getting sick and feeling listless and very drowsy. I asked my sister-in-law why I was feeling so sick. She said, *"Haramzada to chhor ke chala gaya, ab tujhe kya bataun"* [the bastard has left you high and dry, what can I say?]. You are with child.'

'So, what was your husband like?' I asked. I started from the deep end since she was in prison for killing her husband and we needed to know what her marital life was really like. We had to know just what happened with this apparently simple woman, who after producing 13 children and losing ten of them, killed her spouse and landed herself in this terrible mess.

Her reply was a sad 'You don't want to know.' There was such a long pause that we began to think we had lost her and she really didn't want to talk about the murky past. But we have learnt to be patient. And there is much that she still wanted to say.

'Funny, isn't it, that my husband sold vegetables like my father had. That was only a façade though. My father slogged day in and day out to make ends meet. My husband however was actually a *chor* (thief). He did nothing to keep the home fires burning. I survived because there was a father-in-law and three brothers-in-law in the house and so there was a joint kitchen. My mother-in-law passed away soon after I was married.'

'His "beat" was not just in the village where we lived. He covered a wide area, supposedly to sell the vegetables. The vegetable cart, however, was a cover for his other antics. Sometimes he would just pick up bicycles belonging to other people, sometimes a wristwatch, or he would snatch gold chains from women's necks, and so on. Because they were stolen goods, he would sell them at whatever price was offered and that was his *amdani* (earnings). But this money he spent on himself. I was never given anything and just as well, for I didn't want to partake of his ill-gotten gains.'

'He went to the nearest towns to steal — Kota, Sawaimadhopur, Alwar and other places. On a few occasions, the police caught him and brought him home and I had to go and get him released, pleading with the constables that he would never do it again. Sometimes, a lawyer would have to be engaged and surety provided, which was a financial drain. But nothing changed — this was a way of life for him.'

'I had to take work on construction sites, carrying bricks and other materials, which was a strain for me — but then there had to be some money coming in. By that time, I had conceived 13 times, and produced 13 children, but all except three had died either at birth or in early infancy. My first pregnancy was when I was not even 15. It was a harrowing experience and I hated it. As soon as I was a little recovered from one pregnancy and childbirth, I was pregnant again. The man was a brute and no one ever advises women in such cases. It was obvious I was not healthy enough to produce healthy children and they were either stillborn, or died very young. There was no money to feed them — I don't know how three children survived: God's wish, I suppose.'

Shobhavati's story was similar to the tales of woe one hears from women like her, not necessarily incarcerated women but those with backgrounds similar to that Shobhavati had: poverty, destitution, archaic social practices, lack of education, lack of guidance, wayward husbands, gender biases, an environment that has no features that are conducive to even the semblance of a silver lining anywhere and a general powerlessness of these women that accompanies their situations.

'I would die in such an environment,' I have the nerve to say softly and perhaps all too hastily to Shobhavati in one of my conversations with her. She hears me and says, 'I heard you, ma'am — you said you would die if you lived that way. Yes. We do die. My children died, and I lived a slow death every day. So it is dying. You are right: *'hum guzar to nahin jate, par har roz hum marte zaroor hain* [we don't all pass away, but we do die a hundred deaths].'

Where does their hope come from? This is a question we ask ourselves all the time. Without hope, life is really not worth living. What keeps such women going so courageously? They are plucky women and sometimes we wonder who is learning from whom.

At this point, we haven't even heard the story of what led to her offence. I shuddered to think what it was all about. Sometimes I wish we were able to have conversations with the husbands of these women, but that has been possible only once in the women's prison in Hyderabad.

Shobhavati continued her story: '*Mera gharvala poora randi-baaz tha* [my husband was a womanising lout].' The neighbours used to tell me he is a lout, and has women all over the place. But which wife wants to believe that? Once he left home and didn't come back for three years. Can you believe it? I had no idea where he was — people told me he was in the *shahar* [town], and living with another woman. People who travelled to Jaipur told me they had seen him with her and knew exactly where he was — but I was the one who said "can't be" and let it pass.'

'There were occasions when I did feel that there was something very wrong in my house. My things (good clothes, jewellery) would suddenly disappear and I would wonder where they went. For some time I thought he was selling my stuff and spending the money on himself. If I had brought it up, he would have thrashed me, so I kept quiet. Then the neighbours and relatives started taunting me — that I was a fool and was deliberately blind to the reality of my life. I had a three-week-old infant in my arms then and perhaps that determined my inability to face reality. But day after day, when people tell you that you are gutless and don't want to face the fact that your husband has left you for another woman, something snaps. So, one fine day I decided to check for myself.'

Shobhavati asked her brother-in-law (her husband's brother) and nephew (her sister's son) to take her to Jaipur. She had her infant in her arms on the train journey. They had some leads about where her husband was and after wandering around the city for some time, arrived at the address given to them.

A woman opened the door and they asked, 'Where is Tejpal?'

'He has gone to the Ganesh Temple, which is just outside the city, and won't be back for a while. And who are you?' the woman asked.

They didn't reveal the truth just then: 'I am his sister-in-law and this is his brother. We just came to find out how he is doing — we hadn't heard from him in a while and just wished to check that all was well.'

The 'other woman' accepted their story and asked them in. They sat down and she said, 'I'll just go and get some milk from round the corner to make tea.' As they waited, Shobhavati spotted an item lying on the bed that was hers. She was dumbfounded. She and her brother-in-law opened a chest lying in the room and she was horrified to see that the stuff she had been missing all of these years was in that chest — her new clothes, jewellery and many other personal effects.

'I was in total shock. I just couldn't bear to stay there a moment longer and asked my brother-in-law to take me back. So we left.'

'You didn't have tea and didn't wait for the woman to return?'

'No, I just couldn't. I felt so cheated and was almost physically sick. I have no clue what transpired once the woman returned and found we had gone. Or for that matter what happened when my husband returned from his so-called visit to the Ganesh Temple. There was silence from that end for over a year. Can you imagine that?'

The neighbours and relatives were usually the ones that incited her to make a move and not just sit around as if nothing had happened. 'Your husband is gallivanting all over the place: we have seen him with other women. Why can't you take this whole thing more seriously? Are you going to spend the rest of your life this way?'

Shobhavati told us that she had asked her brother-in-law to take her one more time to Jaipur. He refused, saying he didn't want to get involved. So, she sought her sister's help. The sister asked her own brother-in-law to escort Shobhavati. He was not too keen, but was not able to refuse either. Shobhavati took her youngest child with her and they took the train for Jaipur. Midway, the brother-in-law got off the train under some pretext and left Shobhavati alone on the train to Jaipur. She was petrified and alighted when the train stopped at the Jaipur railway station. She was crying all the while and an old man asked her what the problem was: she told him that she needed to go to an address she had but had no clue how to get there. He took her to the lane where the house was and left her there. She had a rough idea about the house and knocked on the door. The same woman opened the door and this time there was recognition in her eyes. Shobhavati felt that this time she was aware that Shobhavati was Tejpal's wife and had come to confront him.

She said abruptly, 'He's at work. He won't be back till the evening.'

Shobhavati left quietly with her child and parked herself at the end of the lane on which the house was located. In the evening when her husband returned, she confronted him and there was a scene that Shobhavati was not really equipped to handle. There was abusive language from all sides and the 'other woman' was a full participant in the quarrel, declaring that he dare not leave her because he had taken her as a wife. Shobhavati could not do more than that because this time she was alone and had to reach home by herself.

'I had no money to return home; my sister's brother-in-law who had abandoned me halfway had all the money and I didn't know what to do. So, I went to the nearest police station and sat on the verandah and started crying. I couldn't narrate my personal tale of woe and said that someone had stolen my purse and I had no money to return to my village. They were sympathetic and had me escorted to the station and told the guard that I needed to be taken to the village. I was given a pass to my return journey to the village.'

Personally, I am amazed at her guts: someone who had not travelled by herself and was dependent on others for decisions most of her life was actually able to conduct herself the way she had — that was something really courageous. It clearly reveals the capabilities of a person who, had she been given the opportunities and guidance in handling her life, might have managed to deal with her problems much better.

She decided then to ask the panchayat of the village to intervene. The 'village elders' decided that Tejpal would be brought back to the village and told to stop his philandering and carry out his family responsibilities. He came back all right, but did he stop his philandering? That was another question altogether. It didn't take long for him to go back to his old ways. The second wife may have been forgotten, but there were other women with whom he had associations.

The worst was still to come. Tejpal actually started eying his daughters: as Shobhavati said, '*Ab uski nazar betiyon par parhi.*' It was this that led to the unfortunate event that led to her being imprisoned. One day, he was trying to rape his daughter when Shobhavati was not at home, but fortunately, she arrived in the nick of time to save her daughter. There was a scene — Shobhavati screamed at him and he pushed the mother and daughter — but because he was inebriated, they were able to control him.

Shobhavati was quite upset as she narrated all this. It was an ugly scenario and one that she would rather forget. '*Beti ki izzat lootna* [shaming his own daughter]', as she called it, was not just disgusting and horrifying, she said it was traumatizing for her. For days she could not sleep and was vigilant all the time to protect her daughters.

'But,' she said, '*bheria to bheria hi rahega* [a wolf is after all a wolf].' He tried raping the girl again when Shobhavati was outside the house. This time both the girls took a *lathi* and beat him up to ward him off. By then, Shobhavati heard the screams and came running. He was bleeding and lay unconscious on the floor. He had been hit on the head and had had a concussion.

The neighbours were called for help and after examining him, realised that Tejpal was dead.

'I was cold and trembling and didn't know what to do. This was not something I had ever envisaged would be happening in my house. All his antics so far had been outside the house and now this! I think I was hysterical and the neighbours and relatives tried to calm me down. They said, "It has happened now and we need to see how to handle this." They called the panchayat immediately: the members of the panchayat said that since there was a dead body in the house, we had to inform the police. But before the police arrived, we needed to sort a few things out. The young girls were defending themselves and had hit their father. They did not know that he would die. But he did. They asked me, "Now do you want to ruin the girls' lives by involving them in a criminal case?"'

Shobhavati was weeping as she narrated this part of her story. We gave her some water and asked her to calm down. She was silent for a long time. So many thoughts came flooding in our minds, too: she has just given us gory details of how the daughter's clothes had been ripped off by the father and she stood there half-naked while the two of them struggled to shake off the father. It was certainly not an experience any mother should be subjected to, we thought. But there it was — and if that was not bad enough there was now a crime on their hands for which someone had to pay.

'I told the panchayat members that I would take the blame. The panchayat then calmly told me what I should say that he was drunk and was getting violent — he was beating up me up with the *lathi* and in defending myself I struck him with the same *lathi* when it fell from his hand and he fell unconscious to the ground.'

Sure enough, when the police came, they made a report based on her statement. They took her to the *thana* and she spent all of the next day there while they filed their reports and the charges against her.

'I was in a daze. What was happening to me, I thought? What had I done or not done? Tejpal had hardly been much of a husband to me and yet I tolerated it all as best I could. But this I could never accept — molesting his own daughters. It was like a horror story for me.'

'I was charged and while the trial was on, I was a pre-trial prisoner in Ganganagar jail for eight months. It was unbearable — I was a spouse-killer and since that jail was attached to a male prison when the male staff took their rounds, they never ceased to remind me about my offence. They never know the details and the history of a person; they just brand people and that really hurt.'

We (Nina, Kiran and I) stare at each other in amazement. This is the stuff that nightmares are made of. Again and again, we are faced with horrific details of people's lives, evoking a sense of shame in us that we are privileged to be free of such anxieties that persist like running sores in a life, leaving no room for even a modicum of normality. What is surprising is that there are not more symptoms of depression and anxiety-related disorders among these women, who show a resilience that never ceases to amaze.

The law takes its course: a woman is charged with an offence and she must pay for it. The rulebook prescribes the punishment and it is meted out by a due process that we are not in a position to question. It is immaterial that she is taking the rap for someone else — that is her prerogative. And why she is doing it? The law is not concerned with that — it is as clinical as that. We are powerless in the face of the law for it is the same law that we invoke when we want justice for those who don't get it, one of those paradoxes, among many, that has to be accepted. And so we move on from case to case, from woman to woman, from victim to victim, from offender to offender.

This case made us feel a frantic urge to confront Tejpal — to get some answers to the complex questions surrounding the lives of the relatively simple persons in his family. But he is not around anymore. Only the children are left to vouch for things that actually happened. For a while, we actually considered asking Shobhavati if we might talk to her children when they came to see her.

She said, 'No, I don't think I want them to relive the trauma they went through, especially the girls (the youngest, my son, is too young, anyway). Once when I was telling someone in the jail about what happened that got me in here she said "*Arre gaon mein to ye sab hota rehta hai* [Oh, these things happen in villages all the time]." I was so peeved; I thought if it had happened to her, I wonder if she would have made such a careless remark. It is assumed sometimes that there is a sub-strata of humanity that lives in the villages and "sub-standard" things happen to them. That is not so. We too have emotional states, sensitivities and feelings that get hurt just as yours would, ma'am. Don't you think so?'

Shobhavati will spend her time in the prison and then be released. It is assumed by the 'system' that the day she walks out of jail would be a happy day for her — she will go home to her family. Has anyone really checked whether that entry is as smooth as they would like to believe? The fact is — it is not. We followed another 'Shobhavati' to her village after she returned. She tried to settle down, but life was a nightmare for her there. She was staying with her sister in the first instance, but clearly, it was a problem. The sister's husband taunted his wife each day and said if 'Shobhavati' was not thrown out in a week he would take drastic action. So this 'Shobhavati' took a hut not too far away and thought she would do something to generate an income. But she had had no education and was only fit to do manual work. No one would let her work in their fields and it was tough being accepted — she had to live with the label that defined her: '*Jail ho ke aayee hai* [she's been to prison]'.

How does one deal with 'labelling'? It's not possible to preach to people who believe they are right in ostracising a 'jail-bird', or to compel people to change either. So we decided to step in and ask a local girl's hostel to employ the woman as a cook. The owner was a benign woman who was told all the details and she agreed after taking all our particulars should she need to contact us. 'I am not going to reveal her past to anyone else,' she added, 'and I would request you to do the same. It will spoil her chances of settling down and also it will spoil our prospects of getting girls to come to our hostel.' That seemed fair and we shifted 'Shobhavati' to the hostel where she was given a room and began her job the next day.

She had to leave the village, but it was really not a home for her anymore, and for all practical purposes she had left it years ago. We visit her from time to time and it is most comforting to see her children going to school and getting the education that she never got. She asked us to take a photograph of her with her school-going boys. They all said 'cheese' and we clicked our cameras. As we left she said this was the best thing that had happened in all her life.

◫

Note

Shobhavati was one of many women we encountered who were married as children (at about the age of ten). That there is a law against child marriages is of no consequence at all: this is a practice followed for ages, whereby families tie up relationships between them and ensure what they consider good ties and safe-keeping for their children well in advance.

Child marriage is a phenomenon that has existed in Hindu custom as well as other faiths (Judaism, Islam). Forging political, financial and military ties that were of advantage to parents and families was one reason for such marriages as also the security of ensuring a daughter's future while she was a child so that the risk of not finding a suitable groom (from the same background, or caste) later could be avoided. It is also believed that the practice became more prevalent in the medieval period of India's history when invading forces settled in India and established their own cultural and political roots. For the local population, the protection of their women was paramount and apart from the *ghunghat* (veil) and supposedly also *sati*, considerable thought was given to protecting girls from the threat of abduction and invasion. Marrying off daughters into families that were acceptable as early as possible would ward off the danger to a growing girl's virginity. Regardless of these alleged historical reasons, the concept of women as property is not a small part of the continued existence of many customs that relate to women.

As with several social and customary practices that the colonial administrators considered odious, child marriage was on their 'to be abolished' list. Like *sati*, or the plight of widows in some regions of India, child marriage was regarded as abhorrent and unacceptable and would be addressed by making the practice a crime and laying down the punishment for the different actors involved. The Child Marriage Restraint Act, 1929 (19 of 1929) was passed to restrain the solemnisation of child marriages. It was amended in 1949 and revised in 1978 to become the Child Marriage Restraint Act, 1978.

Under the Child Marriage Restraint Act, the legal position was that it was the policy of the state to discourage child marriages. Those promoting or engaged in the act of marrying under-age boys and girls were liable to punishment. The new spouses, however, were not liable for any action; the marriage, despite either or both parties being under the prescribed age, was legally valid and enforceable; and there lay a proper civil action of the enforcement of conjugal rights from such marriage — rights which are a concomitant of a legally recognised marriage.

The raison d'etre behind such a policy (under the 1929 Act) was that it was in the best interests of the girls involved in such a marriage for under the existing cultural and social ethos of the land, a married girl was no more considered a part of the family of her birth and instead, a part of the family of the groom. More importantly, since non-recognition of such marriages would imply that the offspring of such marriage would be illegitimate (a stigma which the law seeks to avoid), it was considered important (at the time of framing the Act of 1929) to consider such under-age marriages valid. So, they were illegal but not void.

Under the later 2006 Act (the Prohibition of Child Marriage Act 2006), the parties to an under-age marriage were given rights to get their marriage declared void (thus essentially making child-marriages voidable at the option of the under-age party to such marriage). In any case, the right to maintenance of the girl was protected, i.e., even if such marriage was declared void, the girl had the right to maintenance from the husband till the time she got remarried. Further, under the new Act, the punishment for encouraging or facilitating, or solemnising such marriages was increased. Nonetheless, the policy of not holding women liable for solemnisation of such marriages was continued even under the new Act. But (as it happens in most cases), it seemed to the Law Commission that the 2006 Act was not a panacea to the ills of child marriage, and therefore, it took up the issue to examine the various facets relating to it in greater details, which resulted in the 205th Report. The Report analysed the provisions of the Act and made further recommendations:

> We need to examine whether the new Act addresses all the concerns relating to child abuse, health and human rights which are inevitable consequences of child marriage (Report 205 of the Law Commission of India, 2008).

Criticisms were levied against provisions of the Act that lays down (Section 3) that a child marriage would be rendered void only if legal proceedings were filed by the children or their guardians. Given the social environment in which they occur there is little chance that that would happen. Child marriages will be void only in cases of 'compulsion' and trafficking (the law is silent on the status of the marriage if it is not under compulsion or for trafficking).

While making punishments more severe and providing for the intervention of courts through stay orders, the Act does not provide for registration of marriages. Some states such as Karnataka, Rajasthan, Maharashtra, and Goa have instituted the practice of registration and certificates, and child marriages would be recorded without the issue of certificates. Areas where such marriages take place are under the administrative jurisdiction of officials who could be held as responsible for the breach of the law as the family of the children were. Parents often go in for such marriages for economic constraints (avoiding the extra expenses of adult marriages and the dowry system). They need to be made more aware of the negative consequences of such a practice rather than just be subjected to penalties and punishments. Informing the society about the trauma to a girl child (psychological and physical) is more important than a purely punitive approach. Most of the girls become mothers within a few years. Despite the practice of *gauna*, Shobhavati had sexual intercourse before she menstruated and became pregnant before she was 15.

The Act contains certain welcome provisions. It provides for the intervention of courts to prevent child marriages through stay orders. Punishments have been made more severe. It provides for the appointment of government officials as Child Marriage Prohibition Officers.

The Law Commission's Report entitled 'Proposal to Amend the Prohibition of Child Marriage Act 2006 and other allied laws' suggested amendments making 18 the uniform age of marriage for boys and girls, thereby declaring child marriages involving either party being under 16 illegal for the first time. Marriages between the ages of 16 and 18 should be null with an option to the minor to repudiate the marriage after he or she attains the age of 20. (The present marriageable age under the Hindu Marriage Act is 18 for girls and 21 for boys.) The Commission did not address separately the position of girls under the Muslim personal law where the 'marriageable age of a girl is when she attains puberty', suggesting by implication that these provisions would be applicable to all girls in India regardless of religion, region or cultural practice.

The Report also stipulated that the exception to the rape Section (375) of the Indian Penal Code be deleted. 'This would ensure that the age of consent for sexual intercourse for all girls whether married or not is 16.' (Section 375 has an exception clause: 'Sexual intercourse by a man with his wife, the wife not being under 15 years of age is not rape')

Between the PCMA and the 205th Report of the Law Commission on the Act, some changes came about but not strong enough to help those who were still subjected to the vagaries of the social system. Marital rape was still not directly addressed: its first recognition as an offence came with the law on domestic violence which suggested in its clauses on emotional, verbal and economic abuse that spousal cruelty could be extended to include 'forced sex'. The husband would then be tried under Section 498 A. The only mention of punishing 'intercourse by a man with his wife' in the Indian Penal Code related to a couple separated under a decree of separation.

The journey is still a long one for most women and for the less informed and helpless; a big push is still awaited by law and by society.

8

Urvashi:
'In a Woman's Body'

◫

'There are two things that are a part of my fate that I curse most: one is that I was brought up without parents and the other is that I was born a girl and in a woman's body. Both those aspects of my life are responsible for my being here.'

These words were spoken by someone who was only 20 years old, but looked too sad and solemn. Her face could have been pretty if she smiled but clearly, as she says, 'there is nothing in my life worth smiling about.'

'If you start life "in care", you are condemned forever,' Urvashi laments. 'Some people say, a child's personality is almost half-made when she is in the womb. I don't know much about that but this I do know, that the lack of security as a child (including emotional security) determines many things that happen later in life.'

'My childhood was spent in an ashram (care institution) in Bombay. I have no recollections of any other environment: how would I? My father was in the army and died just before I was born. My mother died shortly after I was born. Even these details I learnt from the ashram people. They said that my relatives sent me there because no one wanted to take charge of me.'

'So where were you born?' we ask. 'Did someone tell you that?'

'I have no idea. My own memories are only those of being in care in the ashram for girls who had no one to care for them. Someone said I was born in a village somewhere in Maharashtra, someone said just outside Bombay city. But no one could tell me for certain where. I only remember the ashram and that is all.'

'What was the ashram like? Were they good to the children? Were you well looked after?' I ask, thinking about the two girls' ashrams I had recently visited that had given me nightmares for days when I saw the conditions.

'What can I say?' she replies. 'If I should be grateful that I was given two meals a day and a bed to sleep on at night, then I suppose I should say "yes", I was looked after. But is that all that life is — being fed so that one can be called "alive"? Then it may have been better if I had died when my parents died. These places are called "shelters", and "care homes" and when visitors come to visit or inspect them you should see what a show is put up for them! If only there was a way that they could see what really happens inside. No one has any idea.'

Oh, but I do have an idea, I think to myself. I have seen 'homes' and though not all are condemnable, there are some that are in dire need of scrutiny. We made an unannounced visit to one such home (because the magistrate with whom I was doing prison work had an emergency call to make at the 'home'). He was going there to retrieve a young girl who had run away from home and because her parents had reported the matter to the police and the magistrate was asked to assess the situation and determine whether she was a minor and whether she could be forcibly brought back to the parents. It was a pathetic place — dingy and dreary, in a crowded part of the city, and had barely any facilities worth talking about. I went in the evening, when there should have been a bustle of activity for dinner. But there was nothing going on. The lights were dim and the girls were sitting in the verandah doing nothing. When I asked to be taken around (there were only four largish rooms, two with rows of coir-string beds and two that served as a kitchen and pantry) I could only ask what was wrong for there was nothing that explained itself. The kitchen lights were off and when I asked, 'what about dinner tonight?', I was told 'Oh, it will be prepared shortly!' But there was nobody in the kitchen and no ingredients that awaited being prepared for cooking. Nor was there a fire that was being lit on the coal stove. Clearly, there wasn't going to be an evening meal! I pushed for an answer to the question about the evening meal and the 'in-charge' told me that because the girls had had so much food at tea-time, they would eat a little late that night. What a load of nonsense, I thought!

'Don't they have a television they can watch?' My question sounded like a 'let them have cake' joke. But I was not being so foolish. It turned out that the television that was in the 'in-charge's' room was really for the girls, but was being used by the 'in-charge' for her own entertainment.

This was a 'home' in Uttar Pradesh (one of the largest States in the country), housing girls from different places and of different ages, roughly between 7 and 17. The magistrate had come to 'rescue' a girl who claimed she was 18 and therefore not a minor and protested against being taken back to her parents. The parents had sent a certificate to the magistrate stating that the girl was 17 and had run away with a young man she was involved with. But she had no place to stay since his parents had also protested against the relationship, so she had sought shelter in the 'home' and the police had been duly informed. The police, in turn, informed the magistrate, and he had come to verify the particulars and decide what needed to be done.

While we were in the 'home', we saw a very young girl (not more than ten years old) who had chopped-off toes and could scarcely walk. She had bandages on her feet. It turned out that she had been kidnapped by people in Agra and sold to some shady women who ran a disreputable joint where girls were taught dancing to entertain equally disreputable men. Once the girls were older, they were used in the sex trade. This little girl had tried to run away and to prevent that from happening, the women had actually chopped off two of her toes. Fortunately for her, a kind soul who had seen her running away and then being forcibly hustled back to the 'shady' house, reported the incident to the police who raided the place and rescued several minors who had been abducted from different parts of the State.

And that was not all. The 'care home' was next to the local police station and the boundary wall of the home was scarcely four feet high. Far from being protected, the girls were often 'supplied' to the constables who had the power to file complaints about the 'home' if they were not kept happy — so much for shelter.

So, I had had some exposure to 'homes' and what they are all about. If I don't seem too horrified at Urvashi's plight, it is only because I have seen worse and I certainly don't want to minimise her predicament. I couldn't help thinking that at least she got her meals since I knew that only one meal was given to the girls in a 'home'and the rest of the budget pocketed by the staff.

Getting inside information about these places is not difficult even though the residents are petrified of the 'in-charge' and wouldn't dare speak about the place because they would be thrashed if they squealed. However, there is always some employee or resident who has some signs of a conscience, some sense of ethics, who wishes things were not as lousy as they are. They make an effort to seize the moment when they can say something to a visitor who they think might make things better. Not to me, of course, but to the magistrate whose presence was a godsend that particular evening. So, while the 'in-charge' painted her rosy picture of the place and how her heart bled for all those in her charge, the truth lay elsewhere. A young boy who did chores at the place came to the magistrate as he was leaving and asked if he could meet him in our car and talk to him. The magistrate noted all that the young fellow said and promised to take some action. I returned many months later to the city and was told that the place had been shut down and the girls were sent to another place; disciplinary action was taken against the 'in-charge' and she was suspended from her job.

To come back to Urvashi, I ask her, 'So what happened that made you leave the ashram? Clearly, you did avail yourself of some minimum facilities there and received some education worth the name. And now you are here — in another State altogether. How come?' I am wondering at how a long distance she has come, not just regionally but in life generally.

'Oh yes, I passed the Class IX examination and so you could say I have had a basic minimum education. This is a large ashram for orphaned children and is run by a trust that supposedly has a good reputation. But an ashram is an ashram and girls are a vulnerable species anywhere. The ashram has a policy that if someone wants to adopt a child from here, they allow it after checking the credentials of the person. But there is also a rule that once you have left the ashram, you will not be taken back, no matter what.'

'But I don't quite understand how you left, if all it did was land you here. What happened?'

'Well, it was not entirely of my choosing. A person came there one day and that visit sealed my fate. He appeared to be a well-to-do person and seems to have convinced the committee at the ashram of his bona fides. He was between 45 and 50 years. He had no children and said that he and his wife wanted to adopt a girl whom they could take care of, educate and bring up and that it would also mean companionship to his wife who was alone most of the time, a situation that was getting to her. The ashram people were obviously quite taken up with the man and agreed to help him. It was quite pathetic because they actually made all the girls stand in line like a parade. He chose me and I was petrified. I really didn't want to leave the place and start an unknown journey. But the staff worked on me and said that I would be educated in an English-medium school and maybe that would enable me to have a good future. "They will find you a good match and you will be happily married one day: take this opportunity and build your future. They will be your parents, your guardians, your everything. So, don't leave their home because remember the rule is that once you leave this ashram, you cannot be taken back" the staff said to me.' (See Notes.)

Urvashi looks out of the window pensively. She is clearly reliving that fateful day when everything changed for her. We almost know what she is thinking: "If they made the decision for me that I should go with the man then it was not *my* choice at all. How could they have said to me then, "Once you *decide* to go you can't come back"? But I didn't *decide*, did I?'

'I packed whatever few things I had,' she continues. 'The staff said to me, "They will give you many more fancy things, Urvashi. You will probably discard all this — all this from your past." My past! Little did they know, people like me never leave their past, any past. Even the future they have is so tinged with some past that that too becomes a tainted past for yet another future.'

I dare not question that view. She has reason to believe that everything in her life has been like a rotten apple and that eventually everything would continue to be the same. I would have to wait for her to tell me how bad things kept getting for her to even give any comment. My colleagues seem to have a clue about what is coming, but we want to stop ourselves from stereotyping personal experiences that are, even when they appear similar, so uniquely intense for each person that carelessness in our understanding of them could be soul-destroying for the person.

Urvashi was taken to Ahmedabad where the man's home was. So, she had already crossed one State boundary, already in an unfamiliar territory. 'It was a largish house', Urvashi says, and at first she was impressed by it. She had never been in a real home, a family, and this appeared something different. The trepidations she had had about leaving the ashram seemed misplaced and she thought she might even like her new residence. But clearly, there was more to it than met the eye.

'There was a woman there and a young girl about my age. When I entered I assumed that woman was the man's wife who, it had been said, would treat me like a daughter — as if I had any idea what being treated like a daughter really was. However, even then right at the start I did wonder who the young girl was since he had told the ashram he was adopting me because they had no children and his wife was lonely. He explained that a relative's daughter was staying with them for a while, and I was gullible enough to believe it.'

'You were only 19, girl, why would you doubt anything?' We try to be reassuring.

'I had a pleasant couple of weeks and everyone was friendly and warm. I was well-fed and well-looked after. I had plenty of time to myself and I spent it embroidering and stitching and watching television. I got to know the other girl a little, but she seemed to be hesitant about getting too close to me. Actually, we had adjacent rooms and shared a small bathroom. But she didn't come knocking on my door to talk and I was too new to approach her. I didn't see much of her for days and then when I would bump into her she was friendly but a little aloof. As for the lady of the house — it was not really such a great relationship and all that talk about me being a companion didn't really happen. I asked her a few times about when and where I would go to the new school and she just said 'all in good time, my dear' and that was that.'

There are moments in a narrative when one is waiting with bated breath to discover the flaw in the whole set-up: after all,

Urvashi is here in the prison, so the obvious question is: what happened? Which way did things go to bring her to this?

Urvashi continues, 'One evening, I was making my way to the bathroom and the other girl's door was ajar, so I knocked and asked if I could come into the room. She said, 'Wait,' and then asked me to come in. She was getting dressed and was putting on make-up, so it was evident she was going out. I asked her where she was going and whether we could go together. She looked at me in a strange way, and I think she wanted to say something serious to me but for then all she said she was that she was going out with some friends. I did find it odd though that she was getting dressed so elaborately only to meet friends. I felt somewhat uncomfortable hanging around while she got ready for her outing, so I left her room.'

Urvashi then looks away, stares at the wall and seems visibly distressed. She keeps pursing her lips, puckering her eyebrows, and then finally breaks her silence.

'The girl stayed away all night and came back early in the morning. I was awake when she came because all night long I had this foreboding that there was something not quite right here. But I kept quiet until mid-morning and then went to Veena's (that was her name) room. She knew that this was the moment of reckoning and I knew that that was my moment of ruination. I had had such a bad night fearing the worst and sure enough, my fears were confirmed.'

Urvashi says, she mustered up enough guts to ask her bluntly where she was all night. 'I was trembling all the while that I stood there waiting for her answer. Either she would tell me, or she would shut me up and ask me to mind my own business. But Veena was composed and asked me to sit down. "I think we need to have a frank chat," she said, "and I really don't think you should be deceived any longer."'

'And then the saga that unfolded left me so numb, you cannot imagine my state. "I am not a relative of these people, Urvashi," Veena said. "This is a hellhole and I, too, was picked up from an ashram like you. Isn't it sad that we were both duped and our stories are so similar? When they went to your ashram to get someone, anyone, I felt so wretched. I wished that I could warn you somehow. But in this racket there is no squealing. Any attempt at exposing their schemes means there is hell to pay. So here we are, doomed for life, and there is nowhere to run, believe me. Their tentacles are spread far and wide and we'd be caught wherever we are."'

While Urvashi relives the horror of that moment, we can see that she had suffered a jolt even as she had suspected there was something amiss. We just look at each other with the same thought going through our minds as when other similar experiences were narrated to us, 'Not another hapless victim'. And yet each experience has so many personal nuances that it never fails to shock us.

'I just sat there and wept my eyes out,' she continues. 'I don't think I have shed as many tears in my life as I did that day. Veena kept telling me that the sooner I accepted my fate the better. But how could I? And the first question that came to my mind was whether the ashram people had any inkling of all this? Were they also part of the racket? How could they not have checked these people out? Had they been given money in exchange? All these thoughts kept consuming me all day long. I couldn't eat and couldn't sleep and the lady of the house actually had the nerve to ask me if anything was wrong! What did she think? That I was such a young fool that I would not catch on, or that Veena would not reveal it all to me some day?'

She did make an attempt to escape. 'Early one morning, before Veena returned from her "night out", I packed up a few things (I didn't have that many anyway) and left. I made my way to a bus stop, but before I could so much as enquire about buses and which one went where, there he was, the man who had brought me from Bombay, and he dragged me back to the house. When we entered the house, the lady was fuming in the front room, red with rage. Veena was standing in a corner, trembling. Clearly, she had been given a taste of their wrath. But my share of their anger was still waiting for me. The lady took me inside her room and thrashed me non-stop. I kept screaming and she kept beating me with the words, "Is this how you respond to people who are doing something lucrative for you?" She was shouting and I was shouting back, even though Veena had warned me there was no getting out of their clutches.'

We are stunned into silence. One cannot even utter the obvious words 'we could have told you that' to someone who was already bearing a cross? What do you say to someone who is *now* well-entrenched in the path that she is traversing, albeit involuntarily, a path that she believes is hers to take forever. Short of starting a moral sermon that she naturally doesn't want to hear, what can one say?

Veena then told her that she would now be sent to 'work' in places where Veena went, and 'the best thing I can do for you is tell you what happens there'. Veena also told Urvashi what she had to wear, what she would be told and that there was no way out so she had to come to terms with the reality.

'Come to terms? How on earth can I come to terms with this kind of reality?' Urvashi told Veena. Urvashi is getting quite red in the face and she is a little reticent as she unfolds this part of her story to us.

'That night the man took both Veena and me to a farmhouse. It was a big sprawling place and while Veena moved with some confidence, I was more than petrified. There were three men waiting for us. They were so smug-looking and their all-knowing smiles and sloppy bodies made me feel so unclean and improper. Veena went with one of them almost like a robot. I was left with another. You cannot imagine what I was going through. I thought then: "If I had had a mother, I wonder what she would have said!"' Urvashi starts weeping, wipes her eyes and remains silent for a long time. We get her some tea and ask her to have a biscuit, as if that would ease the pain she is experiencing yet again. Meanwhile, we move aside to talk amongst ourselves.

My young associate look stricken: she had heard similar stories and yet each time a new one comes up, she is incensed — as if this were her first encounter with the seamy side of some girls' experiences down the slippery slope. 'I can't bear to hear these things,' she says quietly to me. 'She is part of a category for all of us, isn't she? My goodness, I have a little daughter and I slog day in and day out to make sure she is protected and sheltered. Ma'am, one day one of my relatives had come to stay in my house. He was a young man and had come for a job interview. One morning when I was leaving for work, he said, "Would you like me to fetch your daughter from school? You don't have to rush back then and can take your time coming back." I agreed. He was family! When I came home that day, my daughter was all flushed and flustered. She wouldn't eat, she wouldn't talk and I had a rough time with her all evening. When I was putting her to bed, I sat her on my lap and asked her why she was so *gumsum* (clamped up). She said, "I can't tell you otherwise he will beat me." "Who will beat you?" I asked her and she said, "Rakesh Bhaiya!"'

'You don't want to know how I tackled that situation, ma'am! It took me an hour to get my little girl to tell me what had happened. The young man had brought her home and tried to rape her! She asked him not to touch her and struggled and struggled but he overpowered her, took off her underwear and lay on top of her. Just then the phone rang, startling him. He got up and my daughter ran out of the door to a neighbour's house and waited till I got home. Since then I have a thing about men and about their no-holes-barred attitude to sex. My daughter was just ten years old. What was the fellow thinking, trying to destroy a little girl's childhood in that way? How disgusting is that? You can see that I can't hear about any young girl's misfortune at the hands of depraved men.'

What a complicated world, I thought. Everyone has experiences that can't be talked about ever, after the event. It's a hush-hush situation and yet it's so close to home and seen and heard by all of us at some point or another. 'Lock up your daughters' is the response of many I know. But can we really and do we want to lock up our daughters? And the sordid fact is that so many cases of sexual abuse and exploitation are within the extended family (uncles, brothers-in-law, cousins) that no amount of locking up really helps. These are some of the dilemmas that I want to highlight through the narratives I am recounting.

Urvashi goes back to the barrack after tea, saying she would come back later. 'Fine,' I say to her. 'Come back just when you like and when you feel like talking.'

She doesn't come back for a day or two and we do not push to see her either. Then she returns, sits down and asks us to tell her our reactions to all that she had said to us so far, candidly. Were we judging her? That was her primary concern — also, when we talk to the people in prison, do we judge them for their offences? When asked what she meant by 'judging', she says, 'I mean that one judge has already judged me and meted out the punishment from a book under PITA (the Prevention of Immoral Trafficking Act). Now are you judging me with some other scale?' We assume she is talking about a moral judgement pronounced on her 'kind'. It is evident that our conversation amongst ourselves the day she had come to us is what is prompting her to ask that question.

'We are trained counsellors,' we assure her 'and have studied the concept of counselling in some depth and with great intensity. A counsellor must neither judge nor even seek to give advice that says "do this or don't do that". We are there to assist you to find your own way and make your decisions yourself. So, we would be failing in our job if we sat and passed judgement on you, and also if we prescribed a path for you that you have not been instrumental in choosing for yourself. So, the answer to your question is "no", we are not judging you. As for our reaction to what you have told us so far: we are not horrified in the manner that you are accustomed to. We find it unfortunate that persons like you who had no intention of going this way were compelled to do so. There are so many words used for what you do, but one that does the rounds of the prison is that you do *dhandha* (trade) and when people look at you that is all they think of. When we look at you, we do not just think of a girl who does *dhandha*. We want to know your history and where you came from. And yes, at the end of it all, depending on how far gone things are for you, we wonder where you will be headed. That does concern us.'

'Well, since you don't know whether I am knee-deep in things or waist-deep,' Urvashi says, 'perhaps, I should take you through the worst parts of my journey. If you think you can guide me, I am happy to listen. But you have to know what happens to us, especially when we are pushed into this 'business' unwillingly and with much pain and remorse. There are always sordid details in what we do — no one is really interested except for sensational purposes. So, we don't talk about the details but believe me, it is the details that shake one's faith. And you need to know them so that you know what happens to us when we are trapped.'

'When I entered the prison I was petrified. It is the last place I thought I would come to. When I was searched and then strip-searched, I was reluctant to take my clothes off and the staff was so crude about it all. They pulled off my *dupatta* and said, "*Arre, itni baar nangi ho chuki hai gair mardon ke saamne, ab kya sharam dikha rahi hai*! [You have stood naked so often in front of all kinds of men, why this pretence of feeling shy]. I can't explain why that remark of theirs really hurt me. But they didn't stop there. "*Chal kapre utaar*," they ordered, and pulled off my *kurta*. They got such perverse pleasure from taunting me that I believed then that there was really no hope for me. And these are women guards, can you imagine? They don't want to know how all this happened — they ride the high moral ground and only see the end result — and I am labelled for life.'

We realise then that in asking us how judgemental we were, she was alluding to how much thought we had given to the question of how and why she got enmeshed in all this. Related to that, she was probably anticipating a question that does arise in our minds every now and then: how far is the reluctant 'sex worker' (as they are called in the prison) able to resist pursuing the 'trade' and just how does she resist. And what is the point of 'no return, that is referred to so often. That thought does cross our minds each time we are faced with girls like Urvashi. So, her query is valid and she feels the need to tell us just how much she was able to and did resist the coercion.

'That night at the farmhouse, one of the three men took me to one of the rooms clearly allotted for sexual activities. He had obviously frequented the place and moved about as if he owned it. He locked the door and the ground beneath my feet seemed to just sink. I thought I would faint. He first poured me a drink and sat down to drink himself. When I said I didn't drink, he said, "Of course you don't, but you will now." He sat me on the bed, took the glass of liquor (whatever it was) and forcibly made me drink. I was dizzy within minutes and he probably knew that. Then he began to undress. I looked the other way — I had never seen a man naked, ever, believe me. He then told me to take my clothes off. When I didn't, he just pulled them off, lay me on the bed and pushed himself into me. Oh ma'am, I cannot tell you how loudly I screamed — from the pain and the shock of what was happening. I shut my eyes and he just went on and on and on. When he was done, I realised I was bleeding profusely and told him so. Do you know what he said? "Good! That's very good. Now you will see you will enjoy sex even more — take my word for it."'

All three of us are totally silent for a while. Sometimes, silence is not a good idea because the person recounting her intense experience is anxious to know what's going on in our minds. But we decide to be silent and soon she continues.

'I was a wreck that night. It is difficult to describe what I felt — no one would understand but those who have had such experiences. Something snaps inside the head and you feel numb physically and mentally. It is as if you are outside of yourself and not inside. I kept telling myself that this was not happening, knowing all the while that it was. I was too numb to even cry. The tears were not coming although God knows, I was so saddened as if I had been bereaved. I just wanted to rush out — even as I knew there was no one I could run to. It is an indescribable feeling!'

As I am about to open my mouth to say something, Urvashi says: 'Don't think that was the end of that night's experience. That man left the room smoking a cigarette and I thought I should get dressed and get out of that place. As I was dressing, believing I was free to go, the second man came in. He saw me buttoning my shirt and said "Arre kahan ja rahi ho? [Where do you think you are off to?]." Oh God, I thought! What on earth is happening here? I will not go into the sordid details of how that man worked on me in my next ordeal. It is not a pleasant thing to acquaint you with what these people do. They are so crude and coarse both in their language and acts that it is not worth recounting the horror of their behaviour. Suffice it to say that it leaves any girl feeling both defiled and dishonoured.'

Our faces must have revealed our shock at the poor girl's nightmarish experience that night. 'To think that in the prison I have to hear time and again "yeh ganda kaam kar ke aayi hai! [she has indulged in dirty acts]." When they say, "kar ke aayi hai," anyone would think I opted for what I had to do. The fact is, I did not, and that day and for many days after that I could not even look at myself in the mirror. I cursed my body and then I cursed my soul.'

Our silence is actually beginning to be an embarrassment all round, even for us. I move my chair closer to her and put my hand on her shoulder: 'What can one say to you that will make it better? Nothing really. That is how helpless we are. But if it's any consolation, we are not looking at you and saying, "She is a defiled person". You think what happened to you ruined your life, but you are so young that it would be foolish to think for a moment that it is the end for you, forever tarnished and irredeemable. Not at all — there has to be another way and it is up to you whether you want to choose it.'

'But that is not the end of that day, ma'am. After the second man left, the third (the one Veena had gone in with) entered. I was so shattered and worn out already, I screamed when he came in. I started running out of the room, but he held me by my hair and pushed me inside. You thought you only see this in the films: well, this was for real. He was the worst of the lot. He made it plain to me that he would do with me as he pleased, so I better "shut up". And he did. Again, I'll spare you the details, they are too rough and raw. I just lay there and closed my eyes, hoping it would end soon. But as I said, he was the worst: out to cause pain and hurt, and he did. I came out bruised and physically injured. I wish I was able to tell you just what he did, but I can't.

We really can't take it anymore and my young associate is actually feeling sick. She excuses herself for a moment and goes out. Urvashi also senses the discomfort of my young colleague and doesn't say much more about that night for a while. 'I feel more than just humiliation — there is no word I can use that captures the emotions I have inside. Today is the first time I have spoken so candidly about my experiences. It is because there was no one I could unburden myself to. Veena already knew it all, but other than her, there was no one who could be told about the horror I experienced. I had this feeling when I saw you people and the way you moved around the women here that you were here for something serious and I mustered up enough courage to talk to you. I have been bursting inside for more than a year now. And I am sorry if I have touched raw nerves all round.' And then she is quiet.

I begin to feel a strange emptiness inside. How many young girls go through this? Probably many. This thought went over and over my mind. And they emerge as not just offenders but sinners too. Other players in this pursuit get off the hook and go about their lives as if nothing untoward had happened. They are untouched by the law and by society's moral code, while those that got enmeshed through coercion live harrowing lives for a long time. How? Why? I felt defeated, unable to find any answers and explanations.

By the time my colleague comes back to the room, I think we all needed a break. It has been a rough ride with Urvashi and maybe the point has been reached where we are so out of our depth, we cannot absorb anymore. It is not just her experiences; it is also the future. Several women we had talked to had found their way as part of the 'trade' and had come to terms with the fact that if this was how they would have to make their living, then so be it. We had fewer problems with them. Urvashi's story, however, is something else, leaving us perturbed for a long time.

Urvashi is tense on the one hand, but also relaxed in a strange kind of way. She wants to get it all off her chest. It is like a dam waiting to burst — we can see she needs this catharsis. So, while my young colleague whispers to me that we can continue the next day, I have to tell her that we would take the cue from Urvashi.

'Do you want to continue?' I ask, 'or are you tired?'

'Oh no, ma'am. I want to tell you more, please. I will never be able to tell anyone what I went through. It is something I can't forget even if I try. And it is something I wish to hide from most people who I know will look at me with a funny gaze when they hear about it. People react to such stories very strangely. But I do want you to know so that some day you will be able to tell the world what really happens to some of us when we get trapped into what is so coolly called "sex work". There is an assumption that women who have done "sex work" go into it brazenly. I want you to know that is not a pattern. And I feel you will be able to give some explanations on behalf of the likes of me without revealing my personal details. There are many categories of women in this business, if you want to call it that. People should know the details of the different categories,' she says, reflecting our thoughts exactly.

Questions start piling up in my mind — two specific questions plague me more than others and I feel the need to put them to her, but I would wait since they may sound pedestrian to her just then, at that particular juncture.

She goes on, 'You would think that by the time that horrendous night was over, I would have returned and got a chance to recover (if one can ever recover from such an ordeal). Unfortunately not. In the early hours of the morning, the man who brought us there was waiting for Veena and me. No, he didn't take us "home". How can I call it home though, for home is where you feel safe. Much to our horror he drove us to a hotel. Can you imagine? And all the while, the one thing I was desperate for was a bath. I had this feeling in me that if I had a good long bath, I would wash away the muck of the night's experiences. "Silly", you may say, but that is how I felt. But this man actually had other plans for us, "*Abhi tumhara kaam khatam nahin hua*! [your work is not over yet!]," he said. We protested and said we wanted to have a bath and rest and he said, "All in good time. You can do that at this hotel. I have arranged that and I will pick you up in two hours."'

'There was a "customer" waiting for each of us there. Once again we went through the same routine. What can I say to you now? It is all so sordid and for you all who are by God's grace so removed from this murky world, it would just be another lot of details. But both Veena and I went through the ordeal again. Then we did have baths and managed to "clean" but not cleanse ourselves. We sat in a lounge and waited and talked. I needed to talk and Veena was patiently listening. Just then there was a loud scream from one of the rooms near the lounge (next to the rooms where the "customers" had been with us). We rushed to the room where the scream came from. It was locked, so we went to the reception and asked the man to open the door, saying "we think someone is trying to kill someone." So, he opened the door. We could not believe our eyes. A father was actually trying to rape his daughter. She was yelling, "Papa, don't do it! Please leave me alone. Please don't do this to me." But the nude man kept on molesting her, taking his daughter's *salwar* off. Both Veena and I picked up a side table and hit the man hard on the head till he fell. We told the daughter to run. And she did.'

'It was time for us to run now. In another 20 minutes we were supposed to be picked up. I hardly knew my way around but Veena did. She took me to a place where she said we would be safe.

It was a teashop in an alley and she knew the owner. We went to an anteroom and asked the owner to give us some tea and biscuits and requested him not to let anyone know we were there. Veena said we needed this breathing space to talk and plan rather than make a dash for bus stops and railway stations where the man would be looking for us anyway. She explained to me that now our fates were sealed and there was no escaping the work we were doing. "We are marked for life," she said.'

The conversation with Veena was what determined Urvashi's immediate future. Although it was disturbing, she found it useful to be apprised of where she stood in this scenario that lay behind and before them. Veena had been in the mire for almost four months and had become numb to the demands put on her. It was not that she had accepted her fate without agitation, but several attempts at getting herself out of the mess had only landed her in more trouble and abuse.

Urvashi recounts the conversation with Veena at length. 'You have just had an intense day and I can see how traumatised you are,' she told Urvashi. 'You haven't seen anything yet. If you think this was shattering you should know the things I have been through. Let me assure you that people in the society we live in have a very ambivalent attitude to sex. After all, we are told by the men we are pushed in with, that is the most natural activity between men and women, so why are we recoiling? One man actually said to me, "Your parents had sex — that's how you were born!" I wasn't about to embark on a discourse with him about voluntary and forced sex. He was trying to mystify the whole subject and I was bewildered by his blasé attitude. That I was caught in a web and he was free to do as he pleased, when he pleased and how he pleased was not a contradiction for him. For him sex was sex and the problem lay at my end. And time and again, I am told by them all, "We are paying for this!"'

Urvashi recounted what Veena said to her, 'I also need to tell you how bad it can get, Urvashi,' Veena said. 'There was this man who I was sent to some weeks ago who suddenly said to me, "Okay, we are going to do oral sex. Have you ever done oral sex?" And he started to demonstrate to me what I had to do. You cannot imagine my utter horror. Of course, I had never done oral sex!

What was he thinking? I flinched and said, I'd rather not. He was angry. He shoved my mouth on to his organ and said, "Get going". I just didn't know what to do. I pulled my wits about me and said, "All right! All right! But please may I request that you clean yourself before I do that and also there will be an extra charge for this — 2,000 rupees extra. He agreed. Yes, it put me in a spot but I had to do it. All these things have made me a little tougher than you are, Urvashi. That is why I wanted to have a heart-to-heart talk with you.'

Veena had clearly learnt to take it in her stride and had made herself numb to all the nuances and complexities that Urvashi was unable to come to terms with. She told Urvashi, 'You see, there is also the question, what will I do to live? We both have the misfortune of not being able to turn back to any family support. Even families don't take back defiled daughters, you know. So, you tell me, where will you hide?'

Urvashi asked Veena, 'Is there nothing that the police does about cases like ours?' She gave a wry smile and said, You really have no idea where you are living, do you? The first thing that most racketeers do is neutralise the local police. That means they are paid off to shut up and ignore such reports. And here is the most revolting bit: very often the police are the beneficiaries of all this exploitation. So, don't dream of involving the police: you're asking for double trouble.'

It was the moment of reckoning for Urvashi. She and Veena both decided that in order to get out of the clutches of 'the man in Ahmedabad', they might have to part and go separate ways. It was an emotional moment evidently, and both wept because a bond was developing between them. But the worldly wise Veena had clearly thought things through a little more clearly. 'Do you know *anyone* anywhere, Urvashi?' she asked. 'No,' came the reply, 'no one.'

'Well,' said Veena, 'I have decided that I am going back to Bombay for the time being. I know some people there. For the time being, why don't you come with me and if you think that will not be safe for you, we can think of some other place. Right now, you can't make your way to any place since you know, no one anywhere. So, that is the best I can suggest.'

Both girls took the train to Bombay and arrived at the place where the people Veena knew stayed. It was a move that seemed fraught with danger for Urvashi. For a few days she stayed where Veena did, but feared being caught everyday. Veena was not so scared. She knew Bombay better than Urvashi and could wriggle out of situations, something Urvashi felt she could not handle. On one occasion, Veena sent her to the local shops to buy something and from a distance she saw the superintendent of the ashram and ran for her life. She was petrified. 'I can't stay in this city, Veena, I am afraid of my own shadow.'

'Don't you know *anyone anywhere*, Urvashi?' Veena again asked almost desperately, knowing this was not the place for such a frightened girl.

'No, Veena, I have never been anywhere and no one knows me. There is a person in Ujjain who had come to the ashram once to teach us sewing and embroidery — I got to know her and she said to me, "if you ever come to Ujjain, look me up." That's all.' Urvashi believed she had reached the end of the road.

'Well then, Ujjain it is! You can stay here a few days and then I will take you to the station and help you board the train for Ujjain. Go there and see how it works out. But, one word of advice. There is no other way you can make a living easily now, except this. I'm sorry it sounds harsh but that is the reality. For any other job that you may try to seek they will ask you about your past and your credentials for the job — even if you work as a cleaning lady. And the moment you refer to *any* of your past, someone somewhere will track you down and you will be accused of all kinds of things. So think hard and then act.'

Goodness me, I think. Another State boundary to cross for the poor girl. It is beginning to dawn on us just how she had landed in this State where we were in the prison — the fourth since she started her first journey out of Bombay.

And she admits, 'Parting from Veena was a very emotional experience for me and I had no money.'

This was one of the questions that had arisen in my mind when she had been talking so intensely about her night in Ahmedabad: the question of money. I seize this opportunity to ask what happened about the 'payment' for the exploitation she had been subjected to by 'the man' (she continued to refer to him that way and so did we). Clearly, he had neither revealed his name to her nor did she seem interested in knowing it.

'Oh, we never got any of the money from these men. "The man" carried out the financial transactions and then gave us a small amount. His contention was that all our expenses were borne by him, so they only needed a little money for emergencies. Veena had collected some from these paltry sums that had been given. I had just started, and then had run away, so I had no money.'

Veena put her on the train to Ujjain and Urvashi was separated from what was the nearest support system she had ever had in her life. Apart from being thoroughly demoralised and shaken up emotionally, she knew there was nothing but insecurity and instability awaiting her life from then on. She arrived at the door of the acquaintance in Ujjain with the very barest of information about her address. When she reached, she realised she couldn't stay there too long. She had to make up a hundred stories about how she happened to be in Ujjain and knew then and there that she would have to become anonymous very soon. She gave the impression she was there only for a few days and managed to find a hostel where she moved as soon as she could. The lady in Ujjain had befriended her at the Bombay ashram and how could she be absolutely certain that she wouldn't contact the ashram to ask how and why she had landed in Ujjain.

Money — that was her greatest problem and the amount Veena gave her was fast running out. What should she do to live? That was the point at which she realised what Veena had said really meant. There was nowhere she could go to work. She tried at one or two shops to ask if they had jobs and, of course, they asked for references. So, she had come full circle.

'I went to a hotel one day and sat there. Frankly, I was trying to size up the place. It was in the evening and there was a lot of activity. I sat in the lounge and pretended I was waiting for a friend. Sure enough, as the evening wore on, I was "approached" by a few men. They first came and sat in the adjacent sofa. Then they smiled and asked if I would like a drink.'

'The men were "*dalals*" (brokers) not "clients",' she says. By now she seemed well-versed in the jargon of the 'trade'. They had sized her up and gradually ascertained she was alone and needed to earn. She was pretty and likeable, and for them she was a good catch. They told her that a lot of rich, important people came to the hotel and if she would give them company in the evening (by which they meant the night) they would pay. At a loss for what else to do, she agreed.

'And that was the beginning of the end. I was back where I thought I would never return. I kept thinking of Veena all the time that day and wondered where she was. From that day I kept going down the slippery slope. Unfortunately, the (money) figures you hear of never came my way. The brokers made the thousands and I was given the hundreds. It saw me through the rough patch, but I always felt frightened of so many things — like getting caught by someone who would expose me, like being physically abused and messed around with, like being handed over to the police. I kept thinking that this was not where I could stick around for too long.'

The two questions that have been gnawing me at the back of my head for so long keet bothering me, so finally, I put them to her.

'A couple of things have been troubling me all this time, Urvashi, and I would like to ask you about it plainly. I wondered about the money they gave and you have already revealed that it was all given to the brokers and you hardly saw any of it. But when you mentioned all the things you were frightened of, there is one that you haven't told us about and it has been bothering me ever since your narration of the night in Ahmedabad when three unknown men had sex with you and you were new in the game and maybe unaware of the hazards. Were you not afraid that if you were not careful, you could contract some infection through these unknown men with whom you were having sex. How clean were they? Did you make sure that they wore condoms? Was there ever a dispute over that subject?'

She knows this is a rough area. 'Yes,' she replies, 'I was afraid. Aside from the fact that I had no clue about where they were coming from and didn't really want any physical contact with them, I was aware of the fact that unsafe sex was my road to perdition. Veena told me I should tell them straight up that I couldn't have any sexual contact with them until they took the measures that

were necessary. I had to hear snide remarks about it from them —
I spared you the details, ma'am, because their language was always
so rough and rude. But yes, there was even that one night when a
lot of rubbish was thrown at me when I so much as mentioned it.
They did eventually comply — I think because they had probably
had experiences with others who had broached the subject with
them. It took me a lot of guts to regurgitate all that Veena had
warned me about — but I did.'

I am relieved and yet saddened that she has already seen it all
from the rough end. There was nothing left to face, except getting
in trouble with the law and sure enough it came.

'One of the brokers was from this town and he asked me if
I would like to move here from Ujjain. I figured that the further
away I am from those who know where I came from the better, so
I did. For many months I worked with, or through him. The experiences were not good. The problems were at two levels and I really
couldn't handle the rubbish I had to hear from both the broker
and the client. It was too much. By then I seemed to know the
ropes and also the contacts. So I decided to go it alone. I took a
place of my own and started working. I had enough information
about things by then and liased with a group of other girls in the
same 'business'. If I wasn't well, I would send someone else and
that is how I carried on.'

Her brush with the law was something she anticipated but
wasn't prepared for. 'Two men contacted me one day and wanted
to talk to me. They seemed to be well-off, with "high connections", and asked me why I did all this, saying, "You should start
a different life and get on with establishing yourself through other
means. You look like a decent person and should "settle down".
We can help you do that if you like. Well, not directly because we
are married men with wives and children, but we are sure there are
ways we could assist you."'

She didn't pause to think whether they were genuine. One
would have thought with all the knocks and jolts she had received,
she would be wary of such offers that were hardly likely to be
selfless and as innocuous as they sounded. They actually made
accommodation available for her to set up a mini-home and for
a while, she was actually relieved to get away from all that she

had been doing till then. Or so it appeared. The question would always be: what would she do to live?

'Then one day, someone contacted me for "business" and I declined. I told him I was not in the business any more. I then wondered whether the people who had made all the goodies available to me hadn't set me up for other purposes. Maybe they had had long-term plans of running their own "show" through me. Had I been duped again?'

'The man on the phone then said, "All right. At least meet me at the hotel — I have something important to divulge to you."' When Urvashi told us the name of the hotel, we were taken back. It is a medium-sized place which we'd booked for one of our project coordinators to stay a few times.

'So I went,' she continues. 'I waited there for a while and he didn't turn up. Just when I was ready to leave, the police came. I nearly sank as they approached me and said sternly, "Come with us". So that was the finale that I had feared and it happened.'

I am not surprised and have been wondering when and how it would happen. The fellow who said he would meet her had obviously snitched on her. Trust was not meant to be one of the corner stones of the business — the knock-back could come any time, and it did. It was certainly a kick in the teeth for Urvashi and frankly, I thought it was better it had happened now rather than later, when she would be so seasoned and *pukka* in the business that she would have a 'don't care less' attitude to everything. She hadn't reached that point yet — that was our educated guess.

She was taken to the police station and kept there for four days. I wasn't about to tell her that she should not have been kept for more than 24 hours. The police force is a law unto itself and can conjure up any number of reasons for detaining someone as long as it wishes; there was little point in telling her just what the police could or could not do. And her unsavoury experiences there didn't surprise me either. 'They treated me with disdain and contempt and asked me all kinds of questions about my private life. It's funny how, having been caught for a legal offence now, there was nothing to me except the Act under which I had been detained — PITA. They kept telling me what PITA meant — for them, I had no life before that and I would have none after that.

Again, Veena was right. I might as well have had a tattoo on my arm saying, "prostitute" because no amount of change could wipe me clean.'

That is the predicament that faces us just as it probably faced her too — except that hers was delicately personal and ours is dispassionate and detached. Can she wipe it all off and begin afresh? Can we actually sit there and tell her that she is too young to make the decisions of a lifetime here and now? And if we do, can we offer solutions?

◙

Note

This story was about several issues. Inevitably, the problem relating to girls landing up in sex work recurs and rekindles the dilemmas and frustrations relating to the wider search for solutions in this area. The traffickers get away once the 'commodity' is caught. Urvashi was a child in a care home, particularly designed for protecting destitute children, and presumably run according to rules and regulations concerning the children's safety and care. Yet she ended up in a prison, the last place she had expected to be. It was a long journey from a care home in Bombay via two other States, to a prison in Jaipur. Having followed the distressing stories of girls placed in these exploitative situations by different agencies (not forgetting Saloni who was pushed into sex work by her own mother) there are other twists in Urvashi's case that are as baffling as her ending up in a sex trafficking racket. Almost as distressing as Soloni's mother's act of pushing the daughter into prostitution is that of the managers of a supposedly reputable ashram (a care home that must remain unnamed) in whose shelter Urvashi had been placed, supposedly by relatives who were not prepared to take the responsibility for her after her parents either passed away or abandoned her, she was never told which. It makes the predicament about the care of a girl outside the family even more disquieting. Where is a girl safe if there is no one in the family to take her responsibility? Several shelter and care homes that we encountered in at least three States were far from safe.

Urvashi was supposedly taken into adoption from the ashram — that is evident from the narrative. Two sets of statutes therefore come into play: the laws of adoption and the rules and statutes that govern the management of care and shelter homes for girls. One reminds oneself that there are rules in place in all the areas relating to the aberrations we have sought to highlight in all these stories. There are two snags here: one, that the law has loopholes and there are people aplenty to take advantage of any ambiguities and uncertainties within the law, and two, that there is corruption within and without and the nexus between the two spells disaster for those in care. Any misuse of a law hurts the powerless who were put in protection in the first place while those with power (any kind of power) go scot-free. Clearly, both these short-comings need scrutiny.

Our concern is how living in care and shelter is and should be defined universally. The child rights organisation, Save the Children, gives us some broad ideas about care being 'a group living arrangement for children in which care is provided by remunerated adults who would not be regarded as traditional carers within the wider society'. The definition is said to imply an organised and deliberate structure for the living arrangements for children and also a professional relationship between the adults and the children rather than one that is parent-related.

An underlying problem for the futures of many women (and children) either bereft of parental care due to tragic happenings, or left without support on account of ignominious circumstances (like prison) is where they should go. The list of 'homes', 'shelters', 'ashrams', 'refuges, 'safe asylums' is endless, and unsupported women and children are indeed sent there when all else fails. But how safe and protective are they? What is the record of these homes in providing a healthy environment for those in their care? Given that the task of looking after the vulnerable is Challenging all the way, good intentions are clearly not enough: there is a need in both dedication and professionalism. Unfortunately, for every one caring 'home' there is another that will be careless, sloppy, negligent and worst of all, exploitative. The plight of children and girls in particular, in residential shelters is clearly not as it should be and one needs to know why.

Not unrelated to all of these is the overriding feature of the lack of clarity about how the law defines and views rape. Women caught in 'sex work' scenarios would have a hard time proving they were raped. (For a discussion on some aspects of the law on rape, see Note at the end of Chapter 3 and judgements relating to cases such as *Tukaram and Another v/s State of Maharashtra* 1978, AIR 1979, SC 185; *Vishakha v/s State of Rajasthan and Others* AIR 1997 SC 3011; *Sakshi v/s Union on India, 2004.)*

What does the state have in place by way of laws to safeguard the security and protection as well as the needs, rights and entitlements of those who are put in care because the primary care system has failed them? The Allahabad 'home' we visited is a state-run home: who do we turn to when the state's functionaries are the guilty party? In this particular case (Urvashi's), four statutes come into play, three relate to *adoption* and the fourth relates to *the supervision of homes and shelters.*

Adoption has no uniform law in India; there are different legislations relating to adoption spread over a period of time: (i) The Hindu Adoption and Maintenance Act, 1956; (ii) The Guardians and Wards Act, 1890; (iii) The Juvenile Justice (Care and Protection of Children) Act, 2000; and (iv) The Orphanages and Other Charitable Homes (Supervision and Control) Act, 1960. The last one is the main statutory provision for running and managing homes and shelters.

Adoption laws in India are woolly and dated. The Hindu Adoption and Maintenance Act (HAMA), 1956, is the only existing legislation that provides guidelines for adoption to Hindus in India. The category of Hindus includes any person who is a Hindu by religion, or any of its forms as well as Buddhists, Jains, Sikhs, or members of the Brahmo Samaj, Prarthna Samaj, or Arya Samaj. Under this Act, a couple can only adopt children belonging to the sex opposite to the child that they may already have. The adopted child is legally considered a natural-born offspring of the couple and has all the rights, including the right to inheritance. The city civil courts handle the adoption cases. The Guardianship and Wards Act, 1890, relates to non-Hindus in India, who are governed by their personal laws, that is, those who are Muslims, Christians, Parsis and Jews by religion. Personal laws of none of these recognise full adoption, that is, the Act only confers a guardian–ward relationship to the adopter and the adoptee. The petition of guardianship has to be accompanied by an investment plan for a certain amount of money for the ward's security. The High Court or Family Court handles the case. Very recently (August 2010), the Supreme Court asked the Centre (the Law Commission, specifically) to re-examine the country's archaic adoption laws. The suggestion came because of a particular case relating to the difficulties for foreigners in adopting Indian children. The Court pointed out that there are at least 12 million orphan children in the country who are forced to beg, work as domestic helps, or languish in the government's orphanages. There is a Child Welfare Committee in charge of the adoption of abandoned children. A coordinating Voluntary Adoption Resource Agency and Central Adoption Resource Authority also exist — mostly in relation to inter-country adoption, that is, adoption by foreigners. The District Court judge, who is the legal guardian of all abandoned and orphaned children, can reject an application for adoption.

In Urvashi's case, the adoption was obviously sloppy and hasty — on the face of it the institution seems to have connived with the adopting party. Were the person's credentials and bona fides investigated? Her description of a parade where he took his pick is not only objectionable, but is also proscribed by regulations. Clearly, wholesome adoption laws need to be put in place to facilitate appropriate adoption. The Juvenile Justice (Care and Protection) Act, 2000, specifically recommends provisions for adoption of a child as an alternative to institutional care.

Institutional care has plenty of stumbling blocks and, unless addressed, can defeat the purposes for which it is set up. The Orphanages and Other Charitable Homes (Supervision and Control) Act, 1960, is the only substantial statute relating to orphanages and shelter homes. The preamble of the Act states that the objective is to 'provide for supervision and control of orphanage and homes for neglected women or children and other like institutions and for matters connected therewith'. 'Children in need of care and protection' here is commensurate with the internationally recommended terminology on the subject and 'control' includes monitoring and quality control and is not about policing.

There is ample evidence of the misuse of power by non-government organisations and state authorities in welfare work, and in the case of people in care, their vulnerability and powerlessness make ideal ingredients for abuse and exploitation. This gives the state the mandate to evolve mechanisms to prevent and penalise the neglect and abuse of children.

The 1960 Act provides for a constitution, a managing committee (and its powers and functions), and the duties of the manager. The compliance with all rules and regulations for the welfare of each woman and child admitted to the recognised home are the duties of the manager and the committee until the woman reaches the age of 18 (Sub-section 1 of [22]).

Sub-section (2) of Section 22 of the Act has relevance to Urvashi and the manner of her discharge or departure from the ashram:

> Notwithstanding anything contained in Sub-section 1, no female inmate of a home shall be discharged or given in marriage or entrusted to the care of any other person unless such female has made a declaration before the Board or an officer specified by it in this behalf that she consents to such discharge, marriage or entrustment, as the case may be, and, if the inmate to be given in marriage is a minor, unless the Board or officer, as the case may be, has, after recording the reasons in writing, given its or his approval thereto.

Urvashi was hardly in a position to give formal consent in her 'discharge or entrustment' with the decision already made for her. The director of the ashram, while promoting the idea that the acceptance of the adopter's offer would change Urvashi's life dramatically and for the better, was more keen to impress on her that once she left the ashram there was no possibility of return under any circumstances. With hindsight, Urvashi believed that the warning was repeated so often that she should have realised '*ki daal mein kucch kala hai*' (that something is amiss). All her retrospection of the events of that day when she was cajoled into deciding to go with the man are of little use now.

9

Lakshmi:
'Long Live the Revolution!'

◫

They do not come to us to talk. If there is a group here that does form a category apart from others, it is the 'Naxalites', and while they are proud to be called revolutionaries, they do have a problem with the 'label' of Naxalite that those 'others' have given them and that betrays, according to them, both an ignorance of text and context. They believe in what they do and also believe that we have no clue about their beliefs. They are probably right and we are kept at a distance because it is assumed that there is no way that any amount of conversation with us, or anybody else would get them nearer the appreciation they think they deserve.

We waited in vain for weeks for at least one Naxalite to visit us: 'They have an attitude problem,' my colleague tells me. 'They think they are notches above the average prisoners here and don't even want to mingle with the rest of them, who they believe have come for such mundane and ordinary offences that there is no common ground nor any reason for them to interact. In short, they are quite arrogant and very condescending towards everyone, including us.'

So much for those who believe in a homogenous category called 'prisoner'. Even a superficial examination of the prison reveals there is no such thing. A more detailed study shows not just individual differences; there are categories within categories that can be classified according to offence, background (family, community and others), age, region, religion, language, personality, problems, and other characteristics (such as beliefs and ideologies) that can't really be dismissed if there is to be a serious attempt at understandings, change or transformation. To look for a 'headlines approach' in the prison is to taint one's findings for expediency, that is, to construct theories and paradigms around superficial findings and believe these can be the basis for change.

Painstaking efforts to study prisoners in depth are depressing and disheartening because they would challenge much that has passed for reality. The constant temptation is to dismiss differences and nuances and carry on with a 'common problems, common solutions' approach, which we know is more convenient than it is convincing. Our findings throw the age-old accepted truths and realities back in our faces over and over again as the reality reveals two and sometimes contradictory pointers: first, that the 'uniformity' approach that slurs over differences would be faulty and dishonest, and second, that even the neutral 'same for all' criminal justice machinery handling offenders and dispensing justice through uniform standardised procedures and processes, *does* accommodate difference (often legitimately) and diversity (often arbitrarily) and cannot really boast of 'equality' for all in each of its processes.

Here, we are faced with a category of prisoners that is going to put us to the test in more ways than one. This promises to be a challenge, one we may not be ready for. Figures of women prisoners at any one point of time are not high, and Naxal prisoners are just a handful, moving in clusters, sticking to and by each other and anxious to present a united front. Their prime assertion at the start of any exchange of views with them is that no one really knows what they are about. 'You people are all ignorant about our goals and aims and to start to tell you the ABC about ourselves is pointless: your minds are made up and we are not about to unmake them.'

'Maybe they are right, Vasudha,' I say to my young colleague. 'Maybe we are so stuck in our ways and so self-righteous in our thinking that we haven't bothered to delve into their perceptions and sensitivities at all. The media maligns them because of the havoc that the extremists among them create and they, in turn, malign everyone else. Whether we agree with them or not, they do have a potent ideology, so if we really want to understand what makes them tick and how they view themselves and the offences they are here for, we would have to put aside our intolerance and get going.'

'We shall begin tomorrow,' Vasudha says somewhat reluctantly. Perhaps, she needs time to think and also do a little homework on the subject to address the accusation about our ignorance. She sounds diffident.

'Don't be scared to face them,' I reassure her, 'they have a lot of fervour and zeal, and just as you have reservations about them, they too are entitled to their reservations about you. And really we shouldn't be going on this way — this 'them and us' posture. Let's work out a way to start a dialogue with them.'

We meet the next day and talk about the 'Naxalite' prisoners. Vasudha says she hasn't really managed to get too much information about them and their cause, even though she reads about their 'terrorist' activities all the time in the newspapers. 'But you know enough about them, ma'am, to get us going. After all, their activities go back to your student days.'

'They sure do,' I thought.

'First of all, why do we call them 'Naxalites'? I understand that this word has origins in West Bengal, but we are now in Andhra Pradesh.'

'Yes, good question, and you need to know the answer so that they don't trip you on facts. Extremist groups everywhere, including here in Andhra Pradesh, have this generic label 'Naxalites' given by others; however, they specifically refer to themselves as the People's War Group. Their revolutionary ideology is common to the strand of extremism that developed in the 1960s in West Bengal. A section of the Communist Party of India (Marxist) led by two leaders, Charu Majumdar and Kanu Sanyal, dissociated from the CPI by developing a revolutionary group that was not satisfied just with the rhetoric of communism. They led a violent uprising in Naxalbari village in Siliguri district in the northern part of West Bengal. They didn't call themselves 'Naxalites' — it was a term that was used by their opponents and was intended as a derogatory description of their work. They created enough terror around to terrify everyone, most of all, the government.'

'What was the uprising about?' Vasudha notes the facts as we talk, keen to be well-informed before she approaches the people she regards as formidable opponents.

'A tribal peasant was attacked in Naxalbari village because he had been granted land by the courts under the tenancy laws. The landlords' hired hands attacked and killed the peasant. The local peasants (mostly tribals) were encouraged to retaliate by attacking local landlords and that was the beginning of their posture of not taking the exploitation of peasants and landless labourers lying down.

'They claim to represent the most oppressed people of India — those who are left untouched by India's developmental plans and often bypassed by the genuine electoral process, even though they are wooed for their votes and forcibly told to vote one way or the other by political leaders and their cronies. Invariably, they are adivasis, dalits and poor landless labourers whose earnings are more often than not below the mandated minimum wages. Ideologically, they deplore where India is going in terms of development — according to them, India may well have obtained 'freedom' from colonial rulers, but it still has to acquire real freedom, the real freedom from hunger and deprivation. The rich classes — landlords, industrialists and traders — they say, control the means of production and they call the tune about which way the production process should go. Profits are shared between the magnates and their political partners. Their final aim is to overthrow the present system, so they target politicians, police officers, forest contractors, etc. The ideology is spread through a belt that is often referred to as 'the red corridor', from Nepal through West Bengal, Bihar, Jharkhand, Chhattisgarh, Madhya Pradesh, eastern Maharashtra, western Orissa, western areas of Andhra Pradesh and parts of Tamil Nadu. They operate actively in inland areas, at a distance from the coastline, and forest regions are their sanctuary. I am told that of India's 602 districts, at least about 170 have Naxalite activity in some form or another.'

Vasudha is already overwhelmed with the information, but is still a bit perplexed. She asks, 'So do they believe there can be no common ground to talk and work things out non-violently with the owner classes?'

'It's about a fight against vested interests, Vasudha. When did groups with vested interests ever give up their interests without being subjected to struggle?'

'Mahatma Gandhi achieved it,' Vasudha says promptly.

'Achieved what, Vasudha?' I ask. 'Freedom from colonial rule. But his other dreams of unity, alleviation of poverty, untouchables living with dignity — many believe those remained unfulfilled dreams. Some also believe that these could never have been achieved even if Gandhi had lived longer because those who have vested interests in continuing the status quo would never give up those interests — unless compelled to do so. That is what revolutionary groups have always believed. That is what the People's War Group believes.'

'So, are they right?'

'Who is to judge them, Vasudha? Neither you, nor I, nor any of us around this table can say we are free from vested interests. That is what holds back change, doesn't it? When we complain about no change in the running of prisons, it's not all about resources as the official machinery tells us: it's also about vested interests that don't *want* change, or they want the kind of change that would suit them. Change challenges the way things have been going on for a long time, and those who have become comfortable with the old ways are afraid that if the boat is rocked there would be a shake-up and all their set routines and patterns of working would be upset and their inertia and indolence would be exposed. Don't you think so?'

'I don't know, ma'am,' Vasudha ponders. 'There are many things that can change here in this very prison, without a lot of money being pumped in, and yes, there is resistance to even minor changes. I am trying to focus on the big picture that affects the lot of people at levels we don't often think about. After all, we are the first ones to say that more than half the women who land up here are victims of age-old practices revolving around issues like poverty, ignorance, lack of education and general patriarchal ways of functioning. And these features of many people's lives just don't alter, no matter how hard one tries.'

Kiran adds, 'And the funny thing is the women in here seem to accept the old ways even as they are hurt and damaged by them. That is what surprises me. Why don't they stand up and protest in their communities and in here? When we tell them they should not be so submissive and yielding, they simply mock us and tell us we don't know how it works for them.'

'They are right, Kiran, these patterns have been around for so long that they have acquired a sanctity of structure that is not easy to dismantle. Sometimes, it appears that almost the entire structure would have to come down; the whole would have to be deconstructed to reconstruct afresh. This is easier to suggest in words, but more difficult to implement in actions: that is why we all trundle along with the old and do a little tinkering here and there and call it 'change'. Regimes have been overthrown and revolutions initiated to address these problems of entrenchment, but frankly, unless some security accompanies the changes and alternatives we recommend in our rhetoric, it would be difficult to suggest to unempowered people that they should just throw away the old and adopt a new modus operandi which will give something better. Does that make sense? Or is this sounding like a lecture in political science?' I see heads nodding, but I know I have rambled on too long.

Vasudha gets up from her chair, ready to go. 'Let's give this a try, Kiran. We should begin with that group in Cell 4 — Lakshmi and her mates. They will never come here, so we should go and talk to them casually and try to befriend them if we can, to try and understand why they believe they are so different from the rest of the women here.'

Off they go, armed with pen and paper and a self-assurance and poise about to be tested in the next few hours. I wish them luck, quite conscious of having thrown them into the deep end, and resume tidying up the notes from the previous day's interviews.

And they are back in about an hour.

'What happened?' I ask with apprehension. 'I thought they would engage you for hours.'

'Oh no, ma'am. They weren't keen to talk at all.'

'Oh! You mean you got nowhere? Did they just give you a hard time and baffle you so that you were out of your depth?'

'Well, no,' Vasudha says. 'They weren't quite as offensive as we expected. They just kept asking us questions. They wanted to know about you, and about each of us and why on earth we were so keen to work among prisoners, of all the people. "What," they asked, "do you hope to achieve in this place which no one anywhere is interested in?" And when we said that everyone here was a human being like the rest of us and needed the things that we think are all human beings' basic rights, they laughed. "You don't really think this lot will pay the slightest attention to what you will recommend, do you?" Lakshmi asked us. "Well, we can only hope," I said. "Well, keep hoping," she replied, "We too, are hoping for the things we believe in, but you don't want to know about that, do you?" "Oh, but I do,' I said, 'and that is why even though you didn't respond to our request to come to see us, we have come to you."

Vasudha has acquitted herself well. For a young slip of a girl, she is doing fine, I think. 'But why did you come back so soon?' I inquire.

'Oh, that's because it was lunch time and they told the warder they didn't like the food, so they would not come to lunch and that started an argument between them and the warder. I had to back off and said I would come again the next day and they said, "Sure, and see if you can do something about the rotten vegetables they serve here. They buy them cheap in the market as B-grade stuff and then cook them up for us to eat. Yesterday, we went to the yard outside the kitchen and saw the vegetables: they were rotten and actually had *keeras* (worms) in them." That's when I left.'

This is not the first time one has encountered complaints relating to rotting food in prisons. Relatively, this particular prison in Hyderabad has a better standard than other States. Having seen the storeroom where the vegetables are kept when they arrive from the wholesale market, it comes as no surprise that they are rotting and have worms in them. At a 'Training for Trainers' residential workshop organised through the Prisons Department in Lucknow, I myself was served such food even though we (along with the British Council) were funding the project generously. Corruption is rampant and somehow morally justified because prisoners are regarded as sub-human anyway. If they complain they get snide comments that they are criminals, not state guests, as if that has any bearing on the minimum standards that are the right of any human being that the state puts in its care and custody.

'Lakshmi is clearly the leader of the pack and very articulate,' Kiran adds. 'She chooses her words with care and tries not to be too sharp, but does say it like it is. The other prisoners would never dare complain about living standards. But then she is steeped in the language of rights and is a good spokesperson for them all.'

'Maybe you should come with us tomorrow, ma'am,' Vasudha says.

'Oh no, Vasudha. I think you two can handle this quite well. I'll come once they have opened up to you. You are their age and they will try to convince you about their beliefs — you might respond with more naturalness than I might. We'll take it from there. Let's see how this takes shape.'

Vasudha and Kiran are excited about the next day's interviews. While I am happy for them to take on the challenge, they are nervous, hoping there will not be any fireworks. As I brief them with a few do's and don'ts, I also emphasis the need to go without the prejudices that we are all fed on about revolutionaries and their methods and techniques. 'Don't give them the impression that you deplore and denounce all that they do. They have enough by way of censure each day of their lives: from the system, from the media, from everyone. You want to understand them before you set out to condemn them — if that is what you do at the end of the encounter. They will be hostile when you ask some rough questions because they face plenty of antagonism from those outside their ilk. They are most comfortable amongst their own, and like a few other groups here, they tend to stick to each other. So, go for it and I'm sure you will come back with interesting perceptions.'

While they are away, I am visited by a young prisoner Jayalalitha, who wants me to see an elderly woman in one of the barracks for convicted women. I ask if something untoward had happened and she replies, 'No, but I think you should know about this prisoner even though your colleagues have talked with her and got her history and details in their books.'

Muthamma is almost 70 years old and is in a bad shape — she is old and frail, but that is not the worst of her problems. She is referred to as neurotic and has been put in Jayalalitha's care because she is the only person Muthamma is willing to take help from. She has Obsessive Compulsive Disorder (OCD) and will not let anyone touch her, or her belongings, including the food that is served to her. If someone so much as touches her *thali* of food, she refuses to eat. She misses many a meal as a result and grows weaker as the days pass. Jayalalitha helps her dress and bathe, and oils and combs her hair everyday. As I approach Muthamma, Jayalalitha warns me not to touch her. 'I know you want to comfort her, ma'am, but if you touch her to reassure her she will want to go and have a bath immediately. Sometimes, she comes out of the bath and after a few minutes wants me to take her for a bath again. Even when I try to tell her she has just had one, she insists and we go through the bath routine again. Talk to her, but more importantly, please see if there is a way to get her out of here so that she is treated and attended to both medically and emotionally.'

I sit on the floor near Muthamma — but not too close lest I make her uncomfortable. 'Why haven't you eaten your food, Muthamma?' I ask. No answer. 'Is the food not good? Would you like something else? Milk maybe?' No answer. She is busy folding some clothes and stacking them up as neatly as she can. Jayalalitha does not interfere but seems to be permitted a closer proximity than I am.

'I know her case: she has been here so long and clearly needs special care,' I tell Jayalalitha. 'She keeps talking about her son coming to get her: why has he not come? We could put in a letter to the authorities here for a speedy release: after all, she is over 70 and helpless and there is a provision for ill and elderly people to get an early release if circumstances require it.'

'She believes her son is going to come, but he isn't,' says Jayalalitha. 'She is here as a part of a large family group that was arrested in a dowry death and has been languishing for years. There is no one who is going to come for her, I'm afraid. The 'dowry death' law is all very well to supposedly eliminate a social ill in our society, but it is wreaking havoc as entire families are adversely affected simply because they are all members of one large household. And you know, ma'am, that the law is misused by many families as a sure way to get out of marriages that go sour on other fronts.'

Muthamma in the meantime refolds the clothes already folded and keeps touching things twice almost as part of a ritual. She adjusts and readjusts her *saree pallu* over her head, again and again, till it almost exhausts the onlooker. Her food lies untouched.

Suddenly, she looks up and tells Jayalalitha to take away the *thali*. I extend my hand to remove her *thali* and am immediately told not to by Jayalalitha.

'She will make a scene if you touch that, ma'am.' I back off.

Muthamma is another mentally ill person who became what she is during her prison stint. No one here has really analysed her symptoms as OCD — she has just been labelled 'queer', 'weird', 'senile', or plain *'pagal'*. She should be out of here — but where should she be sent? There is no 'recognised' place where forgotten women prisoners can be sent when families do not 'claim' them.

Two National Commissions in the country have been in existence for more than 15 years to address and intervene should there be human rights violations anywhere and particularly, in state institutions. The National Human Rights Commission is busy with thousands of cases of denials of human rights, makes recommendations and gives restorative and remedial orders almost every day. The National Commission for Women, specifically designed to address all kinds of problems relating to abused and deprived women all over the country promised to be that much needed organisation that could have commanded the respect of women's groups and human rights protagonists everywhere. High-profile persons are in charge of both these organisations. The initial years following their creation saw the human rights agenda placed high on the country's socio-political map, but over the years, the zest and vigour faded with successive incumbents making the organisations their strongholds and platforms for prominence. This is particularly applicable to the National Commission for Women where appointments are political and the appointees too territorial to take advice from experts outside who may know better. The 'headlines' approach to human rights has not helped the invisible and while some of the so-called do-gooders go about fire fighting when they see dramatic violations of human rights, the not so dramatic situations and occurrences go unnoticed. The minutiae of the problems associated with arrests, detention, custody and the release of women and particularly of *prisoners with special needs* got lost somewhere along the way.

Muthamma (here in Andhra Pradesh) and Vimla (in Rajasthan), and others are certainly part of that 'special' group that gets lost easily and conveniently. Their problems baffle most of us, and clearly, scratching our heads for answers is not enough. 'We will write a letter to the prison department,' I say to Jayalalitha and leave in desperation.

Vasudha and Kiran have returned to our counselling room and are discussing their meeting agitatedly. That's a good sign, I feel. I am all ears even though preoccupied with Muthamma's problem. I realise how excited these two are and really need to focus.

'If you hadn't coached us a little about the Naxalites, ma'am', Kiran bursts out, 'we would have made fools of ourselves. These girls are really something. So fearless and bold, it makes one shiver. They have such strong beliefs, they can turn our whole worldview upside down. What can one say? While we still condemn their worldview, I'm afraid one has to say they are gutsy.'

'They were all waiting for us and were seated on the floor in a circle. As we entered their room they asked us to sit and said immediately, "So, what would you like to know about us?" We said, "First we want to know about you as persons and your background and families and then we can move on to your work and activities, if that's all right with you."

Vasudha focused on Lakshmi first. She had asked Lakshmi, 'Where were you born and what was your family background? Apart from factual details we would, of course, also like to know some subjective details like how happy you were as a child and how harmonious was your family life. I hope you won't mind telling us that.'

'Have you seen the film *Mother India*, Vasudha?' Lakshmi had asked. 'It was made well before any of us was born, including you. I am sure you have, but perhaps if you were to revisit that film you would see it with a different vision. I relate quite intimately to some features of that film. I lived in a village almost like the one depicted in the film. My father owned some land and he laboriously cultivated it each day from morning till night and fed and clothed us and we even went to the village school to become literate. My mother helped in the field off and on, particularly when it was harvest time, and when the crops were good there was joy in our family. Yes, I think I was a happy child. I had two younger brothers and as they grew older they, too, pitched in to work the fields.'

'Those who live by labouring on the land have a different attitude to earth and nature: land is everything to them and any severance of that relationship is like a loss of life, not just of livelihood. Earth, trees, water, animals, the sun, the moon, the winds and rain — these are sacred and holy for us, almost divine. People in our part of the world worship all these elements and not the deities at the big elaborately constructed *mandir*s at Tirupathi and Jagannath. Land is not a commodity, it is life and we call it mother earth. It is an altogether different perception, unfathomable for city dwellers.'

'My father's land adjoined the land of one of the big landlords of the village. For a long time the landlord had been telling my father to sell his land (assuring him that he would pay a large sum and also license him as a tenant who could keep half of the produce of the land and give him the other half after each harvest). My father had refused the deal for many years, even as neighbouring peasants had been cajoled into selling their lands. The animosity that followed was very unpleasant for us all and particularly me and my mother, because women are always the weak links in a family that can be harassed in ways that the men of the household cannot.'

'Each day we went to the field, the landlord's goons would pass lewd comments and threaten us with dire consequences if we didn't accept their *maalik*'s offer. On one occasion during harvest, when my mother was helping in one part of the field, one of the landlord's goons abducted her away forcibly. My father lodged a complaint with the *thana* in the village and went from door to door in the village to ask people to protest and enable him to get our mother back, but there was too much fear among the people and no one came forward. They all felt they had too much to lose — land and life. The power play in the village was heavily tilted against anyone who held out. The constables did not register the complaint either and instead advised my father to accept the landlord's proposal relating to his land for the sake of everyone's safety and the peace of the village. They said that might be the only way to get his wife back. But my father was adamant. Two days later, my mother's body was found in the field: she had been raped and brutally murdered. I was 12 years old at the time and my brothers were nine and six. It is not easy for me to forget the sight of my mother's mutilated body lying in the field half-naked and covered with dried up blood. My father covered my eyes when I screamed at the sight — but he couldn't ever cover the mental picture in my mind's eye.'

Vasudha stopped the narrative and looked at us for a reaction. 'I thought Lakshmi, the tough nut we thought she was, was actually going to cry, but she didn't, almost as if she had trained herself not to. She looked devastated but she stayed composed. Imagine the scene — it must have been awful for her. And the worst part of it was that the police did nothing: the landlord's writ ran in the entire region and even the police was afraid of the landlord's henchmen.'

'Lakshmi told us that her father didn't have the strength to fight back on his own. No one investigated the rape or death of his wife and he didn't push hard enough. He compromised and sold the land and accepted the landlord's offer. Nothing was the same again. The children were petrified and the father was no longer the giant figure that Lakshmi always believed him to be. When harvest time would come, he was always under pressure and also swindled out of his half of the crop under one pretext or another. She said she always squirmed at his obsequious responses. She felt as if the whole family was being humiliated everyday. "I think inside me there was something that told me that I should fight back some day," Lakshmi said.'

'I wonder what the village headman and the village elders were doing when all this happened.' Kiran queries. 'After all, they are village people and have titles with responsibilities like *pradhan, mukhia,* and what not. Don't they have any affinity with their brethren?'

'Welcome to the world of power and sycophancy, Kiran,' I say. 'Have you heard that saying "knowing which side one's bread is buttered"? It shouldn't be difficult to understand why and how the alliance between the powerful landlords, the police and the village heads would serve the interests of each. Not to mention the element of force and violence that is used for extraction and reprisal. These are the links of the entrenched that are then sought to be broken by those who decide to take the law into their own hands.'

All this now appears to make sense to Kiran and Vasudha, who have had such reservations about the revolutionary friends. They feel they have been given a reality check and are now keen to understand what really made this category of offenders tick. Not that they have come anywhere near being converted to their ideologies, but they do now want to carry on the discussions that have made them wiser to the world the Naxalites or PWG members come from.

Kiran becomes pensive, 'We all live life so cocooned in our own worlds and simply choose to forget that for some people life is a daily struggle on another plane. It is not just the struggle of poverty. It is the power equations in society and state that are so devastating. I don't think I would want to be like them because I am not sure I approve of the means that are employed to achieve the ends they believe in. And yet I have a hidden admiration for them. I wouldn't have the nerve to go out there and fight for collective rights, even if I believe that groups and communities in our country have got totally missed out on the road to freedom and development.'

I probably look noticeably surprised at their *volte face*, and they feel the necessity of explaining it to me. 'The issues are too complex,' says Vasudha. 'It's one of those chicken-and-egg situations, isn't it? How much power does the state get and how much must the society retain, and for whose benefit all this is done are issues that we discuss in our political science courses at the university. Lakshmi reminded me that these questions retain their importance and can't be decided once and for all at one historical moment. She's quite intelligent, this Lakshmi.'

It appears that Lakshmi hinted that she would come to see us in our counselling room. Vasudha and Kiran aren't sure, but feel that she would come, if not the next day, then certainly in a few days. Now that the ice has been broken, they are almost looking forward to it.

That Saturday Lakshmi comes to visit us with Humra. Lakshmi is tall and dark with long braided hair, and neatly turned out in a cotton saree. She appears alert and confident and has a lively, vivacious look about her. She exudes confidence and her 'no nonsense' attitude is written all over her face. Humra is light-skinned with light eyes and is charming and demure, but a little reticent about how to approach us. They greet us and we ask them to sit down. One of the prisoners has brought some tea for us (the superintendent had asked her to) and we offer it to the visitors, telling them we have just had some. They are clearly appreciative of the gesture and drink the tea.

'Vasudha told me your life story, Lakshmi,' I begin. 'You've had a tough life. But I know that it is not your personal angle that you want highlighted: that is not what the 'People's War' is about, is it? We still wanted to know more about you than the revolutionary fervour that is evident — surely both these features, the personal and public, make you what you are today.'

Lakshmi says, 'You asked me the other day what my agenda was after I leave, ma'am, and I retorted by asking what *your* agenda was. I think I was a bit sharp and didn't quite realise that all of you are part of quite a dedicated group that has made prison work a priority. I have now been seeing all of you function and see where you want to take the institution of the prison although I have reservations about whether you will actually be able to achieve what you intend. There is so much doublespeak here and there is no end to hypocrisy. They tell you one thing and us another. They appear to you like butter wouldn't melt in their mouths and they want to show that their first priority is our welfare: well, the fact is they care two hoots about what happens to prisoners. The little they do is prompted by a fear of getting into trouble if they are found to be careless or harsh. We see them day in and day out and because we are a little bolder than the other prisoners, we point things out that other prisoners would not and they hate us for it. We have a nuisance value here.'

'And what about your value outside, Lakshmi?' I ask. 'How do you view that? Do you think you have a nuisance value there, or do you think you serve a different larger purpose through your activities? I'm sure you know you are dreaded because you resort to violence to achieve your goals, and not for any other reason? It is the fear that surrounds you that gets you the attention that it does. Is that a good idea?'

'This is not really about a simplistic view of good and bad. We do what we believe needs to be done. Why is it assumed that those in top positions of authority and power have the country's interests at heart and those who are simply citizens don't? The big shots don't have a stake in improving the lot of the general mass of people, why should they? It's hard work. I wish we could demonstrate some of the frustrations of the villagers to those who do not live in them. Those who do not have wealth or power are doomed and there is no way that equitable living can ever be brought to places where there are strong vested interests at play. It has never happened in history and it will never happen. Is that good or bad? You tell me. Generations of villagers have been promised a lot of things that just haven't come their way and never will. This is not just about my life. It's not about my mother getting raped and killed and the landlord getting away with it. It is a common tale across the whole country: those who live docile lives and play the tune might manage to eke out a living, some living. Those who do not accept the rules of the game of the powerful: woe betide them, for they will continue to suffer. If there had been a few fiery persons around that day the events happened in my family, maybe they would have let all hell loose on the landlord's goons. But there weren't and see what happened.'

'I share your frustrations, Lakshmi,' I say assuredly, 'but I wonder if you understand that there is this big question about means and ends. Do you believe the end justifies the means? It is a perplexing question that has agitated thinkers for centuries: do you really believe that you have found the answer?'

Lakshmi is already getting red in the face, believing that I am not on her side. I am not about to tell her that I admire her guts for that would make her complacent about explaining the logic of her life to us.

'Surely, you must understand what makes us the tough ones we need to be,' she says promptly. 'We sound brusque and irreverent to people and it is said we have no heart and we are hard-hitting. We are called extremists, terrorists, rebels, fanatics and even seditious anti-national traitors. Is fighting for one's cause when no one else is bothered about it, treacherous? And by one's cause I do not mean a personal, or individual cause: I mean the cause of large sections of deprived people of the country who do not live even half decent lives because certain others have always had it good at their expense.

And yes, it is at their expense because once the powerful are entrenched in their positions they always wish for things to stay that way. Who wants to give up power, ma'am? Not rulers, not the rich, not those holding high positions of authority, not anyone. There must surely be a day when someone gets up and says, "enough is enough"! There is always everywhere a last straw that does break the camel's back and people say, "Oh, but it was only a light straw that we put on the camel," forgetting that there were thousands of straws already on the camel's back and he had reached his limit of load carrying.'

They sound so cogent that we are almost converted to their cause and to the means they deploy, forgetting that we claim to have espoused the cause of democratic institutions through which we believe justice should be sought; and we tell them as much.

'What justice machinery are you talking of, ma'am? The one that looks at the elites and non-elites so differently that one wonders at the concepts of rule of law and equality before the law!'

Humra, who has been sitting silently so far, smiles. She has read my thoughts and says: 'I suppose you think that is quite a mouthful for a young girl of 25. But some of us have been educated as much if not more than the staff that pushes us around here, or the police constables that bully us at police stations and deal with us so rudely when they get the slightest opportunity. Yes, ma'am, we are not the scum that we are made out to be, believe me.'

'Did you have bad experiences at police stations?' I ask, feeling stupid almost as soon as I have spoken. Police station experiences seem to be directly related to the kinds of offences that women (*especially women*) have committed. For sex-related and drug-related offences, police attitudes are predictable. They vary from taunts and snide comments to actual sexual abuse in police lock ups. In terror-related acts, the offender presents them with a confidence that they find cocky: that is met with harsh words and sometimes an unsavoury physical handling that would be uncalled for according to the rule book.

'We didn't keep our mouths shut when taunted by the constables, so we got our fair share of manhandling. It's all so closed and opaque, they are aware that no one will ever know the details. Your colleagues told us that they had worked at the police stations to assess how things happen there, but they will never know. They would have to be invisible to get to the truth. The innuendos, the crude, abusive language the constant reminder about what will happen if someone steps out of line: "*tum aurat ho, zyada boli to ham tumhe kya kya kar sakte hain maloom hai?*[you are a woman, if you talk too much do you know what we can do to you?]." One would think they don't have mothers and daughters in their homes. And let me tell you, ma'am, the women at these stations have also learnt to abuse in the most 'chaste' abusive language you can think of. It is sickening because they are the people in charge of good behaviour. You would never know these things because you are not likely to be a *victim* at a police station.'

She is right: the chances of me being arrested and detained and then locked up are slim. That is a reality in societies like ours where class and caste, privilege and position ensure that some will never experience what many others do. I can't pretend that that is not so. These girls have made us revisit so many of our established beliefs that sometimes we are speechless, even when we do give rejoinders.

I feel compelled to reply anyway. 'Yes, Humra, you are right. I don't think I would be faced with your experiences. I am privileged and sometimes almost ashamed of that. My life is comfortable and I can't say I wish it otherwise. I am sorry that there is no chance that people would have the patience to hear you out. They would just dislike your type if there were a type. But speaking for myself, I am willing to accept that there are two sides to this very long story. I was your age when the Naxalite movement was at its peak. And I lived in West Bengal for some time when the countryside was shaking and quivering with a lot of violence and the government was exasperated by, and desperate about the turn of events. I was definitely influenced by the happenings and am a product of those tumultuous times, and as the phrase goes, 'some of my best friends' were revolutionaries, and believed in the movement. But none of this resolves the dilemma that many of us face about exploitation and how it should be handled.'

They are so passionate about all their convictions that it is difficult not to give some credit for their beliefs. But the reality is that innocents that are caught in the crossfire also get killed and ruined. I didn't expect my acknowledgments and admissions to have any dramatic effect on them, but they were a little less dismissive of my colleagues from that day on. They actually greeted them when they passed by and said they would come again to talk. That was a change.

And they did come again.

'We have a court hearing tomorrow, so let's see what happens. Perhaps we will get bail, perhaps not. It depends on the judge and the way things are presented to him, and his predisposition. Most of them are so stuck in their ways and have no time for people who "disturb the peace". One often feels like asking them, "whose peace are you talking about?"'

'So, at least you get to appear before a court. In 1970, when there was President's rule in the state of West Bengal, the centre appointed a governor who had leftist leanings and was an exjudge. The logic was that his leanings might bring some dialogue with the leftist revolutionaries. Meanwhile, the state machinery kept arresting troublemakers; they were simply locked up and detained without hearings. The requirment of producing them before the courts was dispensed with and jails were full of Naxalites and others who were their associates and friends. Appointing a judge as governor didn't work out for the government — they had probably forgotten that a judge needed to uphold the due process of the law and appearing in court (*habeas corpus*) was an essential part of that process. The governor packed his bags and made room for a more compliant functionary who then went on to become Chief Minister of West Bengal. Unlike today, there were governors in those times who refused to be puppets and would not do the bidding of the centre, regarding the upholding of the Constitution as their primary function. So, you see, there are people who stand up for their beliefs even if they are not out there fighting on the streets.'

Lakshmi, who has been listening very carefully to this long narrative, thinks that matters have worsened since then. 'No change of heart on either side,' she says, 'and, of course, there was violence on both sides. But our violence is black-marked far more and we draw more flak because the other side is the state machinery and they have a right to kill!'

We could go on forever with the polemic on both sides. 'There is one thing though that does perturb me endlessly,' I say quietly. 'Your quarrel is with the haves who prosper at the expense of the have-nots, and your fight is with the state machinery that combats you when you transgress and violate rules and laws. You use violent means because you say that the former (with vested interests) will never give up anything without being forced to and that the latter (the state establishment) is out to get you on the slightest pretext and they use violence to put you down. But tell me, why do you kill tribal people and peasants simply because they find themselves unable to support you because they fear reprisal from the government machinery? If you are championing their cause, how can they be made to pay the heavy price they do if they don't actively support you?'

'No, that is not true at all, ma'am. We are not out to kill people indiscriminately. Some of the peasants are so cowardly they turn into "informers" and we have set up Jan Adalats to determine whether they betrayed our cause by turning against us and snitching on us. The state punishes those who turn traitors, doesn't it? Why are there separate standards for them and us?' Lakshmi gets hot and bothered when the very premise of her cause is being interrogated. I can see I would eventually have to back off because it is really not my intention that she should go back to her cell ruffled and agitated.

'How and why were you arrested and brought here? Was there a raid somewhere in which you were hauled up? I am assuming that since there are quite a few of you here, you form part of a specific group.'

'Did you hear of the incident when there was an anti-PWG raid in some of our village strongholds when a government official had been kidnapped by the PWG because he was passing orders against the farmers' interests? The "raiders" didn't just arrest and beat people from the village, they also raped several women and burnt the houses of several villagers. No one did anything about it even when the errant police constables had been identified. There was a counter attack on some policemen by the PWG. A few (policemen) were beaten; one of them lay dying in a hospital.

There was outrage in the State. Another raid was carried out, not just in that village but in adjoining villages as well. We are from that adjoining village, and we protested violently against the incident. So, here we are.'

Vasudha, Kiran and I are silent for a long time. This is not easy to understand. The predicaments and experiences of prisoners that we have encountered here in the prison are something we are unlikely to experience directly, ever, but this occurrence is something else. There is no regret, no qualms or compunctions and no signs of going back. The road has been taken and it will be traversed till the end, consciously and purposefully. It is evident that we are on different sides of the divide, and there will be no crossing over. And yet these are such smart, sharp girls with such strong beliefs that it is difficult to take the superior road and tell them they are wide off the mark and will only suffer at the end of it all. Their logic is so irresistible, their courage almost laudable and yet one holds back from saying something positive to them. It is a dilemma: how does one laud a courage in which the lines get blurred and there is no difference between the innocent and guilty? There is violence and killing in what they promote. But there is violence and killing in what the state does too, and yet, we back the state each day of our lives.

'Suppose, you get killed one of these days: won't that be regrettable for your near and dear ones?'

'Oh, ma'am, you are so off the mark even after showing us so much patience and understanding in hearing us out. Do you really think we are afraid of death? As for our near and dear: we have no near and dear. And why should near and dear stop at the family frontier? Do all the gains and benefits have to be for one's family only? I think we have to have pride in wider causes. What pride can one have in our country, of which we are an intrinsic part? There is constantly a boast about progress in the country — but whose progress? Those who are already better placed and have the opportunities to avail themselves of the benefits? I know that your blood also boils at the inequitable nature of our society, and the dishonesty and duplicity around us. But you probably tell yourself, "I can't match the power of the decision-makers, and who is listening to my protest anyway?"

Well, we decided that in the first instance voices need to be raised, and when that fails, then arms need to be raised.'

Soon we realise that this discussion isn't going anywhere, on both sides of the fence. Perhaps, the mistakes lie on both sides. If we think they are self-righteous, they probably think the same about us. We aren't getting very far with the resolution of the dilemma. So, we drop that discussion, knowing all the while that this is not just about handling a law and order problem — it is much more and goes deeper than those in charge of the state machinery would like to believe.

I decide to change the subject.

'What do you think about locking up people to punish them for offences they have committed? Does it help them or us?'

'I can't pretend to be knowledgeable about our penal system. But as far as any benefit is concerned, I don't think much benefit comes out of locking up indiscriminately. Some of the women are not likely to offend again. Some have done it in circumstances that were harsh and merciless. But then there are questions that go deeper than any superficial answer I might give. What do you think?'

I try to explain, 'Punishment is based on many theories. They relate to the offender *and* to the society that is the victim of the offences. For instance, in the case of offences that bring terror into the society, the premise of punishment is to protect society from the threat of perils that would result if certain offenders are at large. I believe that your offences fall into that category. Others are not a threat to society, but they still need to know that offences cannot go unpunished. All the women locked up here are not a threat to society, but members of your group are considered a threat. What do you have to say about that?'

This is becoming like a repartee. Lakshmi is bracing herself for an answer. Humra chimes in, 'So, does that mean that those questions, circumstances and issues that *lead* to the crimes that people commit will never get addressed? Poverty will never be addressed as a top priority; corruption will not be the main concern, women will never get the dignity they are constantly deprived of — is that what it will amount to? Law and order is at the top of the list, like a fire-fighting exercise. People will be deprived of land, of their livelihood, or their *izzat* (respect) and we will be told "We shall look into it!" And what does that looking into achieve? Nothing. It is not important because it only happens to the "scum" of our society. No, that doesn't sound right, ma'am. Not right at all.'

She has a point and I can only point to the law, the rules of the game, the state and its promises of justice, which is always too little, too late. I am speechless and not ashamed to admit it.

'I am going to repeat the question I put to you, Lakshmi, when I first met you. Now what is your agenda? Is anything going to make a difference in tactics, or are you trapped in the ideology of the group? Is there no chance of reviewing the strategy at all?'

'No,' she says, 'There is no point. The more the state bullies, and the haves suppress and oppress the poor, the more sharp we need to be. Weakness is not a virtue, nor is excessive patience.'

The next morning, they return from the court, relieved to have got bail, despite their bravado that being in prison doesn't bother them because they have seen worse.

They pack their things and come to say goodbye. 'We have never had a chance to be heard so patiently inside a state institution and we appreciate your patient listening,' Humra says. As Lakshmi turns to go, she says, 'I am curious about one thing, ma'am. How do you know so much about the governor who refused to go along with the state's policy of indiscriminate detention without *habeas corpus*? Were you part of a revolutionary group too?'

'Not really,' I say. 'He was my father.'

Note

Lakshmi proudly called herself a revolutionary. In the prison she was called a Naxalvadi prisoner. In Andhra Pradesh, the revolutionary group to which she belongs is called the People's War Group, even as everyone else continues to call them Naxalites and looks at them curiously but less judgementally than they do sex workers.

The Naxals are a Maoist communist group who were declared a proscribed terrorist organisation under the Unlawful ActivitiesPrevention Act, 1967. The powers of arrest, detention and punishment under this Act have taken several twists and turns since then that have a potential for misuse in a fear-laden, panic-stricken environment, leading to perversions in the course of justice that threaten long-term (ill) effects.

The word 'Naxalite' comes from the village Naxalbari in Siliguri district in West Bengal where the movement for the fight for the rights of peasants and tillers of the land originated. In 1967 there was a split in the Communist Party of India (Marxist), and first the All India Coordination Committee of Communist revolutionaries (AICCCR), and then in 1969, the CPI (Marxist–Leninist) were formed. From West Bengal, the movement spread to parts of Bihar (particularly areas now in Jharkhand), Madhya Pradesh (Chhattisgarh), Orissa and Andhra Pradesh.

Radicals such as Charu Majumdar and Kanu Sanyal, inspired by the doctrines of Chairman Mao, provided ideological leadership for the Naxalbari movement in the 1960s, advocating a forced overthrow of government and upper classes by Indian peasants and lower class tribals. Urban intellectuals with leftist leanings supported the Naxal movement elaborated through Majumdar's 'Eight Documents' that was for a long time the basis of Naxalite ideology. Practically, all Naxalite groups trace their origin to the CPI (ML). There was a Dakshin Desh Group from which the Maoist Communist Centre sprang up, and which merged with the People's War Group to form the CPI (Maoist). Another offshoot was that of the Andhra revolutionary communists, mainly represented by the Unity Centre of Communist Revolutionaries of India (ML) created in 1975 when they broke ties with the AICCCR (CPI [M]). T. Nagi Reddy was the guiding force of this group.

Charu Majumdar's strong presence 40 years ago with an intellectual base in Calcutta (Presidency College) gave a particular flavour to the movement, attracting students and educated elites. Inciting peasants and tribals to rebel against rich landlords, the movement gave the government a hard time. The centre tried different ways to tackle the problem. The governor they sent in 1969 had leftist leanings and the centre thought the problem would be 'handled' hopefully with cooperation and dialogue when the state of West Bengal was placed under President's rule. The strategy did not work as the governor's judicial conscience did not permit his turning a blind eye to the indiscriminate arrests and detention being carried out by the state police and the gross violation of the writ of *habeous corpus*. He did not accept the unregulated (in his view, illegal) suppression of the Naxal movement and the centre brought in a new functionary to do what they wanted. They created a new charge for one of its union ministers, Siddharth Shankar Ray — the charge of minister for West Bengal. So, while the governor packed his bags and left, over the next couple of years after a shoddily conducted state election, Siddharth

Shankar Ray as Chief Minister was able to do the political bidding of the centre. He gave a free hand to the administration and the police to deal as they deemed fit with the Naxalite movement. Extremists were regarded as dangerous criminals and records of the period reveal the use of excessively cruel methods used by the police in dealing with all political opponents and those who threatened peace. Deaths in police custody and fake encounters resulting in a systematic killing of rebels and radicals were a part of the programme of the Congress government of the time and as the new Chief Minister, Ray was able to turn a blind eye to these acts which were no less violent than those supposedly committed by the extremist groups.

Heavy counter-measures were taken against Naxalites and their supporters with little regard for the niceties of the law: the argument being that there was no reason to be civil with the uncivil. Splinter groups were encouraged to question Majumdar's leadership and in 1972 he was arrested, and died in Alipur Jail shortly thereafter. Gross human rights violations by the West Bengal police were alleged by Naxal supporters who were told by the political leadership that the state was effectively fighting a civil war and democratic pleasantries had no place in a war, especially when the opponent was fighting undemocratically. The seeds of heavy-handedness on the part of the police were taking deep roots.

In Andhra Pradesh, the PWG as the most important Naxal outfit (there are five or six others) accelerated the people's war from the 1980s, particularly in the northwestern parts of the state and dispensed 'justice' in 'people's courts' where police informers, and all those deemed oppressors and class enemies, including village leaders are condemned to death if they have collluded with the state system. Casualty figures for both sides, which include hundreds of policemen and suspected Naxalites, vary according to the source. Decades of guerrilla-style conflict have led to serious human rights abuses on both sides. Human rights groups allege that 'encounters' between police and the PWG resulting in the deaths of hundreds of Naxalites are usually faked by the police to cover up the torture and subsequent murders of Naxalite suspects, sympathisers, or informers. The evidence of these fake encounters is the refusal of police to hand over corpses of suspects killed in so-called 'encounters', which are often cremated before families can view the bodies. Andhra police have contributed to the establishment of an armed vigilante group known as the Green Tigers, whose mission is to combat Naxalite groups in the state. The National Human Rights Commission (NHRC) is investigating some 285 reported cases of so-called 'fake encounter deaths' allegedly committed by the Andhra police in connection with anti-Naxalite operations.

Alternating between extreme violence and unconditional talks, the interaction between PWG leaders and the State's representatives has been mercurial and inconclusive at the best of times. The fact that civilians form a part of the heavy casualties on both sides has an effect on public perceptions, and attitudes towards the PWG as well as the police force are unsympathetic and sometimes even indifferent. In 2005 (only months after a period of cease-fire to allow for talks), of the 700 killed in the violence a third were civilians. The AP State machinery believes it has a good and effective record in tackling Naxalites and that their methods have been successful generally.

Other States often believe that the AP model of handling the Naxal problem needs to be replicated. Sometimes articulate Naxals candidly suggest that that would only be possible if some confidence is built up among the tribal and landless peasant groups, a fact that is awkward for the state actively involved in development projects at the expense of the tribal and backward population. Moderates believe that without taking the tribals into confidence to assist in the collection of intelligence among other things, indiscriminate launching of offensives is counter-productive. Tribals are the only people who can help security personnel navigate the terrain and also differentiate between Naxalites and ordinary tribal folk so that errors of casualties are avoided. Unfortunately, the guiding spirit of the government is still the launching of massive security offensives to establish order *before* making any moves to address the plight of tribals and peasants relating to land and livelihood. For the state, Naxalism itself is the problem, and not those issues that are highlighted by the Naxals as problems.

Enactments that seek to change procedures for trying those accused of 'terrorism' by extending periods of police custody and detention without charges, denying bail to foreigners and reversing the burden of proof have multiplied even after earlier legislations (TADA, 2002 and POTA, 2004) were abrogated. The National Investigative Agency Bill and Unlawful Activities (Prevention) Amendment Act (NIAUA), 2009, is one such recent enactment. The Agency is empowered to deal with terror-related crimes across States without permission from the States. It has concurrent jurisdiction that empowers the Centre to probe terror attacks in any part of the country. Two amendments of the Unlawful Activities (Prevention) Act, 1967, came about in 2004 and 2008 that enhanced police powers of seizures, and made interceptions admissible as evidence, including increasing detention periods from 30 days to 90 days. In the NIAUA Amendment Act, the detention period could be 180 days, if required.

The state's single-minded pursuit of all revolutionary groups and other activists supposedly responsible for disruptive activities and therefore, considered traitors to the sovereignty of the nation, assumes significance for our purposes because of the accelerating proliferation of draconian legislations that seek to circumvent the established legal processes of the 'rule of law' principle. The aim of ensuring a quicker disposal of all cases of suspected terrorism also enables the police force to set in motion the use of excessively strong measures as a first option for routine law and order problems. Giving the police more and more powers for tackling what may well be one of the most universally dreaded threats of the century also opens the floodgates to a wide and indiscriminate use and gross misuse of such powers by those not fully equipped to exercise restraint when it may be needed. Nuanced differences between offenders are slurred over and demonstrators, protestors, radicals and revolutionaries and hard-core terrorists are all painted with the same brush.

There are terrorists and there are revolutionaries and radicals. Definitions and classifications may seem unimportant when issues of security are at stake. But every rebel is not a traitor just as every offender is not a hardened criminal. There is a saying that when one gets used to loud sounds one cannot hear the soft tones any more. In all the (justified) commotion relating to terror, it would be an error to smell a rat everywhere. By all accounts, Lakshmi is a firebrand but revolutionary fervour is a far cry from hard-core terror and not realising the difference can threaten to dent the 'civilised' image of our democracy. Lakshmi is only one of the many who protest to make a difference in those remote places where elites visit either for profitable investment projects, or for quelling rebellions. The language of protest is now either too fashionable, or not fashionable at all.

In a society where economic progress and human development have not gone hand in hand, the language of globalisation is unconvincing. At the level of basic human rights and grassroots survival, images of inequity are a risk and 'a sin against the future' (Stern 1998). Legislation after legislation for more power to the state to combat every manner of protests relating to inequities is not an answer. Legislation by itself proves ineffective if not accompanied by concern, not just for developing metropolises, but also the hinterland where our sustainability is drawn from. Simply arresting and gagging the Lakshmis around us deflects from the need to get our act together — one that will address more imaginatively than before the problems of a society where growth rate figures are not convincing indices of development.

10

Raziya:
'I am Staff *and* Imprisoned!'

◙

'We thought you'd never come to talk to us,' Raziya says to us that morning after we have asked the superintendent of the prison if staff members could be included as part of our study in the research and counselling centre. She continues, 'There is a myth going around that prisoners are the only ones needing assistance and support to cope with the prison as an institution. Prisoners come and prisoners go but we are here forever! It is assumed that because we are the khaki-clad guards in the prison we must be so powerful that we need no support and assistance. Well, let me tell you that that is nonsense. No one comes to inquire about our problems and requirements and believe me, they are many.' Raziya is quite angered with our so-called neglect and has clearly been smarting since we started working in the prison. Her grievance is that we are paying too much attention to prisoners' needs.

Excluding staff has never been part of our programme, so Raziya is a little out of line in believing that we would just walk away from the prison one day without hearing them out. In the film we made about prisons years ago (*The Prison: Does it Serve Them Right?*, 2000), prisoners and staff had been given equal voices to speak and air their perspectives. In fact, the film was a part of a neatly spread out project on the training of prison staff (officers and guarding staff) from all over the country and the whole purpose was that they formed a vital part of any scheme for reform and change. A rather competent Superintendent of a District jail in Lucknow had given us one of the best personal interviews we had ever done and we carried his cautionary remarks with us all through our journey: 'If we really wish for change in the prison system,' he had said, 'then along with prisoners we need to focus on the staff and their problems as well.' He had spelt out the kind of problems that the staff faced, and that to him were fundamental if the staff were to perform professionally. His advice was down to earth and reasonable and made perfect sense. Ironically, within a few days of our having completed our film, we were given the news that he had been shot at point blank range on the streets of Lucknow by the relative of a (mafia) prisoner in his jail who had been refused the extra privileges he had sought. The officer, Mr Tiwari, had paid a heavy price for doing his job.

Staff in prisons comprises an assortment of different classes (a pattern for government employees all over the country). Class 1 are the officers, Class 2 are those that directly run the jails as supervisors and directors; the guarding staff is referred to as Class 3 and Class 4, below them, is the unskilled staff for menial tasks. The structural profile of a prison is usually the same in most States with minor differences in nomenclature. Prisons are a state subject in India's federal system and the prison department is part of the Ministry of Home Affairs. The head of each State's prison department is the Director General (DG), recruited either from the Civil Service (for example, Uttar Pradesh, Bihar, Madhya Pradesh), or the Police Service (Rajasthan, Andhra Pradesh, among others). Some States have an additional Director General (ADG) and an Inspector General (IG) who are State prison officials (there is no national cadre called the 'Prison Service'). The status of even the highest prison service officers is not the same as those of DGs or IGs from the Police Service either in terms of salary or privileges and perquisites. The State prison staff comprises Deputy Inspector Generals (DIGs), superintendents, deputy superintendents, jailors, deputy jailors, head warders, warders (called constables in some States), doctors, nurses, a teacher (sometimes this role is entrusted to a 'senior' convict), and cleaners. Many posts are unfilled for many reasons, such as cost reduction and dearth of applicants and/or qualified persons. A 'Superintendent' is the equivalent of a 'Governor' in the prison service in the West. This women's prison does not have a full-fledged superintendent directly in charge; the superintendent of the adjoining men's jail is in charge of this and other prisons in the area. The deputy performs the functions of overseeing and decision-making in the day-to-day running of the prison.

Needless to say, we have had more than a fair share of tales and stories about staff from the prisoners: how vicious and villainous they could be, how greedy they were, how partisan they were and how some were actually informers even as they appeared to befriend prisoners every now and then. That there was beating and bullying was not new and accepted, alas, as part of the disciplining process. While we weren't about to grant credibility to all that we heard, some of the accounts were repeated so often that it was obvious there was some truth in them. In any event, we had already prepared Assessment Schedules for all the staff that had been filled in during information-gathering interviews with them. The feedback from the questionnaires that my colleagues had meticulously prepared and filled in after long sessions with the staff helped tremendously in knowing about work schedules and attitudes of the staff at different levels. One of the crucial features of our questionnaires was: 'Why did you decide to work in a prison?' The answers were a revelation and told us more about each staff member than anything the prisoners may have said.

The guarding staff (constables or warders) is the largest group and does the most basic and mundane work in day and night shifts. The duties of constables range from gate duty, filling in forms for new prisoners, keeping the registers safe, kitchen duty at meal times, head counts, locking up, ensuring cleanliness, bringing (prison and prisoner) problems to the notice of the deputy, and all in all, being the links between prisoners and officers. They have the maximum contact with prisoners for better or for worse.

As things stand, it seems it is for the worse. One can use a multitude of adjectives to describe their performance and attitude; but that might be unsound logic. Why are they the way they are? That is the question that needs an answer and that is what we wish to address. Surely, they don't come to the prison with the attitudes we now see in many of them — clearly they get tough and hardened with time and circumstance. It's our job to know why.

Taking Raziya's complaint in our stride we planned out our talk session with every member of staff as painstakingly as we could. Raziya was the first and probably the most cynical (as if we were not cynical enough!). It is not her fault — it's the way things are and continue to be in most Indian prisons. A prison is a little world unto itself. Huge fortress-like doors shut tight most of the time, a claustrophobic environment, no let up, no levity, no appreciation or commendation anywhere, and everyone inside interacting chaotically with one another. Still, in India it is a shade better than many prisons in other parts of the world, particularly the West, where despite all the electronic razzmatazz, those who are inside might not see the sun for days on end and could walk from corridor to corridor almost unaware whether it's day or night!

So, we start with Raziya. Strangely, her personal story is almost like that of many of the prisoners we have talked to. She is 31 years old, married with two children and has worked in the prison for eight years. She is one of nine children (there were 11, two died from illnesses, and she now has six sisters and two brothers). The father first had an ordinary job in the army, then left the army to cultivate his land. The problem of marrying off seven daughters was almost a nightmare for him. Why he fathered eleven children was a question we didn't have to ask. Raziya expressed her unease herself.

'Why do those who can't afford to bring up large families have so many children, I often ask myself. So much must surely be lost as a result; but no one advises people on these things in our part of the world. It's so embarrassing really!'

There is a lot of resentment in Raziya's mind. She is not at ease with herself at all — she never smiles and is always tense. The first thing we need to do is to put her at ease, which is not an easy thing to achieve in this environment, and more difficult as everyone gets into a groove as time passes.

'Look Raziya, there is something that needs to be said here before you continue. You have reservations about us and we understand that well. You think we are here just for the prisoners and their welfare. That error needs to be rectified. Prison is an institution that is unreal at the best of times. It is not natural that one set of human beings should lock up another set of human beings like animals in a zoo and we are aware of the ills and harms of this practice and the problems this creates for all concerned. Locking up people damages them, most importantly, in unnoticed ways that relate to their minds and personalities. This needs to be understood and highlighted. Our aim is and will be to get on with making this a better place for all concerned *including and above all* for those who work in them. How can a place be congenial if those who work in it are not happy? So, that's the start — does that make sense to you?'

At the time, Raziya and the other staff members are so stiff, nothing seems to work. The mindsets are stubbornly set in one groove. Contact with a changing world outside is so limited that it is difficult to suggest that they should move with the times. It's as if the good things that have happened in the world have just passed them by, so suggesting that they move with the times seems almost silly on our part.

'We had eight *bigha*s of land and our home was our own,' Raziya continues. 'I was married off when I was 11 (*gauna* was at the age of 13). My husband was still at senior school and quit when he failed his matriculation examination. This was a joint family and although my husband had no job, we survived on the collective earnings of the family. My parents did not give dowry, just some kitchenware as a gift. I was not satisfied with our lifestyle: the atmosphere was claustrophobic, with everyone expecting that duties needed to be performed for them. I was the youngest daughter-in-law, the newest entry into the household and needed to prove myself to all. With an unemployed husband, my status was one of the lowest of low and I didn't stand a chance. I wanted to work but a non-working husband always has a greater complex about his wife working. He was idle for a long time and drank excessively and shouted at me at the slightest pretext, almost as if he was trying to prove his manhood to the rest of the family. Sometimes he would get violent and the worst part is the humiliation that all this brings in a joint family. Everyone is watching you and you feel so discarded and dejected.'

My colleagues and I look at each other, asking ourselves the same question: is this a prisoner's or a staff member's tale of woe? It is the same sad, familiar story — child marriage, violent husband, joint-family problems. That *khaki* uniform conceals an injured human being almost as vulnerable as those locked in here as prisoners. The sullen expression and general bitterness become comprehensible and the cynicism seems almost justified.

She says, 'And you thought only the prisoners have sordid life stories. There is nothing as miserable as being married off so young when you don't even know what marriage is. And then to be told by your parents to be happy, but discovering soon enough that married life is a nightmare beyond belief. But I decided the way out was work. I had seen my father in *khaki* and wished to adorn the same uniform — I dreamt of some job, any job, in the army or police. But beggars can't be choosers: I neither had the required education (only did eight years of schooling) nor the "influence" that could give me a job of my choice. I was told about jobs in the jail and filled in a form without telling the family. When I was called for an interview, they were livid. I thought my husband would thrash me to death. But I was adamant and went ahead and was selected as a constable in Udaipur. I went there for two months and then requested a posting in Jaipur, which they gave me.'

'Didn't you need to have training, considering you had no idea about jail work?'

'Yes, after I came to Jaipur, I was sent for six months training to Ajmer (there is a training school there) and that became the cause for further skirmishes and scuffles in the family. By then I was pregnant and you can imagine what a furore that caused in the household. I had to split my training time in two parts: one done during pregnancy and the other after the child was born. When I look back at those times I shudder — no one was there to cushion me and everyone thought I was a neglectful wife and mother. Each day I went to work or training, I left after everyone had had their fill of showering abuses on me. My husband even said once that perhaps I was having an affair with someone at the job. When I returned from training he greeted me with awful words that still ring loud in my years, "Did you enjoy sex with him then?" Men certainly know how to hit below the belt. I was horrified at him and gave him a mouthful back, only to be struck in the face with a heavy, hard hand.'

What can you say when you think you might have been mistaken about someone? Not much. You feel stupid and learn the lesson of your life: not to judge people without any basis. Not all the statistical information we had gathered about staff could have given us the insight that her spoken words did. Her bitterness then was not unjustified: all the consideration that prisoners were getting from us was almost, she believed, at the expense of the staff. Point taken. But let's see where this is going.

'In between all these happenings, I lost my five-year-old daughter. She was very sick with high fever and although I took leave and stayed home to look after her, she died and I was devastated. My husband accused me of killing her by neglect. You would think that with him being home without a job he could just as well have been taking care of her. But it was easier for him to blame me, one more way to make me numb — I think I became numb permanently after that. People tell me I am a dull, boring and morose person. Perhaps I am, but who knows about the wounds I carry?' Raziya is in tears, a sight we never thought we would ever see, but see it we did — and it evoked pangs of guilt in all three of us. We did misjudge her.

'Now he has a job in a private business; his take home pay is lower than mine and that too is a reason to dislike my guts. I don't think that men can ever accept this principle of equality for men and women flouted around in your human rights agenda. That is why I don't believe in it, no matter how hard you all work at it. I hear you talk of men and women having equal status, needing equal dignity, being treated with equal respect — that is all a load of rubbish. Sounds good on paper, but the reality is something else.'

What never ceases to amaze us is the expressive mode into which these women are capable of gliding when encouraged to do so, rendering all our beliefs about their inherent 'voicelessness' into total disarray. We think we may have been viewing Raziya from a perspective that could be wide off the mark; it only takes all of an hour for us to feel we need to revisit some of our views. The exchange is perhaps as much about us as about her, and we need to wait till we actually form our conclusions.

There is a knock on our door and I ask Neena to tell the visitor to come later — we have to shield a teary Raziya. Exposing a vulnerable Raziya to the prisoners who are in her charge will be, by all accounts, unfair. So, as Raziya wipes away the tears from her eyes we tell her to go and come again later; she knows why and after she leaves, we let in Preeti, a prisoner who has been to see us before and wishes to say something.

'So, what brings you here, Preeti,' Kiran asks her, putting away her notebook. 'Come and sit down.'

Preeti is a middle-aged woman who is quite sick and, like
all prisoners with the slightest physical ailment, believes she has
a serious illness that needs more attention than it gets. It is the
same story, the atmosphere and ambience contributing to making
people worse than they might otherwise be. The doctor believes
that half of them are hypochondriacs; perhaps she is right where
a few of them are concerned, but somewhere along the line fails
to see that anyone in an environment such as this is likely to seek
attention one way or another.

'I'm sick, ma'am!' Preeti complains. 'My body aches all over and
I feel as if I have a slow fever all the time. Sometimes I can't move
and then I am in trouble. Not moving is just not a luxury that is
allowed to prisoners. I am not shamming it, you know: but the CO
in our barrack is after my life. "*Nakhre mat karo* [don't fuss],"
she keeps telling me! But I'm not fussing — I really can't move.
I'll collapse one day and then they will realise that there was
something really wrong with me. I went to the doctor and even
she said, "*Chalo hato! Bahut ho gaya!* [Move on and don't fuss]!"
"There is nothing wrong, you are just feeling low. So are many
other women. So what do you expect me to do, examine all the
women everyday to attend to their imagined ailments? What
shall I do?'

This is a recurring problem. Women are depressed and they
are seen as phonies. It's all about the mind. How can they control
their states of mind? It is understandable that in the hierarchy
of responsibilities the staff have, the mind is not likely to be of
high priority.

'Look, Preeti. It's like this. Perhaps, you can't really be given the
kind of attention that you should get. You do have aches — it's
probably not imagined — but because you are sad and anxious,
each pain is amplified in your mind and becomes unbearable. No,
you are not faking it. But there are so many women in your state
that the staff gets fed up and shows impatience with you. You
have been here for a year and can't see any light at the end of the
tunnel. It is despair that you are feeling. Try and remember the
times that you must have felt despair at home too. How did you
surmount it? You probably went to your neighbours, had a chat
with them and told them about your problem. But this is a

depressing place and there is no one that has the patience to hear you out because everyone has her own problems. That is why we have asked for the setting up of a counselling cell in all prisons — so that you can talk it out and if there is something that really needs attention, it should be addressed.'

'My husband has stopped coming to see me and he is not sending the children either. How can I not see the children? It is not fair. I have a teenaged daughter and I have no idea what is happening to her. I can't just pretend that it is not a problem. It is, and I feel so helpless that my whole body becomes numb and I can't move. I really can't,' she says.

Kiran puts her arm around Preeti's shoulders and tries to comfort her. 'Shall I ring up your home and ask what is happening? Could we contact anyone we can talk to and ask about your family?'

'I only have the address,' she says. Kiran takes it down and assures Preeti that she would get in touch with the family and ask them what is going on. In the meanwhile, she needs the strength to carry on. How should that be administered? I wish there was a pill that could provide that strength — but there isn't.

'I'll take her outside and talk to her in the courtyard,' Kiran says, probably thinking that being cooped up in a room and talking may not be as productive. They go out to chat, but Kiran returns in half an hour, looking perturbed. 'Goodness,' she says. 'What on earth is happening? We can't really absorb the spill-over from each life here.'

'What's the matter?' I ask.

'Preeti has an inkling that her husband is carrying on with another woman and that is eating her up. Once a woman leaves her home, the husband seems to think he is free. That there are children whose responsibility he has to take is not an issue for him. That is prescribed as a woman's job, so it's not even on his radar-screen. Her husband is a drunk and she believes that when he's inebriated, he may even make advances on the daughter. *That* is what is consuming this woman. I have promised to contact the husband and talk to him. Fortunately, he lives in the city and I may not have a problem. But imagine if he were far away — I wouldn't be able to do a thing.'

Over the months Kiran has learnt to grapple with some of the undetected problems of the women in distress and to find the simple solutions that might improve their states of mind. This is no ordinary achievement, given the general proclivity here to slur over what we call the 'personality predicaments'.

This is the same Kiran who was hauled up by the Deputy for taking in her mobile phone (see Chapter 4, Hasina's story).

When we highlight personality needs, the staff often believe we are being over-caring about inconsequential features in a prisoner's life. 'Sometimes you tell us that their basic needs are most important,' Raziya has often said. 'Why do you rank personality needs so high on your agenda? *Hum unke khane peene ka khyal rakhen ki unke aansoo pochhe?* [Should we pay attention to their food and bodily needs or wipe their tears?]. *Hamare aansoo kaun pochhega?* [Who will wipe our tears?].' Certainly, this is not an easy question to answer and is very much part of the balancing act we strive to do each day.

Raziya visits us later that evening after the head count and lock-up duty. It's a relief for the staff when the imprisoned women are locked up for the night (it's actually early evening and the sun is still bright in the sky). From this time on till the next morning, no one is allowed to enter the prison or go out, leaving only the prisoners and staff inside, which is respite for the staff but claustrophobic restraint and restriction for the prisoners. Usually, we leave around this time too, but since no one pushes us out, often we linger, partly because the day's work is not yet over. These are the moments of doom and gloom for those inside, the time when their darkest thoughts get free play.

Raziya sits down, saying, 'Another day is over,' and we wonder at her remark.

'Not a happy time for those locked up,' I say, trying to think how I might feel if I were caged while the sun shone outside and the birds still chirped.

'Perhaps not,' says Raziya, 'but how many hours can we be on the alert? We have lives to live too. There are so many prisoners and not enough staff, so we do long and erratic hours with unplanned leave or time off. Last week I was on duty for so long each day, the clothes in my house remained unwashed for the whole week. Our own lives are affected. When we return home we are so tired and irritable that our family members, especially the husbands of the married staff, grumble and complain. My husband thinks I do sub-standard work anyway: if I take the problems of the prison home either to get things off my chest or vicariously in my mood-swings, there is hell to pay. You have no idea what happens to us at home. No one is proud of the work we do, not our husbands, not our children. "It is a ridiculous job," my husband says, "do it and stop talking about it. You deal with scum and you are becoming like scum!" How can one give one's best when the job itself is regarded as worthless?'

'I see from the work schedules that you have three work shifts in the prison, including the night shift. The day shifts, 6 a.m. to 12 noon and 12 noon to 6 p.m., means a six-hour working day. And then there is the night shift. How is that too long? In Hyderabad they have just two shifts, 8 a.m. to 5 p.m. and 5 p.m. to 8 a.m., somewhat longer than the shifts here.'

'It's not just about hours of work,' Raziya points out. 'It is the nature of the work that is exasperating. It's not that six hours really ends up as six hours; if something needs to be done we stay longer. And while we are here, there is so much *khich-khich* (chaos) all the time. Our workload is a mixture of so many un-related duties, we can't attend to any of them properly.'

That's strange, we think. Many a time we find half the warders sleeping on the job, and when they are not, they don't appear to be overworked. Clearly, they don't enjoy the work (our survey data sheets show how some of them begrudge the time they de-vote to prisoners who have problems or complaints). One warder (proud to be a Brahmin), who clearly indicated she hates her job and does it only for the money, said unabashedly that she does not talk to prisoners. '*Yeh sab neechee jati se aati hain. Aise log yahan ka mahol kharaab kar dete hain* [most prisoners come from low castes and spoil the atmosphere of the prison].' The same warder heard a Muslim prisoner creating a ruckus and said, '*In Musalmano ne saari jail kharaab kar rakhi hai* [these Muslims have spoilt the entire jail].' Yet another said [about prisoners in general], '*Yeh achhi auratein nahin hain* [these women are not decent].' The survey interviews had already told us something about these attitudes of the guarding staff, so Raziya had an uphill task trying to convince us that the staff is the underdog.

'What is it about prisoners that gets them more sympathy from you "reformers" than we get? They have done wrongs and are criminals. Why this fight for their rights? We also live challenging and tough lives. We also face harsh and hard realities — personal and financial. We also have domestic problems where there is violence in the home and taunts all round in the home and outside. That doesn't mean we go around killing people and stealing from them or trafficking in drugs. So, why are they the focus of your attention? What about us? You just walk past us, and want prisoners to come and unburden themselves to you so that you might bring relief into their lives — why?'

I know this is not a question that can be brushed aside or taken lightly. Why are prisoners' rights of such importance that we spend hours and hours each day trying to get to the bottom of their lives, their offences, their minds and indeed, their souls? This is not the first time we have had to face this barrage of questions. Out there, the public demands the same answers and also their pound of flesh for the wrongs that offenders have committed in society. We do owe explanations and explain we do, day after day when faced with such attacks. A well-placed woman (Mrs R) in Andhra Pradesh once asked me why I travelled such long distances to work in prisons in the south. 'Surely,' she said, 'you could be working on securing human rights for more needy people nearer home.' And then a few months on, I had a call from her, 'I need your help,' she said. 'I know most of your work is in women's prisons, but my husband has been arrested and is in the men's prison across the road from where you are. He is being denied visitation rights and home food, something that is permitted for pre-trial prisoners. He also has high blood pressure for which proper medication is not being given and he will collapse if that is not provided. Please tell the superintendent that all this must be attended to. After all, it's all in the rulebook. He can't be denied his rights as a human being, surely.'

It's funny how the tune changes when the shoe pinches. 'You are so right,' I said immediately. 'It is a prisoner's right to be treated like a decent human being — the rulebook says so and humanity demands so. I will certainly talk to the superintendent about your husband's medical condition and visiting rights. I'm sure there should be no problem. The superintendent is a reasonable man and there must have been a slip up somewhere in the information provided to him.' The husband got his home food, his medication and his daily visits from immediate family and she was happy. She rang to thank me and I said, 'Don't thank me, thank the superintendent who received his human rights training from us last year and does believe in the rights for prisoners. And I hope this will also answer the question you put to me a couple of months ago relating to why I bothered to work on prisoners' rights when there were so many other needy people in society that required help. When the State puts away people behind bars, they are forgotten about, their basic rights as humans are forgotten and they are helpless inside. It is the State's responsibility to care for those whom it has decided to lock up. Locking up is the punishment not any other deprivation.' She was sheepish in her response and fumbled for words. I couldn't let her go without asking her what her husband was in for. 'Well ...,' she said quietly, 'he is in for fraud, in the bank scam that you have been reading about in the papers. He borrowed money as did so many others and didn't pay back. But you know, he only took twenty five lakhs — there are others who have taken crores and gotten away with it.'

Raziya, too, needs some reality checks at her own level. For her it is a simple 'them versus us' equation: 'Why do prisoners deserve rights when we don't have them? We slog day and night for them and have tough lives all year round. Our lives are not cushy and smooth. Why them?'

'Because you are *free*, Raziya, that is why. You have not been deprived of your liberty like the prisoners have been (albeit legitimately). One doesn't know the value of freedom until it is taken away. If the State has decided that locking them up is the way they must pay for their alleged offences then while they are locked up, the State has to take full responsibility for meeting their basic needs. Being imprisoned is their punishment. No more, no less. In all other matters they are the same human beings they were when they were outside and have to be treated as such. You can't remind yourself of their offences all the time: that has nothing to do with you. Coming here and being caged in here is their punishment and once they are here, they are entitled to all that a decent human being is entitled to. There are standards formally laid down for the care of those we lock up — these cannot be flouted just because we don't like the persons we are dealing with. They can't be starved, or unattended when they are sick, or made to live in unhealthy surroundings, or deprived of contact with their loved ones, or denied all that makes for decent living. That is *not* part of their punishment. And if they are to go back to their homes, it is befitting that they go back bettered not made worse by the institution. Does that make sense?'

I was sounding like a preacher and certainly did not intend giving her a lecture on rights and duties, but there we are. The staff has to be made to realise that this is not the scum of society that has been put in a warehouse for storage. Mrs R also thought all those in prison are like rotten apples until her husband was sent in. Then everything changed. He was a special case for her, but then, so are all these people here for their families. Logic fails us here. We find ourselves opening up layers and layers of the baggage everyone (including us perhaps) carries: our class and caste perceptions, and the fake morality that we all subscribe to. Raziya will carry her baggage with her to her grave and I am sure all this preaching will be like water off a duck's back. But maybe, sometime, somewhere the penny may drop. Something may happen that needs a change of attitude. Heaven forbid, I thought, but if her son were ever to be nabbed by the police even for vagrancy (still an offence in this part of the world), her position on many things may change.

Kiran and Neena deal with every member of the staff day in and day out and see them close up: they see that the staff become ungenerous and almost mean as they get more seasoned. They have managed to justify all that they do or don't do, blaming it on the wretchedness of the system, on the prisoners, on the *mahaul* (atmosphere) and sometimes their *kismet* (fate). It is not easy to refute their assertions, but address them we must. So, we decide to point out some of the complaints commonly made about constables or warders.

'May I be frank and talk to you about some of the allegations made against the lower staff?' I ask Raziya. 'It is alleged that you people take away rations of food that come for prisoners from the kitchen, that you give the prisoners only half their quota of sanitary napkins each month and keep the rest, that you extract money out of them to enable them to meet their families, that you pocket the goodies the families bring for prisoners, and even bully the visitors into providing you with things you want to facilitate their visits. You say prisoners use bad language, but the prisoners asked us the other day whether we had ever heard the vile language that the staff uses towards prisoners, including four-letter words and ugly references to their bodily parts. I'm stating it plainly and hoping that you will give me an answer that will be truthful.'

Raziya turns red with rage, and angry enough for me to revisit my somewhat indelicate questions. 'I am only passing on what is said all round. You don't need to be mad at me, or at my colleagues. This is neither my personal opinion, nor a tirade against you. It's about what most of the staff supposedly does around here. Tell me if all that I am saying is untrue. The place here runs on your shoulders, and your strengths and weaknesses affect everything that happens here. I know there are problems that you as staff member face that just don't seem to improve. But prisoners are not to blame for that. They appear to make your job difficult because they are bursting at the seams with their own problems and have no relief from them. That they come from poor backgrounds is no reason to take out your frustrations on them. If you are not paid enough, or your life is unsatisfactory, it's not their fault. What do you think? Is there a connection between the prisoners as persons and your grievances relating to the terrible lives you live?'

Raziya is unrelenting. 'You come here to ensure that the prisoners get what they are meant to have so that they can live half decent lives. You were quoting the Constitution of India the other day at a meeting and said that an article of the Constitution that spells out the right to life also says 'life with dignity'. Is that just for prisoners? Is there any dignity in how I live? Have you ever been to my quarters? Have you seen what passes for decent living there? I have a family that uses a cramped toilet and when it breaks down, I don't have the wherewithal to have it repaired. When there is a breakdown of the water supply, no one rushes to put it right. I have to beg the people in charge of maintenance here to set

things right and I am told, "first the prison work has to be done."
Can you imagine? So, what if I am free — the point is I cannot
get these things done privately for there is no money. So, just how
free am I? What is this freedom that can't ensure decent living for
millions of us? And you talk to us about prisoners' rights? I grudge
them all the facilities they get. They get free board and lodging,
medical care, oil, soap, sanitary napkins, educational facilities,
and more. If you people had your way you would send them on
holiday!' I don't have the nerve to tell her that in Lucknow we
had actually requested the department to enable women to be
taken in groups for picnics with their children so that the children
didn't grow up without a glimpse of the world outside.

Clearly, Raziya has been smarting about this ever since we
came to the prison. Maybe there are others among the staff who
feel the same way. It seems like our failure to me — we thought
they were failing in their duties by not responding when prisoners
needed compassion, but now *we* feel unsuccessful. Not winning
the confidence of those who are at the interface in prisoner–staff
relationships seems like a fundamental breakdown in communication. All three of us at the counselling centre meet to discuss
this problem. And then I learn more about Raziya.

'Ma'am, do you remember that last January a prisoner gave birth
to a baby girl in the prison? We wrote about it in our reports,'
Neena says excitedly. 'Tara, who had come to jail in an advanced
state of pregnancy, suddenly went into labour. There was no
vehicle to take her to hospital, neither at the women's jail, nor the
adjoining men's prison. The doctor had gone home. The jailor
was called but took a while to come and Tara was in a bad shape,
so the women from Tara's barrack asked the constable on duty
to assist them in delivering the baby. The constable didn't help.
Tara's labour pains became acute and she was bleeding rather
profusely. One of the prisoners said she had delivered a baby
before, so she took charge and asked the constable for help again.
She refused outright, saying, "*Ham kyon karen? Yeh hamara
kaam nahin hai.* (Why should I do it? It is not my job)." Several
prisoners tore up their sarees to procure enough cloth to mop
up after delivering the baby in that half-open enclosure in the
freezing cold. There were no surgical gloves and nothing to cut
the umbilical cord with, so someone ran to the men's prison to

get gloves and a blade. Hot water and antiseptic were procured from the infirmary. The confident prisoner played midwife as best she could. She cut the umbilical cord, and cleaned up the mother and baby as they shivered in the cold in the open space inside the gate enclosure. The naked baby was taken to the infirmary to get cleaned properly and there were only a few gauze pieces available. Some prisoners brought their blankets to wrap the mother and some baby clothes belonging to other infants in the prison. The constable on duty just stood there and watched the *tamasha*. Some prisoners rebuked her for not assisting and she blurted out, "*Is neechi jati ki aurut ko ham nahin chhooyenge* [I won't touch this low-caste woman]." Who do you think that constable was, ma'am? It was Raziya!' Kiran was all worked up about it even though the incident had happened months ago. Raziya's present hostility made Neena resurrect the past almost to remind herself and all of us that it was Raziya who was failing, not us.

So that was a dead end. We were somewhat peeved with Raziya's outburst, not having had any such experience in the women's prisons in south India. The regional variation approach seems too simplistic. Our deliberations begin to point to some link, however tenuous, between the attitudes of senior officers of the department and the lower staff. Where seniors are informed and aware of the debate about rights for prisoners elsewhere in the world, there is some effort to put their own houses in order and look around for answers. Not all the senior staff care to be informed. The old logic about security, law and order was a primary concern for many. 'Nothing should be done to compromise order in a prison' is the oft-repeated mantra for most. But one, even one, senior officer who thinks otherwise can make a difference. That is fine, if we take it at face value, and yet, a personalized approach that depends on individuals is surely not an answer.

Hema, another constable, comes to us a few days later and asks what we had said to Raziya. 'She is so put off with all of us, as if she had been ticked off by someone. She is not pleased with her session with you, ma'am. I just thought I would check exactly what happened here.'

We look at each other, my colleagues and I, and smile. What can one say? Without divulging what our exchange was about, we still have to give an answer that would assure Hema that we aren't exactly the villains Raziya may have portrayed us to be.

'Look, Hema, while we are not at liberty to reveal all of our conversation with Raziya, I wonder if you would like to sit down and have a discussion with us. That may give you an idea about what we discussed. Does that make sense?'

'Sure,' she says, 'I have no problems with that. And if it's unpleasant, then so be it. I am sure I can handle it. I am sure there is nothing that is not known to you. So, what have I got to hide?'

Our chat with Hema is similar to the one we had with Raziya. She resents some matters and accepts others, suggesting that corruption was rampant from top to bottom. 'It's not just constables who behave badly. We are told to do what we do, including corporal punishment if required. "*Ek tamacha mar diya karo!* [just give them a tight slap]" is what is suggested to us if prisoners don't listen. It is a difficult job and patience runs out every now and then. The person sitting in the office (the deputy) comes and goes at her whim and fancy. Have you not noticed how often she is not there till after lunch? She has a small child and we are often sent for 'baby-sitting', whether at her home, or if she brings the child to the office, then in the back room behind her office. She relies on us and we probably take advantage of the fact that she depends on us. So yes, we do what we do because we are aware there is only that much the officer-in-charge will do.'

'So, are you saying that there can be no check on you for anything?'

'Not quite. You won't believe who snitches on us if we listen to prisoners when they complain to us — the COs who have been assigned duties in each barrack. And by the way,' Hema adds, 'even when you people get sympathetic to prisoners and listen to their woes about the staff, the CO promptly goes and tells the officer. The other day Kiran *didi* here promised to write a letter for a prisoner and also said she would post it for her, and promptly the CO went to the jailor to report it. I think Kiran *didi* was called to the office and asked why she did such a thing, am I right?'

She is dead right. We had slipped up there and I had already told Kiran she should not volunteer such favours to avoid breaking rules here. And we did wonder how the jailor got to know, but

now the mystery is solved. We were never happy about this convict officer business: putting them in charge of fellow prisoners
sometimes was a disaster and often made for murky politics.

This prison is like a pond covered with weeds, its intertwin-
ing internecine politics dangerous for those caught in the murky
waters. We are sitting on the edge and dare not try to pull out too
many weeds — we run the risk of getting trapped in the tangles
and wouldn't know how to extricate ourselves. Someone with the
right implements needs to do this job of handling the complex
issues of the staff who find room to manipulate every situation
to their advantage.

'It's a job, ma'am,' says Hema. 'We do it the best way possible
and surely, turning it to our advantage is not such a sin. It's a
battle for survival for us too, you know. Why do you want to
believe that those who undertake this task must do so out of a
sense of commitment in what they are doing? Commitment to
make prisoners' lives better? No one here believes that, no matter
what they have said in the questions set out in your schedules.
It's a mere job and at the end of the day a balancing act, a sort
of endurance test for the fittest. Many flip over and make a hash
of it. The knack is to do it so that one doesn't go overboard. As
they say, "*apne pair kulharhi na marein* [don't hurt your own toes
when you use the axe]". I would go further and say, "*kisi ke bhi
pairon par kulhari na maro* [don't hurt anyone's toes]".'

So, she does draw the line somewhere, thank goodness. But some
of the staff members have become so brazen they just go right
ahead with their self-interest. Perhaps, we may get somewhere
with time and a little patience, but understanding it all has been
difficult.

'There is a need for some radical rethinking here,' Neena says,
almost profoundly. 'With the prisoners it is usually a straightforward arrangement: they need assistance and even when some
pretend they don't need it, after some exchanges they are glad
to be helped in even small ways. This lot — the staff — doesn't
want personal help although God knows they have any amount
of problems. They would rather go along with the politics here
and consider us a stumbling block. We have to think of some way
to we show them we are not.'

'The self-esteem is low in this environment anyway. Winning their confidence is not easy.' We scratch our heads in despair, but Kiran thinks she has an idea.

'What about the eye and dental camps that we have organised for prisoners next week? Well, maybe you already intended it that way, but I figured we should get all the staff to come too, and get their eyes and teeth examined and then get their spectacles and dental treatment, if needed.'

I didn't want to dampen her enthusiasm and had indeed intended to get the staff to avail of the camp facility as well. 'Great idea,' I say to Kiran. 'Why don't you take a round tomorrow and tell all the staff to enroll and make the lists — let's get that going.'

The eye and dental camps were held for over four days at the prison. The specialists from the local hospital came with all their equipment and there was a great hustle and bustle in the prison. The staff members on duty managed the prisoners' queues, ticking off, pushing, shouting instructions as each prisoner came to the room assigned for the camp, and they felt quite involved. Then it was their turn. Kiran and Neena already had their names and called them one by one, including Raziya, to get checked, after which prescriptions and treatments were arranged for all. Some got spectacles, some had decaying teeth pulled out and got the follow-up antibiotics and painkillers. Some older prisoners didn't want to sit in the dental chair and had to be persuaded like infants by us. They had problems with their eyes and teeth but feared invasive treatment. Once it was done, however, they were relieved and days later we were told they really felt comfortable and were glad the nagging pains were gone.

After the four days of hectic activity, I say, 'So that's done — now what?'

Kiran says, 'Ma'am, Raziya came this morning and wanted to talk to me.' Kiran does inspire confidence among many. Her skills are different and she believes that a little holding of hands, an arm around the shoulder, a few smiles do work. She goes on, 'Raziya was clearly a little more mellow than before and said the staff were all quite glad to have been a part of the proceedings this week. She has been given a pair of spectacles and one can sense a little contentment in her attitude. "I never told anyone," she says, "but I was having difficulty filing out forms and checking the register everyday and felt angry because I had problems with my eyes; but now I see better and don't get those headaches I used to." So, there's a start, I suppose.'

'It's that old story about the stick and carrot, Kiran,' I say, 'always a difficult one to decide — when to use what. How long will Raziya's present appreciation last, I wonder. Keeping up the morale around here is not really our job: it's an internal institutional matter. Senior functionaries, unfortunately, don't see 'morale building' as part of their jobs. They just do the prescribed rounds and off they go. The divides in the workforce go deep like our class and caste divides outside. We can play out a few games to believe there is a unity at work here, but there's no such thing. The conflicting divides come right back because that's how things work each day and everyday. I'm afraid the general lack of interest in this institution generally enables all these power games to thrive. Our most challenging task is to keep alive a basic interest in this place even when we get flack from all sides — of which there is plenty as you know — whether from "outside" or "inside".' Kiran and Neena know all this more than anyone else.

No one wants to hear about prisons and prisoners unless there are some sensational stories of beatings, or deaths inside, or escapes, or 'mafia' stories about gangs with mobile phones who carry on 'businesses' from inside, or even engineer killings of enemies from their cells. There is a stir — journalists come and ask us what we think about these incidents and if we say this is not all that the prison is about, they just give wry smiles and leave. They want the juicy news. I have actually been entertained to a tea party in a jail in Bihar where *samosa*s and *pakora*s and *elaichi ki chai* were prepared for me right under my nose in the barrack as I sat interviewing these VIP prisoners who had been involved in scams and who took such pains to tell me either that they were innocent or that they had been framed. They had plenty by way of patronage to dole out to the really poor prisoners, or to the staff even while they were in jail, and people did their bidding without wincing. Nothing happens without staff connivance, I was told, and the proof was right before my eyes.

Kiran says, 'But these stories are about men's prisons. Do people know there is a world of difference between the goings in men's prisons and the ones for women?' Kiran has seen the goings inside of both, and it angers her.

Kiran and Neena have become seasoned cynics over the years they have worked with me, which is not a good thing, I think. They are too young to be so pessimistic. But then it doesn't need a genius to ascertain that with a big chunk of the problem 'inside' being disgruntled staff, the burden of finding solutions and answers is a heavy one. 'By and large, the staff hates this place,' Neena pronounces. 'So do the prisoners, but the staff believe prisoners deserve what they get, when the truth is they really don't. The senior staff is looking for promotions and public recognition and citations, while the juniors are looking for the best ways of surviving. Ma'am, even Mr B. isn't quite what you think he is with all his tall talk, moral pronouncements and supposedly bleeding heart.'

She is right: rhetoric and reality are abysmally mismatched in the prison. The senior staff members mouth all the jargon they receive from us or other human rights groups — but their real interests lie elsewhere. The senior superintendent, Mr B., whom we had enabled to go abroad for human rights training for the prison management in an earlier project, is so preoccupied with promotions and postings, and awards and medals for his prison work, he just can't get himself to understand the concept of teamwork. Me, myself and I — that's all he can think of. He cites Sanskrit *shloka*s of goodwill at every opportunity he gets to demonstrate that with his piety and righteousness he is naturally predisposed towards the prisoners' welfare, and no one can fault him on his rhetoric. His desperate efforts to shift from the (lowly) prison department to the (elevated) civil service (a procedural possibility for 'good senior officers'), with all the prestige and perquisites it brings, reveals something else. '*Et tu, Mr B.?*' we query. If he can abandon the ship after more than 20 years in the prison department, how can anyone blame these miserable constables and warders for pursuing their short-term gains, and for the consequent inadequacies and imperfections that accompanied their work ethics. There is a dearth of exemplary seniors to guide lower staff, and there is no training that places emphasis on characters or personalities — not staff's and not the prisoners'. The word 'personality' is not in their dictionaries. Talking about fractured minds, therefore, makes little sense to those whose preoccupations lie elsewhere.

◻

Note

Some of the laments made in earlier chapters relating to the obsolete nature of the statutes and principles relating to criminal law and justice are equally applicable in the area of penal administration, and more particularly, prison management. The structure and organisational aspects of Indian prisons have not altered much since colonial times. If changes are made, or contemplated they are simply tacked on to the existing system, sometimes clumsily and awkwardly, without any change in the ethos or culture of prison management. Staff attitudes reflect the old beliefs in managing prisons and the women staff reveals deep-seated frustrations of which inevitably, prisoners are the main victims.

As part of the legacy of British rule, the prison administration also reflects the colonial idea that the best criminal code is of little use for society without an effective machinery for the infliction of punishment. The earliest attempt at reforming prisons, initiated in 1836 at the instance of Lord Macaulay, resulted in the Prison Discipline Committee submitting its report (1838) wherein the recommendation that prisons need to be run with strict and rigorous rules and *not humanitarian principles as their guiding force* (emphasis added) still forms the underlying principle of prison management. The sentiments were echoed by another Commission of Inquiry (1864) even as it suggested some improvements in the amenities of the prison, such as food, clothing and medical care. Inching their way towards a special enactment for running prisons, jail commissions were concerned about jail offences and punishments for indiscipline, and finally produced a draft bill that became the Prisons Act of 1894. The present jail administration in the country is guided for the most part by this Act, based primarily on the theory of punishment as deterrent.

The 1894 Act is the only statutory document providing the framework for running prisons all over the country. Some exemptions are set out for the vulnerable — women and civil prisoners are excluded from such punishments as handcuffs, bar fetters or whipping. For offenders who are guilty of specific offences in the prison — wilful disobedience, assault, use of criminal force, insult, immoral or indecent behaviour, refusal to work, causing wilful damage, tampering, false accusation, and conspiring to escape — punishments range from warning, seven days labour, handcuffs, fetters, confinement, and a penal diet, unless the offender is declared medically unfit for any of these.

Moves for any all-India reform (such as the Indian Jails Committee, 1919–21) were not able to go too far as the federal structure of the government was being drawn up (the Government of India Act, 1935) transferring jails from the Central to the Provincial List. A uniform national prison policy has posed a problem to this day as the States exercise their prerogative to be in charge of their territorial powers and obstruct the task of a uniform prison policy for the whole country.

From Walter C. Reckless's report for transforming jails into reform centres, to the All India Jail Manual Committee (1957) that submitted its report (1960) suggesting a uniform policy for jail administration, the attempts for revamping the 1894 Prisons Act are numerous. *The Model Prison Manual* (1960) was made the guiding document for prison management thereafter and the States included features of the *Manual* into their rules as and when they wished (for example, recommendations relating to classification of prisoners and treatment of offenders). The need for uniformity arose again and again and the 1983 Justice Mulla Committee's report provided some new guiding principles and rules for prison reform, covering almost every aspect of prison management that far-sighted reformers had envisaged over the years. Its fate was similar to that of the many well-meaning committee reports (the Police Commission, 1978, the Justice Iyer Committee Report on Women Prisoners, 1987) that are consulted when accusations of malfunction are made, but generally adorn the shelves of libraries and offices, exposing the State's inability to move beyond old (colonial) ideas of punishments that instil fear and awe.

Prison management requires an ethos that differs from that of the police or the civil service and yet the top jobs in the department are reserved for police and civil service persons in the hope that the department would then be highly regarded in the general criminal justice structure. Managing prisons must have its own philosophy and importing senior staff from other services cannot be a substitute for the culture that needs to be in place to guide the department. Lower staff is variously recruited and trained in different States, and contemporary thinking about prisons all over the world is out of their reach. Adding more scattered and fragemented laws cannot substitute for an updated national prison document with inputs from State functionaries and informed members of the civil society who realise the gravity of assigning prisons to the warehouse status that it has had so far. Insignificant attempts by particular States to improve prison practices merely to earn acclaim as (progressive) winners among competing States, have proved to be counter-productive and misleading for an ill-informed public.

Fussing over prisoners is resented by staff at the best of times. Not being well-provided and only marginally better off than prisoners themselves, staff frustration and anger is exacerbated when volunteer agencies look into prisoners' welfare and better management of prisons. Transparency and better independent monitoring of prisons are clearly needed to take the institution forward as an important component of the criminal justice machinery.

A frequently made observation by prison staff to the question of why they joined the prison department is that they wished to be in *khaki*. It is the colour of the uniforms of police and army personnel, the more prestigous all India services whose officers take the service examinations and become part of a national force. Prison is a *ghatiya* (inferior) service, says the staff, and the *khaki* uniform gives a small amount of prestige in the eyes of the public who look upon *khaki* with awe, even if not respect.

Conclusions and
New Beginnings

◙

This book was never intended as an emotional response to the plight of *women* locked up as opposed to *men* locked up. The object has been to demonstrate some failures in the hallowed uniformity that the State's (legal) punishment system wishes to boast — a uniformity that frequently misses the essence of the purpose of punishing those who violate State-made laws of criminality. Some of the issues raised could have equal validity for vulnerable groups in a men's prison where juveniles, elderly and mentally ill need to be de-slotted and de-labelled. Our understanding is that women still constitute the special category of prisoner and/or offender that needs a more than exclusive focus, and the nature of the stories reveals why this is so.

This treatise has been as much about those inside who are part of the 'system' (prisoners or staff) as it is about volunteers, reformers and researchers who go inside to learn about and understand an apparently innocuous institution — the prison — and come out wondering at one's naivete in believing that this is the best we can do and that it will work forever, for everyone and everywhere. The system's failures as they affect vulnerable groups are a matter of particular and grave concern for reformers.

Pursuing the thread of our argument in the Introduction relating to the two facets of the prison that we have chosen to highlight — 'the body' and 'the spirit' — the emphasis in our narratives has been more on 'the spirit of the prison' for a very fundamental reason. Prisons and other custodial institutions have for some time been bombarded by human rights spokespersons for falling short of international standards in managing places of confinement. The knee-jerk response of State functionaries to the criticism has been to set in motion some semblance of physical improvement to keep further censure at bay, but without any fundamental change or re-thinking about imprisonment as punishment. A few more TV sets, less watery *dal,* a cup of milk for infants (sometimes withheld for unknown reasons), a more regular supply of sanitary napkins for women may pass off as welcome improvements but would still fail to address the essential issue of locking up people and figuratively throwing away the key. Accustomed to addressing particular shortcomings as and when they are pointed out, the prison administration fails to see how else it can improve the system. After all, if confining people is clearly accepted as the best way of punishing offenders, why then should that basic premise of prison as punishment be questioned? As a tried and tested system prevalent the world over, it has not really elicited any loud protests about its existence, except in some cases. There is evidence that our refusal to review and revisit the practice of locking up people is intensively and extensively destroying and damaging people, some more than others, far more than we are able and willing to concede/realise, is not a major consideration in penal thinking.

The suggestion that has been made in this book through the lived experiences of incarcerated women is that these are individuals (not *categories* of criminals divided on the basis of statistics) who, for a multitude of personal and social reasons, acted as they did (and this is not an exercise in condoning), that they may already have fractured minds and broken spirits, and the last thing they need is a place where there is a likelihood of further damage to their personalities and self-esteem. The premise has been that not everyone housed inside is a risk to society and punishment needs to take account of that reality. The book has set out some aspects of that reality, including the shortcomings of the law.

A word of caution here: While making a strong case for proper *treatment* (to be read here as 'decent handling'), at no point does the argument set out in these stories of imprisoned women's lives endorse the view that prisoners are *sick* persons and need hospital-like *treatment.* Labelling prisoners as sick individuals is an easy way out of the very complex issue about offenders, their offences and their prison experiences. Such a view attacks some very fundamental premises of the crime/punishment discourse by not addressing: *(i)* the underlying principles related to punishing, and *(ii)* the evidence that most prisoners are ordinary persons gone astray for specific (albeit non-condonable) reasons. These principles, persons and problems need a focus if the various and varying goals of punishing are to be addressed, and without clumsily mixing in issues about sick and healthy, good and bad, moral and immoral.

There is criminology and there is penology — the former being the study and analysis of all issues relating to the formulation of crime, and the latter to forms of punishment and the exercise of the power to punish. Our chronicles fall essentially within the framework of the discourse on penology, sometimes spilling over into the debate about crime formulation resulting in criminalisation — an issue that then gets attached to penological issues. Debate, at least some debate, about penal issues and more specifically the prison is alive in more than a few countries (particularly in the West) where rigorous analysis considers the use, misuse and possible disuse of the prison against existing theories of crime and punishment that are constantly reviewed and revisited to determine their theoretical and empirical validity. Such a debate about the prison as an institution in the penal system that forms a central part of the criminal justice system is almost non-existent in all of South Asia. The prison, a vital component of our sacrosanct historical, colonial punitive baggage, has acquired an unquestionable inevitability, making a search for alternatives superfluous. Deconstructing the package to reconstruct our theories and practices cannot be avoided, arduous and tedious as the task may be, and the belief in alternatives cannot be dismissed lightly. This is the direction our stories have tried to point towards.

What is the most elementary component of the logic of punishment? Simplistically perceived, it has been first about 'payback' — something was taken away and it needs to be returned — whether it relates to property, life, injury, etc., and wherever there is a perpetrator and a victim. Historically, punishment based on the principle of 'an eye for an eye' and 'a tooth for a tooth' emanates from such simple justifications. With time, the repertoire of offences expands as the state decides that offences do not always have to relate to a (personalised) victim. Without embarking on a long inventory of these offences it can be stated that we gradually arrive at unending lists of transgressions, some of which we are familiar with today and which continue to be added to the state's directory of 'offences' and 'crimes'. This is probably not the place to unravel the complex history of crimes and criminality, but a quick reminder might be in order: an ever-increasing and expanding state list of offences is dictated by ends that supposedly serve societal *and* state goals which may conflict. 'Drugs', deviancy related to personal or social 'morality', violations of state-made rules for greater control of non-conformity, and other aberrations associated with anomalous and unconventional behaviour are some of the examples of what feeds into the ever-enlarging list of offences created by the state and which individuals and groups can scarcely keep pace with. In traditional societies, yesterday's customs and mores may become today's offences and crimes if the state wishes to make them so. The logic of 'payback' may be irresistible from one point of view; from another, it smacks of inconsistencies, irregularities and contradictions because of the overarching role of the state in determining the modalities of payback. In our stories we have tried to see how these contradictions play themselves out in real-life situations, making the task of simple indictment and punishment problematic.

Apart from the 'payback' logic, the other rationale for punishment is the quest for order and organisation in society (the stability and security imperative) — one of the defining features of the modern state. Innocuous as this pursuit may appear, it seems to spill over into areas of control and management that are the stuff that manipulation is made of. The language of punishment plays a crucial part in this logic and its claim and assurance of the welfare and well-being of subjects actually has an outreach that is selective, self-serving and expedient, belying its rhetoric of equal justice. Its potential to serve privileged interests has been demonstrated by several (Western) authors and analysts in empirical accounts of punitive processes and imprisoned populations. These accounts show how the justice machinery has enough space to play out racial, communal, class and other discriminatory acts towards its unwanted populations (warehousing), making a mockery of the principle of equal justice for all. This loophole or flaw is addressed by adding public safety as a vital component of incarceration wherein the risk to society posed by offenders at large is portrayed as being in direct proportion to the intensity and duration of the punishment they get.

There are subtexts that underlie the expositions contained in the texts that deal with the theoretical formulations of punishment, alluded to perhaps somewhat simplistically in the above logic(s). It is these that we need to focus on in order to understand how the 'logics' become problematic when particular institutions (police and prisons), and particular persons (minorities, women, the elderly, mentally challenged and non-conforming groups) are the subjects of the dispensation.

A soaring crime rate and an escalating fear of crime (engineered or otherwise) become the site for a hyperactive interplay between state and society. The capacity of the state to enhance the fear of crime and create both criminal subjects and the exceptional measures to deal with them is underscored in much of the literature on the subject. It is able to achieve its two objectives, simplistically stated, *(i)* it is capable of classifying society into good citizens and bad ('demonisation' of individuals and groups), and *(ii)* it has the capacity to extend and intensify the space for state intervention for a larger good (which, paradoxically, becomes a much smaller good than is suggested in the aims and purposes of punishing). How this plays out on the ground is a cause for grave concern as the above objectives are linked and intertwined at will to strengthen the case for tightening state machinery to punish deviants. The underlying suggestion here is that societal malfunctioning and the effective (result-oriented) functioning of the legal order become inseparable. The fallout is a range of hastily created, convenient constructions of the social fabric that are detrimental and injurious to vulnerable groups (listed above, of which women are one). Stereotyping, ideological slotting, intolerant grouping, condemnatory exclusion, bigoted labelling, prejudicial discriminations — they all form a part of the armoury used to weed out (socially and then legally) those who do not fit the picture of the 'good citizen' and become the 'suitable enemies' (Christie, 1994).

So, how do the pictures of women that we have drawn in the chapters address these paradoxical positions. In privileging women with a special group status, are we risking the same stereotyping that we are condemning? Is this a category that is ideologically constructed out of sex and gender considerations? Or has the empirical evidence produced a category strongly dissimilar and distinct as a group with specific and special needs, both in society and in any system constructed by society/state for them, so much so that it becomes imperative to revisit the ossified logic of general imprisonment that seeks to fit women into an all too male an institution. A remark often made by our researchers as they worked in women's prisons was, 'except for the absence of urinals this could well be a men's prison!'

Between two somewhat extreme positions of prisoners being regarded as sick, or portrayed as demons is a range of positions that we have tried to explore theoretically and empirically. Our attempt in these stories has been to show the persons in focus in their entirety, warts and all, referred to variously as 'prisoner profiling', or 'individual pathologies'. The idea behind this was to get away from the notion of statistical collectivities, or subpopulations, a notion based upon and created either out of the criminal acts performed ('*all* offenders who commit any crime have attributes that are the same'), or on supposedly scientific knowledge that addresses the risk potential of a prisoner ('*all* prisoners who have committed murder, or are sex offenders are a risk to society and should not be allowed to be free'). Our goal was simple enough even as the efforts to achieve it needed painstaking methods constructed out of multidisciplinary concepts: *knowing the prisoner*.

Prisoners as persons are neither the homogenous group we try and fit into a category simply called 'prisoners', nor are they the abnormal bunch of evildoers tailor-made to fit the policies we engineer (theoretically) for their management. Perhaps, the only shared feature is the socio-economic vulnerability that makes most of them targets and easy prey for the system. On other points they differ as much as their counterparts outside and they are as 'normal' (not an appropriate word as it belies a preconception) as those of similar background who are 'outside'. Something goes dreadfully wrong in their lives and they are locked in prisons as if they were another species and needed to be caged. Some *may* be the 'demons' that 'the new punitiveness' would have us believe. Most are not. There is an incident (an offence, with an offender and a victim perhaps) that triggers the somewhat phlegmatic machinery of criminal justice into motion. In terms of praxis, one part of the system (police) is able to pick the most vulnerable (vulnerability being defined by their class, race, religion, gender, *and* the soiled tags given them for the 'appalling' offences they have allegedly committed), and then subject them to the vagaries of the rest of the system. Their handling is also determined by this vulnerability; more often than not they are locked away pending decisions by the rest of the system that determines their guilt, treatment inside the prison, etc. How they are viewed and/or handled can be labelled a somewhat capricious exercise and needs to be questioned and commented upon; we have tried to do this in our 'cases' of the 'offending' women that form the subject of this scrutiny by suggesting that there is more to it than meets the eye.

Each story has tried to suggest what is the *more* here *than meets the eye*. Life's promises that passed them by, the challenges for survival, the (misguided) decisions, the desperate measures, the trajectories of their personal experiences before and after they entered the 'justice' system, and the sheer bleakness of their pasts, presents and futures is the stuff that these narratives are comprised of. Why does Hasina get the label 'husband slayer' before any other descriptive tag? Why is the fact that she was not the offender and was covering up for a minor son not the defining feature of her status in the prison? Why has Saloni gained notoriety as a 'sex worker' and no attempt been made by *anyone* to delve into her reasons and compulsions? Does anyone know what role her mother played? How come the long arm of the law is not able to reach those who run the scams associated with sex workers? How did Rukhsana spend three years as a *convict* in this adult prison when she was neither involved in the offence, nor was she an adult when the sentence was pronounced on her family? Whose convenience was it serving? And if Rukhsana's entire family is in prison for a dowry death despite revised laws on dowry and dowry deaths, what does that say about the power of the law to combat social ills? Is sending more and more people to prison actually helping in the fight against dowry demands?

Or is the law now being misused by women and their families for other agendas?

If Vimla had post-traumatic stress disorder and other glaring symptoms of increasing mental instability, why was no attempt made to address her malady? Why was she turned into a *'tamasha'* and made an object of ridicule rather than a person in need of medical intervention? The prison clearly failed her as much as her ruthless husband. How is it that the one feature about mentally disturbed Bina's alleged action of throwing two children into two separate wells that scarcely finds mention in her record is the role of the *ojha* who had been guiding her actions through her son's and her own illness? The prevalence and power of *ojhas*, spiritual healers, witch doctors and exorcists cannot be minimised just because the urban educated are relatively free from it. The ignorant and uninformed are constantly being exploited in villages, remote tribal abodes and small towns where charlatans advocate the need to appease or combat the power of evil spirits to avoid further disasters. Maharashtra's Black Magic Bill of 2005 is a case in point where the damage being caused by charlatans and sorcerers was sought to be addressed. And then there was Lakshmi, forever dubbed a Naxalite terrorist. Instead of outlawing her and condemning her fellow prisoners as dangerous criminals, why did no one bother to find out how they got enmeshed in socio-economic conflicts with the State in the first place? How come no one knows that Shobhavati (who was married at ten and produced 13 children) was married to a man the whole village called a *randibaaz* [philandering scoundrel]and who even tried to rape his own daughters who then (not Shobhavati) killed him (in self-defence)? And then there's the staff, especially those who are labelled Class 3 and Class 4 employees in the system (the nomenclature itself tells the story). They are at the interface of the prisoner–staff relationship. What about them? What are the life-stories of those on whom the system relies for managing prisoners? Why do they take away prisoner rations? Why do they steal the sanitary napkins meant for women prisoners? Why do they resent the idea of better provisions and facilities for prisoners? Why do they hate reformers who suggest schemes that they hope will make the lives of prisoners better? Has anyone viewed the lives of the staff members from close quarters?

The easy answer to all these questions is usually a disclaimer that it is not the responsibility of the penal machinery to go into the minutiae of prisoners' lives. Our rejoinder is two-fold: one that these are neither the minutiae nor the trivialities of these women's lives — these are the stark realities of which their lives are constituted. How far these realities may be ignored, or cast aside as vital considerations for the criminal justice system is not a superfluous question and needs an urgent answer: our stories have suggested that ignoring the before and after of prisoners' lives makes a mockery of the task of delivering just justice. The institutions of the criminal justice system then become the ends of the justice process rather than the means. The second issue is how far the penal system and more importantly the prison is required to be an enabling institution in order to mend the fractured lives of the women inside. If 'human repair' is a goal, then the staff's burden of asking appropriate questions about prisoners and about their own role in the system and the lives of already damaged women cannot be brushed aside by the declaration, 'it's not our job'. A pertinent counter-question would be, 'What is your job?' The answers to this question lie scattered in local, national and international documents, some updated some obsolete, constantly having to be interpreted for prison systems by reformers and other change-agents.

While advocating the necessity of understanding the totality of prisoners' lives, their pasts, presents and futures, and suggesting that they are not merely the sum of constructed parts that we may dissect at will to handle as we deem fit, some apparent contradictions do arise in our expectations. The plea to staff for more consideration towards already damaged prisoners includes the expectation that they should not take (moral) positions on the nature of the offences committed by them. Snide comments about prisoners' offences abound within these walls; drawing a distinction between addressing a prisoner's difficult past to help them tide over the bad patches, and confronting them with unpleasant details about their offences in a derogatory manner is a sensitive issue. Sometimes, staff needs to hear it as it is: that it is not their business to deride prisoners for their offences, and not their place to suggest that they be deprived of basic decent living because they are offenders. They are paying their dues through imprisonment for months and even years. Indeed, the priority of the staff should be to keep prisoners safe and enable them to get back to society. This is a tall order for prison staff in this part of the world because their lives are as difficult as those of the prisoners whom they have to care for are and whose futures are not exactly as promising as their uniforms suggest. That they resent every positive move made for prisoner welfare becomes the reason for many of the malpractices that are an intrinsic part of most Indian prisons.

Emphasising that imprisonment itself is the punishment for prisoners and that no more punishment should be inflicted in the prison also means explaining the meaning and significance of imprisonment being a deprivation of something vital, i.e., 'freedom' and 'liberty'. The general inability to understand the import of these intangible deprivations in a democracy lies at the heart of the quandary faced by the prison management for whom dispossession of a prisoner must be physical, material and visible, and who believe that any other alternative is a mockery of imprisonment as a punishment. That the deprivation of freedom for long periods of time is the punishment and that it can be quite harsh in itself is difficult to explain to a society and to a state that believes that the manner of safeguarding a society's safety is directly proportionate to the degree of incapacitation caused to those who transgress society's rules. The nature of the damage caused to prisoners by months and years of incarceration can only be gleaned from close-up shots which show the horror they experience in living in a virtual zoo. These prison narratives have taken us as close as possible to the negativities of incarceration for those who were already disadvantaged before they became prisoners, a fact either forgotten, or deliberately dismissed by a system more preoccupied with the rule book and its nuanced procedures and processes. That the rule book needs a hard second look seems, unfortunately, to be out of the question.

The essential logic of prison as deprivation of liberty may contain some apparent contradictions. For women prisoners it is suggested that the deprivation of freedom and liberty that we call the essence of incarceration is not the calamity it may be for others, for in profiling the average woman prisoner in Indian prisons it has been suggested that she does not fit the (ideal) definitions of a free person in her family/community life. If that is so, then the prison experience is less of a deprivation of freedom for these women than it is for others. This logic is flawed, and what we glean from experience is that precisely *because* the women have already lived shackled lives underwritten by complex disabling factors, this is not where they should be if and when they offend against the rules made for them by those with vested interests.

It would be inappropriate to look for closures in the proposals we are seeking to set out without addressing the impediments that constitute the real problem in the quest for a rethink in the area of punishment. This treatise is being completed in an ongoing atmosphere of violence and vendettas that continue to horrify Indian society to the point where it looks to the state for more stringent laws and more punitive measures to address the spectre of 'terrorism'. The fear instilled by this new kind of war (and it is just that) is real and the cry for help from society to the state may be justified. As 'war' in its new incarnation, the steps needed to contain and combat it would need to be extraordinary and cannot be merged with the system that handles *ordinary* offenders who do not pose the kind of threat the perpetrators of the new war of terror do. A specific apparatus that would handle this new war would need to be part of a redefined system. When the perpetrators of this war are apprehended, their handling may also need to be redefined. This may well pose a fresh set of problems in the present atmosphere as any parallel system may well be used for vicitimisation and further vendettas of persons and groups that would ordinarily not be caught in the web. As usual, we are too lazy to draw finer distinctions for the betterment of our social fabric.

The subjects of our narratives and discourse here are not the ones who need stringent laws and procedures: mixing and merging offences and offenders, confusing issues relating to them and then building a common reservoir of measures that do not take stock of the differences at the heart of penal issues represent flawed logic and can have a devastating effect on the entire penal system. It is precisely this confusion of methodology that is our concern.

For the ordinary woman prisoner (she may or may not be an offender) who we would wish to return to society as a decent citizen, this addiction to uncivilised punitive measures is unbefitting. The logic of 'payback' and the concern for the safety of the social order do not justify the hardship they suffer at the hands of the machinery. It doesn't need a Dostovesky to tell us that the degree of civilisation of a country can be measured by looking at its prisons. A thorough informed look inside the human zoo is enough. Bad physical conditions, hopeless overcrowding, inadequate and sub-standard food, monotony and idleness, regimented lives with no privacy when needed, disturbed and damaged minds and personalities often beyond repair — this is what prisons are made of.

It is for this reason that we suggest the idea of alternatives to prisons, an idea that is anathema to a state that is able to demonstrate in any number of ways that its role as guardian and protector necessitates it to be tough and relentless with those who fracture the social fabric. And yet the same state has hardly any reservations about introducing privately-managed prisons, another lesson coming from the West that could spell disaster. Why would profit-seeking private enterprises abandon the very self-interests that keep their engines running to meet some charitable and humanitarian ends spelt out by penal reformers? Unfortunately, we seek privatisation because several 'Western countries' have introduced it in one form or another, forgetting that in the West the debate about prisons does not surface only when there is a dramatic event in a prison; rather, it is fast becoming part of a running agenda that reformers have not given up easily. We have tried to analyse the actual workings of our criminal justice model where all manner of offenders are trapped in a system that believes that 'locking up' is the best way to punish because it is an age-old system that has, in fact, been in existence for so long that people have forgotten its origin. Looking for a more restorative form of justice in which victim and offender are both addressed to bring back that social harmony that was breached in the first instance seemed a more wholesome goal than clinging to a colonial inheritance that was ill-suited to our needs right from the start.

Unlike many other objective and dispassionate accounts of imprisoned women, these narratives have sought to portray these women in more engaging, real and inspiring images depicting her in the fullness of her person with a past, present, and future. This is a group with differing special needs like some other groups we encounter in this same environment — the very young, the elderly, and the mentally disturbed or ill — and together they point to the futility of locking up vulnerable people to satisfy the ever-growing demand for more stringent punitive strategies of punishment. If imprisonment has not worked, particularly for these groups, then advocating its overuse is detrimental to the very ethos of building the edifice that would produce 'good and law abiding citizens' (as the mission statements in some prisons declare). Attempting some minor changes to mollify reformers is also not enough. India's definitive document on prison reform was produced more than 25 years ago (Mulla Committee Report). It was ahead of its time in recommending changes that included alternatives to prison for several categories of prisoners: open prisons where prisoners could/should live with families and other good practices that could have been introduced and developed had the report been officially adopted. The Krishna Iyer Committee Report on Women Prisoners that came a few years later specifically recommended radical changes in handling women offenders in police and judicial custody. Each conference or workshop on police and prisons pays due lip service to the recommendations in these reports. We are unable, however, to let go of the archaic prison structure and the archaic rules and regulations that guide its management, even as we boast of dramatic changes in economic and technological areas of functioning to keep up a global pace that is not always relevant in our everyday lives. The clamour for privately run prisons is one such modern demand that belies an ignorance of who is ultimately responsible.

In consolidating and presenting these narratives as we have done, no presumption of wisdom beyond the ordinary has been claimed. Complex issues and concerns continue to baffle the most ardent scholar and practitioner, and a quest for pat answers would be immature. Practical matters relating to the handling of women in the criminal justice system have not been elaborated in these narratives for they are both numerous and unresolved and not easy to place within the ambit of a study that is still struggling to re-open specific issues relating to the punitive package that does not serve the ends of justice that it professes to. Only when the discourse is vigorous and robust enough to endure the kind of critique that is being suggested here can the finer points be addressed.

One of these finer points is the subject of the children of incarcerated parents. There is a glaring shortage of information relating to these children: neither the criminal justice system nor social systems address this problem because the children of incarcerated parents are not recognised as a group to be studied and addressed formally by any state agency or department. At the most, one will find a bare minimum statistic about how many 'children accompanying mothers' there are in any particular prison, a meaningless statistic if it is not part of a designed approach and official policy that addresses this huge problem. One part of the problem is the children 'inside' with mothers; the other equally grave problem is the children 'outside' who are left behind when their mothers are arrested. Collectively, the two sets of numbers are large, but more than their number is the immeasurable trauma they experience as a result of their separation from a prime carer. Children 'inside' or 'outside' face unique difficulties that have neither been researched nor systematically addressed by the justice system — a grave flaw in a system that claims to protect society. The effects of this lacuna on the mothers inside are equally devastating as the stories revealed.

The subject of infants accompanying imprisoned mothers is a knotty problem the world over. Each society believes it has the solution when it defines the most appropriate age for children to be or not to be in a prison with their mothers. Eighteen months (as in many European countries) or six years and flexible (in South Asia and other parts of the world), there is no agreed appraisal about the 'right' age for children of imprisoned women to be inside. The problem is complex and like many other such questions, it is left to be addressed only when it becomes inextricably difficult. The subject of children left 'outside' poses equally acute problems for individuals, families and the community. At no stage in the justice process (arrest or adjudication) is there a request for information about prisoners' families: how many children does the woman have, what are their ages, gender and locations, what will happen to them when the woman is sent 'inside'. The official machinery that produces draconian criminal laws and equally draconian punishment to protect society fails to ensure the future of those who seem to get punished by default: dependent children — whether they accompany mothers and lose their childhood 'inside' or are left 'outside' — become rudderless adolescents. Equally, the effects on children of fathers in prison have not been analysed in developing countries. The collective effect of these oversights is one of the paramount reasons for women 'inside' breaking down and unfortunately no help is at hand for the problem. Their desperation was more than apparent when they narrated their agony about the future of their children.

Another 'finer point' relates to older women in prison. This is a group that is almost totally overlooked, even in the limited number of studies on women offenders. Older women in society feel vulnerable at the best of times; as prisoners they receive the kind of attention that borders on pity and contempt. The Committee on Women Prisoners (Krishna Iyer Committee) and judicial pronouncements have provided guidelines for prison administrations to release old prisoners when they reach 60 years of age. Prisoners with disabilities related to old age are specifically targeted for early release under these provisions. However, even a cursory look around a prison reveals both the presence of the elderly and the general apathy towards their needs. Frail, wrinkled women with untidy hair and bent backs can be seen crouching against walls or lying spoon-shaped on the floor in many parts of the prison, scared and confused about their future and fearful of dying in custody. That they are in prison is a slur on our society, and that this is accompanied by general apathy towards them in the system and in society itself reveals the complexities of the problem. Continued inaction is neither an option nor a solution.

Making the justice system look neat with its laws, guiding principles, procedures and implementation mechanisms duly in place does nothing for those who face the realities that lie in two worlds — the world of the law *and* the world they live in. The essential question that arises when dealing with the subject of offences and offenders in traditional and relatively ill-equipped social groups has two aspects: what role is the legal system expected to and able to play in helping such groups avoid getting trapped in the vagaries of the (legal) criminal process (that of enabling and equipping), and what role does the justice system expect to play in addressing issues that are a fallout of the process (damage control). A host of traditional practices that were innocuous for centuries become illegal malpractices with time under the assumption that the law has the ability and the capacity to take on the onerous task of a general cleansing of both the (mal)practices and the perpetrators associated with many such traditions (dowry is only one of them). Women were supposed to benefit, but this turned out to be a bad assessment that took little note of the realities of their lives. Under what justice system can the fractures caused to the integrity of the family as a result of the incarceration of mothers be justified? It is time to take a hard second look at the way we punish so that we don't throw away the baby with the bath water.

It may be an accident of history that brought the concept of open prisons to India (open camps were set up for refugees in post-partition India). But the fact that they soon became the unique feature they were is a tribute to those who looked beyond the confines of blinkered thinking about punishment for offenders. In the early 1960s the Gandhian Governor of the State of Rajasthan Dr. Sampurnanand proposed that Sanganer village in Jaipur should be home to a new concept in prisoner welfare. Seeking to address the major drawbacks and drastic effects of punitive and retributive incarceration, he promoted the idea of transferring 'low-risk' lifers to a place where they could be reunited with their families and 'serve out' the remaining part of their sentence in home environs, thereby taking responsibility for their lives and those of their families. The concept, expanded to allow convicts to spend the final (two-thirds) stretch of their terms with their families, to earn and work in nearby towns and even build their own homes in the fenceless jail premises has been replicated in other States in India and speaks volumes about innovative thinking. While still needing some fine-tuning to address certain conceptual and practical anomalies, the idea of bringing a semblance of normality into the lives of otherwise condemned persons, albeit in a transitional phase, does prepare them for the release that society would rather forget about by allowing them to rework their social equations. (See photographs of open prisons in this book.)

It took a while before women qualified for being sent to open prisons: the reluctance came from a fear for their safety and security, the usual reason for witholding the benefits of freedom from women and the children who accompany them into prison. The benefits of open prisons may not be identical for men and women (once convicted, women are abandoned by families and the chances of their families joining them in open camps are slim), but keeping them in oppressive suffocation 'inside' is hardly conducive to building the futures of a nation's citizens.

There is still more that needs to be done to search for alternatives to 'locking up' for women and the children who 'tag along' for lack of care-givers at home. International declarations, charters, conventions, commissions, protocols and national legislations on the rights of the children notwithstanding, little systematic attention has been paid to what incarceration of parents really does to the family unit and to the children in particular. It needs far more research than has been undertaken or indeed deemed necessary. Statistics alone will not suffice when the conundrums relate to real-life issues.

The assumption that the law and the state serve better the interests of societies that are ailing as a result of overpowering traditions takes us back to the tradition–modernity dichotomy so seriously and sometimes simplistically portrayed in the 1960s. Sociologists have come a long way since then, putting tradition's creative potential where it belongs: back into real society to contest in a healthy and constructive manner for the space it lost decades ago. Homogenising society through the hegemony of the state's institutions and legal processes is not the objective of justice systems. Enabling fair and equal opportunities and treatment is. As far as the women in our stories are concerned, the 'system' with all its good intentions failed them at several junctures in their lives. To perpetuate this failure with a 'one size fits all' institution called the prison is surely indicative of a fundamental weakness in the mindsets of those who profess to take society forward in an era of progress and advancement.

This failure needs to be addressed with a little more attention to details and nuances. The dysfunctional nature of laws and law enforcement agencies has demonstrated just how unequal women are in the South Asian region. Constitutions and principles of liberal democracy notwithstanding, the state has not really been able to ensure protection to the woman as person. Being safe has been negotiated through too many intermediaries — family, community, religion, caste, class and finally the state — instead of being a right that should not depend for its negotiation on any socio-cultural or other positioning that women have been placed in through the centuries. Neither the socio-cultural nor the legal agencies are 'granters' of rights and equal status for women: the rights are theirs in the first instance. Institutional frameworks are meant to be facilitators and if they fail to discharge even that function, then they are stealing from women what rightfully belongs to them. These stories are reminders of system failures on all fronts — by society and the state. A long, hard second look is essential if the most fundamental of concepts — equality and fairness — are to find a meaningful place in our thinking about half the world's population that is also the mainstay of society.

Bibliography

◉

Reports and Official Documents

'Model Jail Manual', Report prepared by All India Jail Manual Committee 1957–59, Ministry of Home Affairs, Government of India, 1960.

Report of the All India Committee on Jail Reforms, 1980–83 (Mulla Committee), New Delhi, Ministry of Home Affairs, Government of India, 1983.

Report on the Committee on Prison Discipline (Macaulay Committee), Calcutta, Home Department, 1838.

Report of the Departmental Committee on Prisons: The Gladstone Report, Command 7702, British Parliamentary Papers, vol. lvi, 1895.

Report of the Indian Jails Committee, 1919–21, London, HMSO, 1921.

Report of the Indian Law Commission on Penal Code, 1837.

Report of the Indian Police Commission, 1902–03 (Fraser Commission), Simla, Government Central Printing Office, 1903.

Report on Jail Administration (Chairman W.C. Reckless), United Nations, 1953.

Report of the Law Commission of India Proposal to Amend the Prohibition of Child Marriage Act 2006 and other allied laws (Report 205 of 2006).

Report of the National Expert Committee on Women Prisoners, 1987, vols I and II (Krishna Iyer Committee Report), New Delhi, Ministry of Human Resource Development, Government of India.

Reports (I to VIII) of the National Police Commission (1978–81), New Delhi, Government of India, 1981.

Report on the Royal Commission on Capital Punishment, Command 8932, London, HMSO, 1953.

Standard Minimum Rules for the Treatment of Prisoners (SMR), United Nations, 1955.

'The Stern Review', A Report by Baroness Vivien Stern CBE of an Independent Review into how Rape Complaints are handled by Public Authorities in England and the Wales, 2010.

International Classification of Diseases (ICD-10): Mental and Behavioural Disorders, Geneva, World Health Organisation, 1993.
Diagnostic and Statistical Manual of Mental Disorders (DSM-IV), Washington, American Psychiatric Association (APA), 2000.
Making Standards Work: An International Handbook on Good Prison Practice, The Netherlands, Penal Reform International, 1995.

Statutory Documents

Child Marriage Restraint Act 19, 1929.
Child Marriage Restraint Act, 1978.
Dowry Act 28, 1961 and Dowry Prohibition (Amending) Acts 1984, 1986.
Guardian and Wards Act, 1890.
Indian Code of Criminal Procedure, 1973.
Indian Penal Code, 1860.
Mental Health Act, 1987.
Narcotic Drugs and Psychotropic Substances Prevention Act 61, 1985.
National Charter for Children, 2003, No. F 6-15/98 CW, 2004.
Orphanages and Other Charitable Homes (Supervision and Control Act), 1960.
Prevention of Immoral Trafficking Act, 1986.
Prohibition of Child Marriage Act, 2006.
The Commissions for Protection of Child Rights Act, 2005 (Act 4 of 2006).
The Government of India Act, 1935.
The Hindu Adoption and Maintenance Act 78, 1956.
The Juvenile Justice (Care and Protection) Act, 2000.
The Mental Health Act, 1987.
The National Investigative Agency Bill and Unlawful Activities Prevention Amendment Act (NIAUA), 2009.
The Prevention of Terrorism Act (POTA) Act 15, 2002.
The Prisons Act, 1894.
The Terrorist and Disruptive Activities Act 28, 1987 (Amended by Act 43 of 1993).
United Nations Convention on the Rights of the Child, 1990.
Unlawful Activities Prevention Act, 1967.

Court Cases

Tukaram and Another v/s State of Maharashtra 1978 AIR 1979, SC 185.
Vishakha v/s State of Rajasthan and Others AIR 1997, SC 3011.

Books, Articles and Journals

Bharucha, R. N. 2004. *Shadows in Cages: Mothers and Children in Indian Prisons*, Honesdale, Pennsylvania: Himalayan Institute Press.

Bilimoria, R. 1982. 'The Pattern and Nature of Female Criminality in Andhra Pradesh', *Indian Journal of Social Work*, 41(4): 393–401.

Blackstone, W. 1979. *Commentaries on the Laws of England, 1765–1769*, Vol. 1, University of Chicago Press.

Burford, E. J. and S. Shulman. 1992. *Of Bridles and Burnings*, New York: St. Martin's Press.

Christie, N. 1994. *Crime Control as Industry*, London: Routledge

Davar, B. 1999. *Mental Health of Indian Women, A Feminist Agenda*, New Delhi: Sage.

———. 2001. *Mental Health from a Gender Perspective*, New Delhi: Sage.

Davis, A. 2003. *Are Prisons Obsolete?* New York: Seven Stories Press.

Dhavan, R. 2003. 'Justice, Justice and the Best Bakery Case', *India International Centre Quarterly*, Monsoon.

Fishman, S. H. 'The Impact of Incarceration on Children of Offenders', *Journal of Children in Contemporary Society*, 15: 89–99.

Foucault, M. 1977. *Discipline and Punish: The Birth of the Prison*, London: Allen Lane.

Gabel, K. and D. Johnston (eds). 1995. *Children of Incarcerated Parents*, New York: Lexington Books.

Jaisingh, I. (ed.) 2005. *Men's Laws, Women's Lives*, New Delhi: Women Unlimited.

Jaisingh, I., A. Basu and B. Dutta. 2009. *Handbook on Law of Domestic Violence*, Nagpur: Lexis Nexis Butterworths Wadhwa.

Lombroso C. and W. Ferrero. 1985. *The Female Offender*, London: T. Fisher Unwin.

Morton, J. B. 1993. 'The Older Female Offender', *Female Offenders; Meeting Needs of a Neglected Population*, Virginia: American Correctional Association.

Price, B. R. and N. J. Sokoloff (eds). 1995. *The Criminal Justice System and Women. Offenders, Victims and Workers*, New York: Macgraw Hill.

Shankardass, R. D. 2000. 'Women, Crime and Jail Justice: Theoretical Formulations and Indian Realities', in Rani D. Shankardass (ed.), *Punishment and the Prison: Indian and International Perspectives*, pp. 384–418. New Delhi: Sage.

———. 2012. *In Conflict and Custody: Therapeutic Counselling of Women*, New Delhi: Sage.

Shankardass, R. D. and S. Haider. 2004. *Women and Custodial Justice: Barred from Life Scarred for Life*, Gurgaon: PRAJA.

Shourie, A. 1983. *Mrs. Gandhi's Second Reign*, New Delhi: Vikas.

Smart, C. 1976. *Women, Crime and Criminology*, London: Routledge and Kegan Paul.

Stern, V. 1989. *Bricks of Shame: Britain's Prisons*, Harmondsworth: Penguin.

———. 1998. *A Sin against the Future*, Harmondsworth: Penguin.

———. 2000. 'Alternatives to Prisons: Reflections and Experiences', in Rani D. Shankardass (ed.), *Punishment and the Prison: Indian and International Perspectives*, New Delhi: Sage.

Warner Kevin. 2010. *Address to the 8th Conference for European Directors and Co-ordinators of Prison Education*, 9–12 September, Luzern, Switzerland.

About the Author

▣

Rani Dhavan Shankardass is currently Secretary-General, Penal Reform and Justice Association, India (PRAJA), a non-government organisation working on penal reform, and Honorary President of Penal Reform International (PRI), a worldwide movement based in the UK to improve prison conditions and to promote constructive ways of dealing with offenders. Prior to this, she was Chairperson of PRI till 2010.

Born in Allahabad, Dr Shankardass attended school in Allahabad, Nainital and Lucknow. She then studied history and political science (MA, MSc and PhD) at the Universities of Allahabad, Pennsylvania, Cambridge and London. Her academic pursuits crossed departmental divisions: having started professional life as a lecturer in political science in Delhi, over the years her writings and activities reflect her multidisciplinary background in history, political science and law.

Her publications include *The First Congress Raj: Provincial Autonomy in Bombay* (1982), *Vallabhbhai Patel: Power and Organisation in Indian Politics* (1986), *Open Prisons in India: How Open can Open be?* (2002); and *Barred from Life Scarred for Life: The Experiences of Women in the Criminal Justice System* (PRAJA report, 2004). She has also produced a film entitled *The Prison: Does It Serve Them Right?* (2000) Awarded the Nehru Fellowship in 1996, she published a multidisciplinary volume *Punishment and the Prison: Indian and International Perspectives* (2000) that spanned history, sociology, law, justice and gender. Her recent book *In Conflict and Custody: Therapeutic Counselling for Women* (2012) is based on theoretical and experiential analyses of the need for professional counselling in South Asia and other regions where women are less able to use the legal and justice machinery for redress and empowerment.

She is currently working on 'Children of Incarcerated Parents' to highlight an at-risk population forgotten as a group by the State's justice machinery.

Index

◻